If You Shoot, Shoot to Kill
An FBI Agent's Unusual Career

To Carol Jane & John — I needed you when I was doing this book. You take garbage & turn out a great 302.

By Corbett Hart

Thanks & Enjoy

Corbett Hart

10/15/17

History Publishing Global

Palisades, NY 10964

History Publishing Company LLC
PO Box 700 Palisades,
Palisades, NY 10964
www.historypublishingco.com

Acknowledgements

Thank you first to all the FBI agents I worked with for over 20 years. There would have been no career or book without you

Retired agents who contributed encouragement and memories with me in writing this book are: Max Noel; Jim Williams; Hank Gaidis; Ellis/Eddie Young; Jim Harcum; Burl Smith; Dave Baldovin; Jerry Bastin; and Supervisor Cecil Moses. Two who passed away too soon are Wayne Tichenor and Gene Stevens.

Special thanks to retired agent Hank Hillin who allowed me to borrow heavily from his detailed book *FBI Codename TENNPAR*.

From the U.S. Attorneys office I was helped by retired USAs Hickman Ewing and John Hailman and AUSAs Dan Clancy and Tim DiScenza. Memphis defense attorney Bruce Kramer provided the FBI with information that in the end convicted two of his colleagues, I applaud him.

I never would have had the complete story about Billy Dean Anderson without the use of Kay Wood Conaster's book *Billy Dean Anderson: A Criminal Life* which she graciously permitted me to use.

Thanks for being there to all the members of the OCDETF, especially retired ATF agent Walter Hoback.

Informants could be a curse or a blessing but I wouldn't have been successful in several cases without the help of Art Baldwin and Earl "The Dogman" Woods.

My early readers Verleen Tucker and Amy Hayden asked all the right questions to help me flesh out the stories. Thank you.

My neighbor and friend Larry Barnes introduced me to the wonders of the dictation feature of MacBook Pro. Neighbor and friend John Anarella took my photo for the book. And daughter-in-law Helen MacIntosh gave me the best book ever written on non-fiction writing by William Zinsser.

Without my wife Barbara I never would have completed this book. She did all the typing, editing, corrected grammar and punctuation, researched and added much needed dialogue. She came up with the book and chapter titles. We had many book-related arguments throughout the process but managed to stay married. She is the love of my life and I thank her.

Contents

Introduction

I was born and grew up on various sharecropper farms in Northeast Arkansas. After high school graduation in the small city of Trumann I promptly joined the U.S. Army, there being few if any employment opportunities that appealed to me there. I knew I didn't want to work in a furniture factory the rest of my life like so many of my peers.

The Army was my ticket to the future. I served three years in the Army Security Agency; 18 months of my tour were in Tokyo, Japan.

Upon my discharge I started working for McDonnell Aircraft as a final assembly electrical inspector. It was my honor to be part of the Mercury capsule program from start to finish.

At the same time I was a part-time student at Southern Illinois University in Edwardsville thanks to the GI Bill. I graduated in 1965 with a BS degree in accounting. The IRS recruited me to join the audit section in Springfield IL where I did mostly farm audits for three years.

I got to know an FBI agent in Alton IL where the Bureau had a Resident Agency office. I worked with him and a few other agents from time to time. They described their work to me, much more exciting than audits, and convinced me to apply to the FBI.

I received my appointment letter on June 17, 1968, and entered the new agent class NAC 1-68 in July. I never dreamed I could become an FBI agent and when I did I couldn't have been prouder. I was the first one in my family to graduate from high school let alone college.

In those days classes were held in the old Post Office Building in D.C. with only field exercises and firearms in Quantico. After 16 weeks of training I was sent to my first office, Denver, in October 1968. On August 30, 1969 I was transferred to San Francisco. By my request I transferred to Memphis in August 1972 and served there until my retirement, mandatory then at age 55, in October 1990.

During my 22 years with the Bureau I worked just about all the criminal cases within the FBI's jurisdiction. I qualified as an Expert Firearms instructor in July 1977. A few years later I became a member of the Memphis SWAT team and remained for the rest of my FBI years.

Upon my retirement I went to work as Assistant Deputy Chief of narcotics in the Shelby County Sheriff's Office.

I retired again in May 2001 and now live on a small ranch in Northwest Colorado with my wife Barbara and our dogs, horses and chickens.

Eight years ago my wife encouraged me to start writing my life story. This was a personal account of the years growing up in the Depression, a sort of "we were poor but we were happy" tale.

I always had it in the back of my mind that I should preserve my FBI career in a written form for my family and friends. Like many agents I kept documents, photos and newspaper clippings from significant cases. When I began sorting through these and with my memory rekindled I thought, "Why not try writing a book?" So the task began in 2014. Throughout the process I have contacted agents and prosecutors I hadn't spoken to in years. We go back a long way and have many shared memories.

I hope you enjoy these stories. They are in chronological order covering everything from petty crime to national and international cases.

Corbett E. Hart
June 2017
Spronks Creek Ranch, Colorado

Chapter 1
First Office: Denver

My first day out of the FBI Academy at Quantico was in Denver. It was exciting, just like a movie with bad guy, guns and a chase.

My supervisor John Broughton hooked me up with another new agent Tom Wiseman to track down an Army deserter who lived in town. We were to check out his residence.

At 4 p.m. we began the surveillance of the house, a modest red brick home near the industrial section of town. After an hour an old blue and white Ford pickup truck pulled into the driveway and a broad shouldered white guy in work clothes who fit the description we had got out. We began approaching him. When he saw us he ran behind the house and down an alley. We were 50 yards behind him, running as fast as we could. Tom pulled out his gun and held it in the air and shouted, "FBI, you're under arrest. If you don't stop, we'll shoot you." I raised my gun too. The suspect looked over his shoulder, saw the guns, immediately stopped and went to a fence and put his hands up.

We made the arrest and holstered our guns. Yes, it was exciting. Well, maybe not exactly like a movie but it was exciting.

Not as exciting was a case involving a check protector, a machine used to curb check forgeries, and blank checks stolen from a business. The device imprints the payee, the date and the amount of the check. Stolen checks, each less than $200, had begun to show up at various nearby stores, mostly supermarkets.

Most of the victim businesses had photographed the person cashing the checks. We prepared a flyer with three photos of the subject and posted them in nearby neighborhoods. Several calls came into the office (the number was on the flyer). After I interviewed some of the callers I had an address for the subject but no name. A check with Denver utilities gave me a name.

The subject had a Colorado driver's license which led me to his criminal record. He had been arrested and convicted three times for forged checks and had served prison time. After comparing the photo from his driver's license it was clear the subject in the store photos was the same person.

My partner and I checked out the address. We found a modest bungalow in a low income subdivision east of downtown. A few sparse trees stood in the dusty yard. We watched the house for an entire day and saw a white male we were certain was the subject going to work and returning in the late afternoon.

During our stake out we had seen a young white female with an infant child out in the yard. The next day, after seeing the man drive off, we knocked on the door. The woman peeked through a curtain, then came to the door holding the baby in her arms. After we identified ourselves she let us come in. We told her we suspected the man living with her was the person who was forging checks. She looked at the photos and denied knowing him.

The reality finally hit her when we let her know that if the man was convicted he could get a heavy prison sentence and she could be charged with conspiracy, with possible time in jail. She admitted it was her husband. She said he had become concerned he might be caught and had her dump the check protector in a nearby river.

I requested help from the sheriff's office who had divers and the next morning I met them at the spot the wife had pointed out to us the day before. Three of them went into the murky, although not very deep, water and began searching for the machine. They quickly located the check protector and gave it to me. I sent the machine and the stolen checks that had been cashed to the FBI lab which confirmed the link between the two.

We located and arrested the subject who admitted to his crime. He entered a guilty plea and was sent to federal prison. The wife wasn't charged.

This was my first investigation using all the tools I had learned in Quantico and it was my first conviction as an FBI agent. I knew then that an FBI career was right for me even though it would mean moving my family far away from our roots and long hours of work. I already loved it.

Chapter 2
San Francisco: 1969-1972

The Office

I moved on to San Francisco after about a year in Denver. Over 200 all male agents and a steno pool of more than 50 women worked in the office, a top ten office in size.

I arrived at the Federal Building on Golden Gate Avenue in downtown San Francisco on a remarkably clear day. It was impressive, 21 stories tall with marble steps reaching across the front. The Special Agent in Charge (SAC) was Charles Bates, a very distinguished looking tall, lanky Texan in his late 40s. He was typical of the type J. Edgar Hoover selected to be SACs: handsome, tall, and self-assured.

I was assigned to a squad that worked Bureau applicants, background checks of high government employees, White House inquiries, white-collar crime and deserters.

Each squad in the Bureau was set up the same: a clerical employee maintained the files contained in the Rotor, a large gray metal cylindrical cabinet that held all the active case information. My supervisor, Bob Roby, demanded no less than perfection from agents and staff. He was rumored to have been a secretary prior to becoming an agent and could take shorthand.

Even though I had traveled in the Army, including a tour in Tokyo, I wasn't prepared for the diversity in San Francisco: hippies, gays, cross-dressers and a wide range of people of different colored skin.

The Haight

Hank Gaidis, Max Noel and I worked on military deserter cases. When a member of the armed forces left his post for more than 30 days the military declared the soldier to be in "deserter" status. The FBI's job was to locate and arrest them.

Objection to the Vietnam War was heightened in Haight-Ashbury, a hot bed for anti-Vietnam protesters sympathetic to and protective of military deserters. Hank and I often drove through the Haight searching the faces of people walking the sidewalks and streets. I always drove since we had a stack of 40-60 photos and Hank had a photographic memory for faces. Our clean-shaven appearance, suits and ties, and our vehicles—muscle cars like the Plymouth Fury with black-wall tires—practically shouted "police" to the longhaired, unshaven, hippies dressed in tied-dyed shirts and scruffy jeans. As soon as we drove into the area we would hear whistles blowing. The sound would be picked up block-by-block, warning deserters that the law was on the prowl.

When Hank would spot a deserter on the street we would drive around the block passing by brightly painted Victorian style homes with the ever-present aroma of burning incense filtering through the open car windows. If the deserter was still where Hank had spotted him, we would pull ahead of him a few car lengths, stop, approach him, then arrest him, sometimes after a foot chase. Hank and I made a good team. He was better at faces. I was better at running.

One day I took an agent with me who was fairly new to San Francisco. We were pretty positive that we had good information as to where the deserter was staying in the Haight. We found and arrested him inside his residence without incident.

We walked the handcuffed subject outside and were met by 20-30 people shouting at us "Pigs" and curse words, which was usual, but they seemed to be on the verge of attacking us.

When we got nearly to our car one young man broke from the crowd and charged me as I was holding onto the prisoner. He didn't stop so I straight-armed him to the ground where he stayed.

We were just getting ready to call for back up when someone in the crowd picked the man up and they all backed away chanting, "Let him go! Let him go!"

"Crow"

Hank and I were once looking for an American Indian male deserter named Crow, who we believed was staying in a rundown hotel in the Tenderloin District of San Francisco, more commonly known as a "red-light district," eight blocks from our office. The Tenderloin was four blocks of bars, cheap hotels, tattoo parlors and brothels.

We took the stairs to his third-floor room and saw a padlock on the door, which told us he wasn't home. Door locks in this type of hotel were notoriously faulty so tenants used padlocks to secure their rooms when they left.

We stood there a few minutes trying to decide, should we set up and watch for a while or come back another time? Then we saw two young males approaching us, one of whom appeared to be an American Indian.

We showed our credentials and asked them their names. They both gave us obviously fake names. "Aren't you Leaping Crow?" we asked the Indian. "No, I've never heard that name" was his reply. "Who is the room registered to?" The other male said it was his. "Will you let us search your room?" He said okay, reached around and took the padlock in his hand. He then turned to the American Indian, "Give me the key, Crow, you have it." Crow looked at him like he could choke him. We told Crow he was under arrest for desertion, put him on the wall and searched him for identification and/or weapons. We found a folding knife with a 6-inch blade. He admitted who he was and said, "Okay, you got me."

"If the Shoe Fits..."

Hank, Max and I learned that a deserter we were searching for was living in what was once a grand two-story Victorian house in the Haight now converted into four seedy apartments. We showed the subject's photo to some neighbors, two of whom recognized him and said he was living with a woman in apartment #4 on the second floor.

The next morning two other agents came with us to watch the rear in order to prevent an escape out the back door or window.

We went in through the front door into the foyer that had a long winding staircase to the upstairs apartments. We rushed up the stairs to the door of apartment #4, knocked, and said, "This is the FBI. Open the door." We could hear movement inside and after a few minutes a scruffily dressed young woman opened the door. We identified ourselves and showed her a photo of the subject. "This man is a military deserter. Do you know him? Is he living here with you?" She denied even knowing him. We then asked if we could come in and look around the apartment; she said "No."

We left, convinced the deserter lived there. Later we learned from a neighborhood source that the subject had been in the apartment when we hit it but had escaped down an enclosed stairway we didn't know about on the side of the building.

Two or three days later Hank, Max and I and the same two other agents went back to the house at about 5:30 a.m. This time we had the back and both sides of the building covered. When everyone was in place Hank and I stormed through the front door and headed at a run for the staircase. I was in front. I put my right foot on the first step but couldn't lift it to climb the stairs. A three-foot long 1x6 board was attached to my shoe. I kicked at the board with my left foot knocking it off. I wasn't quite certain what had happened but Hank and I made it up to the same apartment. In the meantime the two agents outside had caught the subject trying to escape down the outside stairs.

Someone had hammered a large number of 4-inch medium sized nails into a board leaving three inches or so of nail exposed on the other side. The booby trap nailed the board to my shoe. Two nails pierced the sole of my shoe leaving holes in my wing tips.

"My CI in SF

While working deserter cases I recruited a criminal informant (CI) who provided valuable quality information on several cases. I first met this person while covering a lead on a deserter case that another office had sent.

Hank wasn't with me this day when I knocked on the door of an apartment in the Haight. After knocking several times a young woman in a flashy Oriental robe partially opened the door. I slid the photo of the deserter through the opening. As usual she denied any knowledge of him but when confronted with information I had she admitted she knew him.

She invited me in and told me this man had lived with her for several weeks but she had no idea where he was now. When we sat down in her living room I sat on the couch and she sat in a chair near me. There was a small table with a lamp on it between us. As I was talking to her I began picking up signals that this was not a "she" but a "he." I noticed a distinctive Adam's apple when she turned on the lamp that had a soft blue glow. As I continued to examine her features I could see the beginnings of a black beard. What I had before me was a transvestite.

When I told her I believed I was talking to a man she admitted she was a gay man who always dressed and acted like a woman. She had even had breast implants and hoped to get enough money to have a sex change operation. She was in her late 20s, tall, slender with long dark hair and very attractive. She worked as a prostitute in the Tenderloin district rubbing elbows with the criminal element.

I convinced her to work as a CI for me and gave her my beeper number. Her job was to call me anytime if she had urgent information. I in turn would contact her on a regular basis to give her assignments, show her photos of wanted subjects and pay her for her work. The arrangement was beneficial to us both.

When this CI was dressed up she was a beautiful woman. I would often take new agents to meet her and after the meeting I would say, "Do you think she is attractive?" A common response would be "If I wasn't married and she wasn't a prostitute I might want to get to know her better." I then would show them a mug shot of her out of her costume. The response, "You son of a bitch, you tricked me."

The Robbery that Never Was

One morning I was driving along Fillmore Street covering leads. I pulled over to the curb directly in front of a branch of Crocker National Bank to consult my map.

I noticed a young black man who was walking toward me, looking around front to back and both sides of the street. I don't know exactly why but he looked suspicious to me. When he got even with the bank door he glanced at me briefly and entered the bank. I saw him go to the counter, take a piece of paper from one of the pigeonholes and write something on it. He took the piece of paper, turned and started toward one of the tellers. He stopped, looked at me through the glass door for a few seconds, then threw the paper in a trashcan and left the bank quickly.

I was even more suspicious now and went into the bank and retrieved the crumpled up paper. I read something like, "This is a robbery. I have a gun. Give me all your money and don't trip any alarms or I will kill you."

I questioned the bank manager who didn't recall ever seeing the man before. The manager told me one of his tellers was what was called a "police teller." There had been so many bank robberies in San Francisco that a plan was worked out for banks to hire off duty police officers to man tellers' windows.

I went up to this teller, identified myself and told him what I had just witnessed and showed him the note. He said, "Let's see if we can find him." I had seen the suspect turn left as he was leaving the bank. He was dressed in a light blue washed denim suit, which would make him easy to recognize. We cruised the nearby streets for about ten minutes and then the officer/teller saw him leaving a convenience store carrying a soft drink. The officer told me to get ahead of the subject and drive onto the sidewalk in front of him if I could and he would get out and approach him from the rear. The plan worked.

We made a quick pat down on the street for a weapon but found none. When the officer did a more thorough search he found what is known as an "Outfit." He had a needle, spoon, wide strip of rubber and a cigarette lighter, the necessary equipment to inject heroin. The officer told the subject who I was, what I had witnessed and showed him the note he had written in the bank. He told him if he would "come clean" he would ignore the outfit and a small packet of white substance that would no doubt test positive for heroin. The subject admitted he was in the bank but the note was only a joke. The officer told him he didn't think a jury would find it very funny.

A few days later the police officer called me and told me the robbery squad had reviewed surveillance photos of some unsolved bank robberies. They identified our subject in two of these. He pled guilty to all three.

A Real Bank Robbery

In late summer of 1972 a call went out that a bank robbery was in progress at the Crocker National Bank on Mission Street with shots being fired.

I was nearby and responded. When I entered the lobby I found two men laying in the lobby, one near the front, and the other near the far wall. A man, later identified as a police teller, was handcuffing the person farthest from me and I spotted a pistol about three feet from him.

The man closest to me was moving around and moaning. There was a pistol on the floor within his reach so I kicked it several feet across the floor, went to him and handcuffed him. He told me the handcuffs were hurting his back. He said if I would turn him on his stomach he would talk to me. I did but he still wouldn't talk.

I followed the ambulance carrying the wounded robber to the hospital and got his clothing from the nurse who was undressing him as I watched. I found a laundry tag on his trousers with the name of the laundry and a number. I drove to the laundry and talked to the manager who identified the tag. From the number he searched his records and gave me the customer's name and address.

I got on the radio, told the dispatcher what I had and asked for two agents to meet me at the suspect's address in a nearby residential area. The woman who answered our knocks at the door refused to let us search after we told her we were looking for a man involved in a crime. The other two agents stayed with her to prevent possible destruction of evidence while I went back to the office and prepared an affidavit for a search warrant.

With the search warrant in my hand the search began. In one of the bedrooms I found a pad of paper on a desk. It had indented writing on it that was legible enough for me to make out that it was a bank robbery demand note, just like in the movies.

One of the agents who was still at the bank confirmed that a demand note had been bagged as evidence. He read it to me. I could make out enough words from the indented writing to establish they were identical.

The agents searching the house had found several pieces of identification including a driver's license with a photo ID that looked like the robber. When he was well enough to be interviewed we confronted him with the evidence. We told him the case was going to be prosecuted as a state crime and he could be charged with first-degree murder. Even though the dead person was his partner in crime and had been killed by the police teller, the law provides anyone who took part in the crime can be charged with murder. Once the robber learned of this possibility we told him we would ask the district attorney not to charge him with murder if he cooperated with us. After thinking about it for a short time he agreed to confess and told us everything.

Three Airline Extortion Cases

(1) The Laundry Chute

In the early 1970s the San Francisco office investigated a rash of airline extortion cases. The typical scenario was for the airline to receive a phone call from an unknown person saying a bomb would be placed on one of its flights unless a large sum of money was paid to the caller. The airline would be instructed to get the money together and await a call with details as to how the money should be delivered to the caller.

I was involved in one such case in which the extortionist instructed the victim airline to take $250,000 in small, unmarked bills to the restaurant on the top floor of The Drake, one of San Francisco's luxury hotels, and wait for further instructions. Morrie DeJonn, the supervisor of our squad, assembled 10 or 12 agents to make and cover the drop. We recorded the serial numbers of the currency and placed it in a duffle bag along with a small transmitter which allowed agents on the ground and in a surveillance aircraft to trace the movement of the "package." All the negotiations were between the extortionist and the airline official who then passed on the instructions to the FBI.

In order to look inconspicuous we filtered into the hotel individually and made our way to the top floor restaurant. About 30 minutes after we arrived the airline representative contacted us with these instructions: when the caller gave the signal, within two minutes the package should be dropped into the hallway laundry chute; if he spotted any law enforcement in the area, he would detonate a bomb aboard an unspecified flight.

The hotel security chief said that the laundry chute ended on a concrete pad in the hotel basement. Four of us were then quickly dispatched to the basement. The call came and the agents placed the bag in the chute and radioed to us in the basement that it was on its way down.

We were all wondering how the subject planned to get the package since we were the only ones in the basement. We covered the entrance and the exits and two agents were concealed in such a way that they could see what came down the laundry chute.

Within seconds we heard a rattling noise in the chute and the duffle bag landed on the concrete with a thump. We made no immediate move to approach it. After several minutes the supervisor advised us that the spotter in the aircraft was no longer receiving signals from the transmitter and told us to open the package to find out what had happened. We quickly discovered the problem: Whoever had packed the duffle bag had concealed the tracking device under a flap of canvas at the bottom of the bag and it was completely crushed upon impact.

Additional agents were called in and we searched the hotel, knocking on doors and talking to guests. The hotel furnished a list of all the guests registered at that time which we checked against the guests already interviewed. We planned to locate everyone who had checked out and interview them. All names would be searched through the FBI Identification Division for any arrest records.

During a physical search of the hotel an agent found a cutout piece of plywood stored behind a panel containing a fire hose and ax on the sixth floor. This board had been cut so that it could be inserted in the laundry chute to deflect an object coming down the chute. We surmised that the subject must have been slow in inserting the board or perhaps another person was in the hallway at the critical time so he couldn't complete the task without drawing suspicion.

We eventually returned to the office and critiqued the operation. The SAC asked the supervisor how he knew the package wouldn't somehow be intercepted on the way down the laundry chute. Without much hesitation Morrie replied that he had thrown a saltshaker into the chute and received a report from the agents below that it had smashed on the floor. I was there and this didn't happen but it makes a good "cover your ass" story.

We were never able to develop any leads to locate the subject despite all the interviews that were conducted.

(2) The Bus Station Locker

We learned, however, this guy was not going to give up easily. About three months after the attempted laundry chute drop the same airline received a phone call from the same person. He berated the airline for bungling the delivery of the money. He told the airline he almost hit the button to blow one of its aircraft out of the sky but decided to give them one more chance to get it right. He demanded the same amount as before, $250,000, and said he would be back in touch with directions for the drop location. The airline called the FBI immediately and Morrie put together a squad of agents to cover the drop if any was made.

In the next call the subject directed that the money should be placed in a locker in the basement of the Greyhound bus station. Again we covered the drop site. At about two that afternoon the caller gave specific directions: The money was to be placed in a certain number locker. The key to the locker would be concealed under an upright ashtray located near the stairs to the basement. He said to get the key, unlock the locker, put the money in, lock it again and return the key to its original hiding place. An agent did as directed and we set up a close surveillance.

About an hour later we saw a nondescript woman approach the ashtray and removed the key. She went directly to the locker containing the money with the key in her hand. She appeared to be having trouble getting the door unlocked. One of our undercover agents, who was working full time as a "hippie" with long hair and a beard, saw what was happening from his nearby place of concealment. He strolled past the woman and then turned to her, "Can't you get that opened?" he asked. "Let me help you." She gave him the key and the agent unlocked it but didn't open the door. He then began walking away watching her over his shoulder. The woman removed the package and started walking in the same direction as the agent. After they were about halfway down the hall, the agent turned around, took the woman by the arm, identified himself and told her she was under arrest.

She admitted that her husband had asked her to pick up the package while he waited, double-parked at the terminal. She didn't even know what was in the locker. With a description of the vehicle and her husband, surveillance agents on the outside easily located and arrested him in his car without incident.

The husband backed up his wife's account. We didn't know if it was true or not that she was innocent of the plan. He also admitted he was behind the laundry chute incident and went to federal prison while she only got probation for her part.

(3) The "Rube Goldberg" Extortionist

I wasn't involved in the early stages of this case but being able to witness the "pay off" was a once in a lifetime experience. No one had ever seen anything like what this extortionist created in hopes of getting a small fortune.

Once again an unknown caller called an airline and demanded $300,000 or he would blow up one of its flights. The subject said the money was to be placed in the trunk of a vehicle parked on an entrance ramp to an interstate highway in San Mateo, which is about 30 miles south of San Francisco. The final instructions came at about 2 a.m., detailing exactly where the vehicle was located. An agent delivered the money, packed in a medium size canvas bag, to the car, placing it in the trunk that had a key in the lock. Agents then surveilled the vehicle from the ground and from the air.

The agent who made the drop said the only place he could put the bag was in a flat area about 1 ½-foot square at the very front of the trunk, toward the passenger side. He couldn't see what else was in the trunk since a tarp had been placed over what appeared to be a hodge-podge of items of varying heights and then tucked around them leaving only the small flat area.

We continued our surveillance until mid-afternoon. We then went to the vehicle and opened the trunk. We could see the bag of money right where the agent had left it. When the tarp was removed we first found a gallon jug of what looked like gasoline with a loaded and cocked pistol on a little stand with a wire attached to the trigger pointed at the jug. We called in the San Mateo Police Department bomb squad before doing anything further. These officers examined the contraption, made it safe and then removed everything from the trunk.

The subject had installed a small conveyor belt at the front of the trunk in the flat area. To the left of the belt, hidden by the tarp, was a small electric motor. It appeared that the electric motor was to be activated by a remote control, which would then supply power to the conveyor belt. If an item were on the conveyor belt it would then move to the passenger side of the vehicle. There a trap door had been cut in the right fender and was held closed by a latch with a spring attached. The latch was electrically controlled and in the subject's mind hopefully could be tripped remotely when the conveyor was activated.

The car was parked on the right shoulder of the interstate on-ramp, slightly over a steep embankment, which caused it to lean to the right. After studying the vehicle's location and the built-in conveyor belt and trap door awhile we believed we had figured out what the subject's plan was. He would wait at the bottom of the embankment, trigger the conveyor belt remotely as well as the trap door, and expect the conveyor to send the money through the trap door which would then fall down the embankment where he could retrieve it. He then would remotely fire the pistol, which he thought would ignite the gasoline and burn up the vehicle. He either got scared and left, or his contraption didn't work.

The contents of the trunk were sent to the FBI lab at headquarters. The lab report stated the pistol could be fired remotely but the bullet would not ignite the gasoline and that the conveyor belt and trap door mechanism could have worked if activated.

Even though I didn't do any more work on this investigation I know every possible lead was followed and the subject was never identified.

Chapter 3
San Francisco: Hijacking of PSA Flight 710

Author's note: I am indebted to my colleagues, retired FBI agents Max Noel and Jim Williams, for sharing their memories of this event with me.

"We disappeared on a cloudless day," Inez McDermott would recall over 50 years later. When National Airline Conair 440 vanished from its intended flight path on May 1, 1961, it was considered lost and missing at sea. McDermott was the sole flight attendant for a Marathon, Florida flight bound for Key West that was hijacked to Cuba. Without any security measures in place, the hijacker boarded the plane armed with a knife and a gun that he held on the pilot and co-pilot as they gave in to his demands and rerouted the plane to Havana. Cuban authorities threatened to shoot the plane down but agreed that for the safety of the passengers and crew aboard they finally allowed the plane to land safely in Havana where Cuban police took the hijacker into custody. The passengers and crew onboard were safely returned to Florida. The hijacking was over in a day. The first of its kind in the U.S., where air piracy was not even listed as a crime, the incident sparked an "epidemic" of hijackings that lasted, confounded and terrified passengers, crews, airlines, state and local authorities as well as the Federal Aviation Administration (FAA) and the FBI until 1972—159 hijackings in all—sometimes over 30 a year.

During that 11-year period, no one could agree on a solution to the problem. The FAA argued with the FBI as to which should be in charge of dealing with a hijacking. The Bureau was very leery of other federal agencies encroaching upon its jurisdiction and risking any weakening of the FBI's power. Director J. Edgar Hoover unequivocally insisted that hijacking was air piracy, interstate in nature, and therefore, clearly and solely under the jurisdiction of the FBI. He won the debate.

My first experience with a hijacking involved the infamous DB Cooper. On November 24, 1971, a man registered for his flight as Dan Cooper—and who would go on to become known as DB Cooper—hijacked Northwest Orient Airlines Flight 305, a Boeing 727 aircraft, from Portland, Oregon, bound for Seattle. While in the air he opened his briefcase and displayed to a flight attendant a device he told her was a bomb with which he threatened to blow up the plane if his orders weren't followed. He demanded $200,000 in exchange for the release of all passengers. When the plane landed in Seattle he was given the money and three parachutes and the passengers were released. Cooper then demanded that two pilots and a flight attendant remain on the plane; the aircraft took off, heading in a southern direction.

When the report of the hijacking reached the FBI office in San Francisco the SAC issued an order that 12 agents, one of whom was me, remain in the office, draft a plan of action and be ready to respond at a moment's notice. In bits and pieces we learned that about 45 minutes after the plane left Seattle Cooper sent the flight attendant to the cockpit. He put on one of the parachutes and jumped from the lowered rear stairs of the aircraft, leaving behind his black necktie and the other parachutes.

One of the most distinctive features of the 727 was built-in " air stairs" which opened from the underbelly of the fuselage and could be opened in flight although Boeing never intended for this to happen. No one knew how lowering the stairway in flight would affect the aircraft.

The pilot of flight 305 said they were aware when Cooper lowered the stairs because of the changes in the aircraft's flight characteristics and he made a note of the coordinates which gave a reasonably accurate location of where Cooper parachuted from the plane. The area below was heavily forested terrain, north of Portland. Knowing then that Cooper had jumped from the plane hundreds of miles north of San Francisco we were told to stand down and go home.

An eight-year boy picnicking with his family along the Columbia River in February 1980 found some of the extortion money. A total of $5800 in $20 bills was located and were examined. Serial numbers confirmed they were part of the ransom. An extensive digging operation by FBI agents revealed nothing more.

DB Cooper became a bit of a folk hero as someone who cleverly evaded the law. His actions set off a rash of nine copycat hijackings into 1972. The hijacking of Flight 305 remains the one unsolved air piracy incident in U.S. history. In July 2016 the FBI basically closed the active case file.

The lack of co-operation between law enforcement and the airlines resulted in hijackers running the "Friendly Skies." Several of the early hijackers were Latino and wanted to go to or leave Cuba for political reasons. At a point, there were so many hijackings to Cuba the FBI considered setting up a fake Havana airport thereby tricking hijackers into believing they had arrived in Cuba.

Even from the very beginning, all hijackers were considered armed and dangerous. On March 17, 1970, a hijacker shot First Officer James Hartley as the plane was coming in for a landing in Boston. Hartley later died from the wounds, the first pilot to be killed during a hijacking in the U.S.

On July 5, 1972, Pacific Southwest Airlines flight 710, a Boeing 737 aircraft, departed Sacramento with a crew of five and 81 passengers, destination San Francisco International Airport, a half hour commuter trip. The weather was good, no problems. Stewardesses Linda Heath and Lorraine Adamski were forward; Stewardess Jacquelyn Stallman was in the rear galley.

PSA Aircraft with author's notes

A man in a dark suit stood up, turned his back on the passengers and showed a pistol to Miss Stallman and forced her back behind the partition. The gunman told her he was taking over the plane. He ordered her to pick up the phone to the cockpit and tell the captain they were going to Russia and he needed two parachutes and $800,000. He then told Stewardess Stallman to summon the other two stewardesses to come to the rear and sit down. They walked to the rear of the plane, unable to believe what was happening.

A passenger, Victor Sen Yung, was seated near the galley in an aisle seat. It was later learned that he was the actor who played the Chinese cook Hop Sing on the television series "Bonanza." As the stewardesses went by he turned his head and, from the corner of his eye, saw a man with his hands crossed and an automatic pistol in each hand. One pistol was pointed at the stewardess standing near the galley, the other aimed at the seated stewardesses. Sen Yung realized a hijacking was in progress, turned his head back and looked straight forward. The other passengers were unaware of the threat to their lives.

Dr. Manuel Alvarez of Sacramento was seated across the aisle and two seats forward of Sen Yung. He ordered a soft drink when one of the stewardesses walked by. He couldn't figure out why it was taking so long and asked if something was wrong. No reply. Then he winked at her and half laughed, "Are we being hijacked?" The stewardess nodded "Yes."

Dr. Alvarez wondered why there hadn't been an announcement from the captain, why wasn't anyone alarmed? He took the paper napkin from his drink and wrote a note, "I think we're being hijacked," and passed it to the woman across the aisle. The woman read the note and turned to stare at Dr. Alvarez.

The hijacker holding the stewardess at gunpoint, said quietly to Sen Yung, "Hey you, move across the aisle." He didn't move and when ordered again still didn't. Stewardess Stallman then came up to him and said, "I've been told to tell you to move across the aisle—very slowly." He moved over to the right side, one row forward that put him four rows from the rear and one row from the hijacker holding the stewardess at gunpoint.

In the tower of SFI airline personnel and Federal Aviation Administration officials had received a message from Captain Dennis Waller: There is a hijacker aboard. The flight was cleared for landing. From the tower the message went to the FBI, the San Mateo County

Sheriff's office and the Coast Guard.

In the downtown San Francisco FBI office it was a normal morning. Shortly after 10, SA Max Noel was summoned to his supervisor's office and told about the hijacking. He told Max to take all available firearms instructor agents and appropriate equipment to SFI and await further instructions. He quickly found agents Ed Sauer and Chuck Latting to go with him to the airport to prepare to intercede in the hijacking.

In the meantime a command post had been set up on the fourth floor of the Central Terminal with the FBI, communications men and Pacific Southwest Airlines representatives. Another FBI agent was sent to the tower with the air traffic controllers to monitor traffic between the tower and the hijacked plane.

Agents Noel, Sauer, and Latting headed to the airport with their sniper rifles, portable radios and other assorted gear. When they arrived at the command post they learned the plane had landed at about 10:45 a.m., parking on runway 19 Left. This was a remote location near the San Francisco Bay. The hijackers demanded $800,000, parachutes, various maps and charts and an internationally qualified pilot. In order to buy time and figure out how to stop the hijacking they were told it would take a while to meet these demands

A short time later the plane unexpectedly taxied back onto the runway and took off. It was airborne by 11. The hijacker told the air traffic controller the plane would return to SFI after the money, maps, charts, parachutes and pilot were brought to the airport.

SAC Robert Gebhardt, additional supervisors from the office and several agents were in the command post. Gebhardt dispatched Max, Ed and Chuck to a small radio communications shack between runways 19 Left and 19 Right. This location was a few yards from where the aircraft had parked on runway 19 Left. The agents could monitor the traffic control tower's communications; they also had their hand held portable radios to communicate directly with the FBI command post. A plan was developed for an agent to assume the role of the international pilot and board the plane with the money, parachutes, maps and charts. Max, Ed or Chuck was to be that person. Once the pilot/agent was on board the plane he would attempt to arrest the hijacker and free the flight crew and passengers. The SAC decided that Max Noel would be the pilot impersonator. However, when the plane returned to SFI at approximately 11:45 a.m. it taxied to a different position at the end of runway 19 Left. There was no way the agents could leave the shack without someone on the plane seeing them. They were stuck there. Someone else had to take the role of the international pilot.

That day my partner Hank Gaidis and I were working the Haight-Asbury district looking for military deserters when the radio call went out for all available agents to proceed to SFI and go to the command post in the terminal.

The command post was crowded with 20 to 30 other agents, supervisors and several airport personnel. SAC Gebhardt described the hijacking situation to us. He said he wanted five agents to go to a Coast Guard installation directly across the Bay from where the aircraft would park and stand by. We were told the aircraft had already landed once and taken off again and was still in the air.

Gebhardt told SA Jim Williams, a firearms instructor, to lead the Coast Guard installation team and select four other agents to formulate a plan to thwart the hijacking. It was traditional in the Bureau then to have a firearms instructor lead in a potential shooting incident since there were no FBI SWAT teams in 1972. We learned the hijacker, while talking to the pilot earlier, said he was the only hijacker on the plane. An airline executive was certain that one time he heard the hijacker use the word "we" indicating he had a confederate. We had to be prepared for two men.

Jim Williams chose SAs Kenneth D. Herman, John Reikes, Donald J. Bechtold and me for the team. We drove over to the Coast Guard installation and met the commanding officer and several other CG officers. We discussed what we knew: There were 81 passengers onboard with a crew of five, demands were for the ransom and parachutes, as well as an aircraft and pilot capable of a flight to Siberia. Also, 18 hostages were to remain on the aircraft, the rest of the passengers released, and the hijackers were armed.

Since the hijacker had asked for two parachutes we considered they might have plans—like DB Cooper—to jump from the aircraft in flight, a plan that surprised me since I knew this 737 was not the same sort of aircraft. Any attempt to parachute from a jet of this size and at that altitude would likely end in the loss of everyone on board. It made me wonder exactly who we were dealing with. The hijacker had told the pilot he thought he would be safer in the air, so the plane departed the airport and went into a holding pattern only to land again at 11:45 am. If the aircraft ever got off the ground again the Coast Guard was prepared to furnish chase planes to follow it.

Jim told our team that the SAC, who didn't give him any explanation as to why, had instructed he didn't want the plane to leave the ground. If it did, at least one of us was to be onboard. Negotiations had been ongoing for close to four hours. While, up to that point hijackers' demands had been largely met by the airlines and law enforcement, at that moment we were keenly aware the game had changed. There was going to be a confrontation.

The SAC said Jim would impersonate the international pilot and deliver a package containing the money, parachutes, maps and charts. We jointly formulated a plan for John Reikes to carry a shotgun. The rest of us had our .38 revolvers. If the plane attempted to leave, John's job would be to shoot out the landing gear. He loaded the shotgun with two buckshot and two rifled slugs. The SAC then changed his mind and said he wanted John to return to the airport with Jim to be his driver. Jim told me to take the shotgun and go with Ken and Donald and get under the aircraft as we had planned. We all were equipped with FBI handi-talkies on an FBI frequency, which would handle only the hijacking communications.

Jim Williams had by far the most difficult and dangerous role in the plan. It takes a brave person to agree to impersonate a pilot and face a desperate, armed man who had already broken enough laws to put him in jail for a long time. Plus the hijacker desperately wanted the $800,000 as evidenced by his actions. There was also the likelihood (we figured about 99%) that a second armed hijacker was on the plane, thus doubling the danger that Jim faced. He took the job without hesitation.

The Coast Guard commander said he could transport us across the inlet of the Bay directly behind the aircraft which was, by then, again on the ground. Although the pirated airliner had been taxied to an isolated northern runway in order to not create a panic, it was business as usual at SFI, with flights taking off and landing. The CG commander said we could approach the aircraft from behind the tail and couldn't be seen unless someone stepped out and onto the stairs that had been rolled up to the cabin door.

Jim and John left us and returned to the airport for Jim to don a pilot's uniform for his role. In the meantime we boarded a CG launch. We had changed out of our suits and, unlike SWAT teams today that go into any potentially lethal situation protected with bullet proof vests, goggles, helmets, etc., we put on olive drab CG flight suits with no protection at all. The skipper of the boat circled around far out in the bay and approached the plane from the rear. When we were within 30 yards of the shore the captain told us it was too shallow for him to proceed.

We climbed down a ladder, dropped into the waist deep water, lifted our weapons above our heads and waded toward shore like in a John Wayne war movie. We crossed a berm and climbed over an earthen bank putting us directly behind the plane. We then bent over at the waist to make us as small as we could and moved quickly under the belly of the plane, huddling under the nose gear.

After about 30 minutes we saw a station wagon driving slowly across the tarmac. It stopped about 25 yards in front of the plane as the hijacker directed. Jim, in a dark blue pilot's uniform, exited carrying what appeared to be a duffle bag, a briefcase and two parachutes. We heard the aircraft door above us open. Stewardess Stallman left the plane and approached Jim. Before he could say anything she told him the hijacker had instructed her to tell the pilot to remove his clothing down to his underwear. She said, "You don't look like a flight captain." He told her he was disappointed he didn't look like a pilot but "I'm an FBI agent." Jim realized that she had seen the three agents under the plane when she modestly turned away as he disrobed. We found out later that Jim told her we were agents and to run under the plane when we came out from the nose wheel area.

We watched until Jim was down to his T-shirt and jockey shorts. I was sure Jim had a weapon but didn't know where he had concealed it. We knew the hijacker had earlier said he would kill a passenger if anyone came to the plane armed. Jim got dressed and walked to the bottom of the stairs with Stallman and stopped. We later learned that Jacquelyn told Jim there was a second hijacker at the back of the plane, how they were dressed and what kind of weapons they had. Jim was surprised to learn about the second one. We learned later that the agent stationed in the control tower knew from communication with the pilot that there were two hijackers but for some reason failed to notify the FBI command post.

We then heard a male voice tell Jim to drop the items he was carrying and board the aircraft. Stallman remained on the tarmac where she had stopped. This was about mid-afternoon and the sun was on the side opposite the open door of the plane. I told the others agents we would be able to see Jim's shadow and once he had gone up the stairs and entered the cabin we would go after him. I said to Ken and Donald, "Anyone we see with a weapon, if you can get a clean shot, shoot to kill."

As I predicted we saw Jim's shadow as he stopped on the landing and we heard the same male voice tell him to go to the back of the aircraft. I then gave the signal for us to storm the plane. I was carrying the shotgun in the hip-shooting position. Ken and Donald followed with their pistols. When I got approximately half way up the stairs I could see the first male subject, later identified as Dimitr Alexiev, in a blue blazer standing alongside Jim with a pistol in each hand, pointing one pistol within a foot of Jim's head. Alexiev obviously heard us on the stairs and made a half turn to face us and started to extend his right arm aiming the gun toward me. I expected him to start firing.

For the first time it crossed my mind that I didn't know the exact order in which John had loaded the shotgun. I knew there were two rounds of buckshot and two rounds of slug. Jim was standing very close to Alexiev so if the first round coming out was buckshot I needed to pull a little to my left to keep some of the pellets from hitting him.

A shotgun round of buckshot contains 12 lead pellets each about the size of a pea. As the buckshot comes out the barrel the pellets begin to spread out, the further they travel the wider the pattern becomes. A shotgun slug round contains one solid lead projectile the same diameter as the casing and about 3 inches long.

As Alexiev extended his right arm aiming at me and I moved up the steps, I fired the first round purposefully holding a little left of the subject and away from Jim. Thankfully it was a rifled slug that hit Alexiev in his right shoulder near his armpit, almost a miss. The blast knocked him back against the opposite bulkhead, a distance of over six feet. His feet flew up into the air about waist high as I hit the landing. I then fired a second round, center mass into his body (rear end was all I could see). I proceeded on and briefly checked Alexiev to see if he was incapacitated, which he was. I also had the thought, "What if he had been a crew member since he was wearing that blue blazer with gold buttons?" But on the other hand he pointed a weapon at me and the plan when we boarded the aircraft was that if anyone with a weapon didn't immediately surrender, we would shoot to kill.

Position of second hijacker, Author's notes included

Inside the plane Alexiev had told Jim, "Go to the rear of the plane," at which time Jim turned and saw Michael Azmanoff, the second hijacker, standing at the rear of the cabin holding one automatic pistol in the "raised gun" position. Jim started moving toward the rear and heard my first two shotgun blasts in rapid succession from the front of the plane—the two rounds I fired into Alexiev. Azmanoff started firing at Jim, who ran to the center section, took cover behind some empty seats and fired two shots at Azmanoff from a kneeling position. He yelled, "Everyone get down!"

Max, Ed and Chuck left the radio shack as soon as they saw us move and followed Ken and Donald up the stairs, after first disabling the plane's nose gear. Max checked the guy in front and got his two pistols. The two auto-loading pistols were cocked in a single action firing position but later we learned neither had been fired. Max told me the hijacker was alive, but barely.

I got up on my feet and moved to the partition between the first class and coach sections. I saw the second hijacker, Azmanoff, in the galley area at the back of the aircraft—less than 100 feet away—with a pistol. He stepped out into the aisle from the right hand side and started firing in my direction. I could see Jim kneeling down behind a seat next to the aisle about 4-5 rows from the front. Azmanoff fired two rounds at me, which hit the luggage bins to my right, triggering all the oxygen masks in the plane to drop, a really eerie sight. I took a kneeling position, brought the shotgun up and saw Azmanoff run back into the galley to my left where I couldn't see him. From the top of the last row of seats to the roof of the aircraft there was a panel that blocked my view inside the galley.

I stayed where I was and knew the next two rounds would be buckshot. Knowing the buckshot would spread as it traveled I purposely aimed near the top of the fiberglass panel and knew the rounds would go through it. I fired the shotgun and could see the pattern of the buckshot in the panel and three or four were in the skin of the aircraft's roof, which meant I should lower my aim some. Then I saw an arm holding a pistol come out from the galley area where Azmanoff was hiding. He began firing a semi-automatic pistol blindly in Jim and my direction. I then stood up and fired into the galley partition again but lowered my aim about a foot. I was out of ammunition in the shotgun so I knelt down and reloaded with the .00 buckshot that I had in my pocket. As I was reloading Azmanoff fired five or six additional rounds in our direction exposing only his arm and the pistol.

My plan was to rush to the back of the aircraft and point my shotgun into the galley and fire two rounds. As I was getting up Jim said, "Hold on Corbett" from his position. Jim was still hunkered down behind one of the seats. I looked at him and saw that he had a snub-nose .38 revolver he had hidden in the pocket of his jacket. I paused and Jim ran to the rear where Azmanoff was hidden. I followed a few steps behind Jim. Max, Ken and Donald were right on my heels.

During all this the 81 passengers were crouched down in their seats so I couldn't see them beyond the rows nearest me. They were crying, screaming, and praying. Jim told me later a stewardess, who was standing by him only moments before we stormed the plane, slipped her wedding ring to a passenger to give to her husband should she not survive.

Azmanoff continued firing from a kneeling barricaded position at Jim who heard a third shotgun blast—again me firing—from the front of the plane. Jim turned and saw me in the kneeling position firing the fourth shotgun blast. Jim then charged to the rear of the plane expecting Azmanoff to be in the galley to his left but Azmanoff lunged at him from the right side of the aircraft with a hunting knife. Neither of us had seen him move from left to right in the galley.

Azmanoff caught Jim off guard. He must have made the move while Jim and I were looking at each other and talking. Azmanoff attacked Jim with the knife cutting the sleeve of his coat. Jim fired three shots into Azmanoff at point-blank range. Azmanoff stood erect and Jim struck him on the skull twice with his revolver causing him to fall backwards into the corner, dropping his knife. He hit Azmanoff so hard with his revolver that it bent the trigger guard making it inoperable.

Max and Ken reached the back of the aircraft while the subject was groaning and attempting to reach his pistol on the floor. Jim took Ken's revolver and fired two additional rounds into Azmanoff's head. He collapsed on the floor ending the lives of both hijackers and the hijacking attempt.

The plane was extremely quiet. Jim calmly walked back to the middle of the cabin, raised his hands over his head and announced in a loud voice, "My name is R. James Williams. I am an FBI agent and the sons of bitches are dead!" Pandemonium broke out.

After making certain Azmanoff was dead I went back to the front of the aircraft. I searched Alexiev and found a small piece of folded paper with words and numbers written on it that I recognized as map coordinates. I called this information into the SAC.

We started checking the panicked and terrified passengers. The scene was complete bedlam. We discovered a middle-aged male had been shot in the back and was lifeless. He was later identified as retired Canadian Pacific Railway conductor Stanley Carter. When he retired, Carter and his wife, Lillian, had sold most of their possessions in Montreal and had planned to find a new home in California. Witnesses stated he stood up one of the times Azmanoff was firing from the rear. His wife had tried to pull him back into his seat but it was too late. He was fatally wounded and pronounced dead later at a local hospital. I had noticed during the shooting that Azmanoff was tilting the barrel of his pistol downward, not level, and shooting into and above the seats. One of these shots must have hit Carter.

We found the Bonanza cook Victor Sen Yung also shot in the back but alive. One of Azmanoff's rounds went through a metal strip running the length of the back of the seat slowing the bullet down that hit Yung. He was rushed to the hospital where he was treated for the gunshot wound and recovered.

Another passenger, Lee Robert Gromley, of Van Nuys, California, was shot through the neck. He was also treated at the hospital and released.

With the battle now over and it was safe to move about the two stewardesses on board along with the captain and co-pilot began to help the uninjured, though still panic-stricken, passengers off the portable steps and the emergency chutes diverting them away from seeing the bodies of Alexiev and Azmanoff.

Six hours and 30 minutes after PSA flight 710 departed Sacramento the hijacking attempt was over.

Later when the dust had settled I replayed in my mind what had happened during the short 6 to 10 minutes from the time we left the nose wheel area and charged up the stairway. I shuddered to think what would have happened if I had missed the first shot. Alexiev would have undoubtedly cut us all down on the stairs. Lucky shot, I guess, but I also attribute it to the effectiveness of the Bureau's firearms training program and instructors.

Alexiev and Azmanoff's suitcases, that were stored in the overhead bins, held rope, several rolls of duct tape, thirty pairs of flex cuffs and many 3" sterile cotton strips. We surmised they planned to fly the hijacked aircraft to a deserted field, tie and gag the hostages and leave them in the plane. That would have been a frightening and traumatic experience.

Dimitr Alexiev and Michael Azmanoff came to the U.S. as Bulgarian refugees in the late 1960s. They entered the U.S., sponsored by the World Council of Churches political refugees program, first living in New Jersey before moving to Sacramento. Both did stints in the U.S. Army. Alexiev married a single mother with three children. One of his neighbors described him as friendly but "not out-going at all." Alexiev had recently purchased his own cab company but had complained on July 3, 1972 "business was slow." It seems that they decided to augment their income with a spot of air piracy.

There was some discussion in the media afterwards that the FBI was responsible for the shooting of the passengers. We knew we had not fired these rounds since they came from the rear. Later examination by the FBI laboratory matched these rounds to the semi-automatic fired by Azmanoff.

A further search of the aircraft revealed the subjects had packed and carried on two inflatable balloons that would look lifelike when inflated. Speculation was that at some point they intended to inflate these objects and throw them from the plane to make it appear they had bailed out.

During an interview with the *San Francisco Examiner* and other media outlets, SAC Gebhardt said that the decision to storm the plane was made when, after four intense hours of negotiations with the hijackers, Alexiev refused to budge on *not* taking 18 hostages with him to Siberia.

In the same issue of the *San Francisco Examiner*, PSA President J. Floyd Andrews conceded to the press that "substantial amounts of tax dollars must be diverted" to prevent future air piracies. "Airlines are not a police force and do not have the capabilities, the knowledge or the wherewithal to act as an enforcement bureau to take care of criminals in any guise. Airline operators, like popcorn stand operators, are not law enforcement officers and never will be."

Using the map coordinates, SA William Stringer discovered the hijackers didn't intend to fly to Siberia but actually planned to have the plane land on a remote landing strip in British Columbia at the exact coordinates on the piece of paper. The coordinate's latitude north 52 degrees, seven minutes, longitude 124 degrees, ten minutes were the location of an airport in the Puntzi Mountains, a remote area of British Columbia, Canada. It had a runway of over 6,000 feet in length, capable of handling a commercial jet aircraft. The military had abandoned the airstrip, now used only for forest fire fighting air tankers.

The FBI gave the coordinates to the Royal Canadian Mounted Police. Within days the RCMP found that a pilot from Campbell River, British Columbia flew a man using the name Cuzzi from Campbell River to the Puntzi Airstrip on July 5, the same day as the hijacking. Cuzzi chartered the plane under the guise of searching for real estate to develop although the pilot reported to the RCMP Cuzzi showed no interest in real estate during the flight. On July 6, Cuzzi awoke the pilot and insisted they return immediately to Campbell River, which they did.

The RCMP discovered the true identity of Cuzzi to be Lubomir Peichev. On July 12, seven days following the attempted hijacking, Peichev was arrested at his job in Oakland, California. He was charged with aiding and abetting air piracy, conspiracy to commit extortion and conspiracy to commit air piracy.

When an article with details of Peichev's arrest was published in the *Vancouver Sun Daily* on July 13, the RCMP received a phone call from an employee of the Dollar-A-Day (car) Rental System. The woman said she recognized Peichev from his picture in the paper but told the RCMP that another individual, not Peichev, returned the rented vehicle on July 6. This information led to the arrest of a second individual, Illia Kelov Shishkoff who professed his innocence at being involved in any sort of plane hijacking. Shishkoff said he took the car back only because his long time friend Azmanoff asked him to. He admitted he was aware that Alexiev, Azmanoff and Peichev were involved in some kind of illegal activity but it didn't occur to him that it was a hijacking until Peichev told him on July 6.

Shishkoff was subsequently released but Peichev went on to stand trial for his part in the hijacking. He was found guilty as charged and sentenced to life in prison.

After the hijacking was over my mind was at ease because I believed the two hijackers would have killed all of us who boarded the plane if we hadn't taken them out first. When we critiqued the incident there was a lot of speculation whether the shoot out would be any deterrent to future would be hijackers. The next day, July 7, we had our answer. There were two attempted hijackings that day; on another flight in California, the other in Buffalo, New York. Both hijackers surrendered when reminded of the fate of the Bulgarians. The shootout with the hijackers of PSA flight 710 became and remains a pivotal moment in history. There were 82 hijackings in 1969 and only four in 1973.

After we all finished our reports the SAC instructed me to take the rounds that struck the hijackers and passengers to Washington, D. C. to the FBI lab. All the rounds that hit the passengers were fired from Azmanoff's pistol. I met the then director of the FBI L. Patrick Gray and assistant director Charlie Bates who was formerly the SAC in San Francisco. Later we reenacted the event in a different 737. It was filmed and the film, along with our account, was sent to Quantico to be used as a training exercise.

The whole incident from Jim climbing the stairs to the end of the shooting probably only lasted three to four minutes. I felt like it was half-a-day. I attribute our success in the shoot-out to the extensive and continuing firearms training we received.

It has been more than 40 years from this writing since this incident occurred but I remember it as clearly as if it were yesterday. And I know, here, in my heart and mind, that Jim and I made a contribution to help change the course of history concerning air piracy. Our actions aided in bringing to an end the "epidemic" of hijackings that had plagued the United States for over ten years.

Jim Williams reenacting the hijacking for training purposes

Chapter 4
Ruthless Kentucky Gamblers

In the fall of 1973 the Bureau issued an alert to all offices of a nationwide bank extortion scheme. A male would call the manager of a bank branch telling him that he and his partners had the banker's wife and children held hostage and demand a ransom in the range of $200,000 to $300,000. The caller always knew the wife and children's names and their approximate age. He'd make threats like, "You wouldn't want to see them on slabs in the morgue, would you?"

At about 1 p.m. on December 12 my partner Burl Smith and I were driving back to the office down Union Avenue, a major east-west artery, from a meeting in East Memphis. The FBI dispatcher sent out a call to all agents to landline the office. Details of a case were rarely sent over the radio since anyone could buy a scanner and listen. When I called from a pay phone I learned an extortion demand had been made to Paul Calame, the manager of the Union Avenue branch of Memphis Bank & Trust. We happened to be only a few blocks away, made a U-turn and headed there.

The first information was that Calame was to make the drop of the money at 3:05 p.m. Before we could get to the bank another urgent message to call the office came in. I called and learned the drop was set for an hour earlier, 2:05 p.m. on Rembert Street, a side street just south of Union Avenue close to the bank. The instructions to Calame were to place a briefcase full of cash on the front seat of his car, drive it to Rembert, park on the west side about 25 yards from Union leaving the parking lights on, and walk back to the bank.

Burl and I happened to know Calame by sight since he was one of the bankers we had met with a few months earlier to alert him of the possibility of an extortion attempt. So when we got near the intersection of Union and Rembert we recognized him walking on Union toward the bank.

Burl parked in the front lot of an office building on the southeast corner of Union and Rembert and stayed in the car so he could watch the "drop" car and maintain radio contact with the office while I ran into the building. I had the idea I might be able to conceal myself in the rear of the offices and see the drop.

I rushed into the office area holding up my credentials and yelled, "FBI. Is there a back door?" The employees were surprised and alarmed but several pointed to a corridor and said, "Right down there." I ran down the hallway to the door that had glass on the top half. I could see Calame's car from my position.

After a few minutes I saw a white male walking from the south, across the street from the car. He was constantly looking around. Just before he neared the car he crossed the street diagonally toward it. I watched him until he opened the driver's side door. I took off at a run, partially hidden by some bushes. He never saw me coming. When I opened the car door he was opening the briefcase. I pulled him out, identified myself and spun him around with the order, "Put your hands on the roof of the car and don't move."

By then Burl was right behind me. He kept his eye on the subject while I patted him down. The only thing I found was a walkie-talkie. We later learned it was tuned to the Memphis Police Department and the Shelby County Sheriff Office dispatches. The extortionists were known to monitor these frequencies. We handcuffed the subject, arrested him for bank extortion and put him in the back of the Bureau car. Then we looked at each other and smiled. I said, "You know who we have here don't you?" Burl replied, "Yes, it's one of the two subjects who have extorted more than ten banks around the country for hundreds of thousands of dollars."

Later the Memphis SAC Ted Gunderson told the press, "It happened so fast. We got the call, dispatched men to the scene and picked the man up within about 15 minutes after we received the call from the bank." That was true. It was probably the fastest Burl and I ever solved a case although there was still more work and another subject out there.

We could find no identification on our prisoner and he refused to give his name. We said, "Okay. We understand members of Paul Calame's family are being held hostage and won't be released until he receives a call saying they are all right. Where are they?" He replied, "There are no hostages, no one is in danger." No matter how many times we asked him that was his only answer.

Burl and I took the unknown man to our office to fingerprint and book him for attempted bank robbery and extortion. While we were in the elevator of the Federal Building riding up to the eighth floor I noticed something odd about the prisoner's hair. I reached over, took hold of the hair on top of his head and pulled a black wig off him. He didn't say anything, just smiled. He was a young man, nattily dressed in a sporty checked knit jacket and black turtleneck.

We put the subject in an interview room, still handcuffed, with another agent. Paul Calame had been reunited with his family and was at his home being taken step by step through his ordeal by other agents.

Burl and I went back to the subject and told him he might as well tell us his name since we were next going to fingerprint him and send a copy to the FBI Identification Division. If he had ever been fingerprinted for anything a match would be made and his identity known. He finally gave up and said his name was Larry Clinton Nein (pronounced "nine") and gave his date of birth. Nein's name and date of birth checked out as true. He also had a criminal record.

Nein agreed to waive his right to an attorney and told us he was on Rembert Street in the victim's car at the direction of a person named Jack Carter. He said he met Carter in Cincinnati about six months before and Carter told him he would eventually have a chance to make a lot of money. Carter called him in Bowling Green, Kentucky about two weeks earlier and told him to meet him in Memphis today.

He met Carter at about 10 this morning on Elvis Presley Blvd. south of the Elvis Presley mansion. Carter instructed him to go to the area of Union Avenue and Rembert Street. After he received a signal by a clicking code on his police radio monitor he should then proceed to a 1973 Dodge which would be parked on Rembert with the parking lights on and the key in the ignition.

Nein said he had waited in the area for almost 1½ hours and finally received the signal code. He went to the vehicle and got inside and was arrested. Carter had told him he was to drive the Dodge to the Holiday Inn on the south side of Memphis where they would divide up the money. He refused to say where he had been staying in Memphis or the location of his car, a yellow 1973 Cadillac, Kentucky license Y28-347.

We had a subject in custody who fit the profile of the bank extortionist other offices were actively investigating. Dallas, Chicago, Cleveland, Denver, Detroit, Indianapolis, Little Rock, Louisville, Milwaukee, Mobile, Norfolk, Oklahoma City, St. Louis and Springfield IL. had open cases. We were the first office to identify and arrest one of the extortionists so many agents were searching for. By late afternoon I had sent out a Teletype to these offices with the details of Nein's arrest.

Early the next morning agents spread out and canvassed Memphis motels for a guest named Larry Clinton Nein. He was registered at the Scottish Inn in south Memphis from December 7 to 12, 1973, having checked out the day of the crime. He listed the Cadillac on his registration and his employment as "Associates Photographers." The desk clerk told SA Ray Phelps that another guest, L. J. Petersimes, from Nashville, Tennessee, had registered at the same time as Nein and the two had been seen together and checked out at the same time, 10:48 a.m. on December 12. This was the first evidence uncovered connecting Nein and Petersimes.

That same morning I contacted an agent in our Bowling Green, Kentucky RA in an attempt to locate Nein's vehicle. A couple of hours later the agent called me back. An agent found Leonard Jerome Petersimes driving the Cadillac and Nein's wife with him. He admitted being in Memphis with Nein and checking out of the motel with him but denied any knowledge of what Nein did after that. At this point we were convinced that Petersimes was Nein's partner in the Memphis crime but didn't have enough to arrest him.

Also on the morning of December 13 the Memphis office, in what was an amazing coincidence, received what came to be called the "Pond Tape" from the Dallas office. It was a recorded conversation of an extortion call made to Douglas Pond, president of Citizens State Bank, Richardson, Texas, dated nearly a year before on December 29, 1972. Burl and I were eager to listen to it and immediately recognized the caller's voice as Nein's, having spent many hours talking to him the previous day, and the extortion plan was identical to the one used in Memphis.

What follows is a transcript of a portion of the Pond Tape. C is caller and P is the banker Douglas Pond. The telephone conversation itself is chilling enough with the words on paper. Hearing Nein's voice is frightening and it is easy to imagine how an unsuspecting banker would agree to carry out his orders. He spoke in a harsh and sometimes loud voice. The tone was threatening as he told what would happen to the banker's family if he did not to follow the instructions. The victim had no idea if the caller would make good on his threats which I think is why the extortionists were successful most of the time.

C: I want you to know what is going to happen to Mary Lou. I want you to stay calm and relax. Pretend this is a business telephone call. Nothing is going to happen if you do exactly what I tell you. I'm going to tell you a few things right off the bat. I want you to get them into your mind and keep them in your mind. If you make any move to notify the guard or anything like that I want to tell you that you are going to have a big explosion in the bank. We have a remote control to set off the bomb. If you do what I tell you nothing is going to happen to anybody. No one is going to get hurt and Mary Lou will be safe. But if you don't do what I tell you to do I will make an example out of you and the Dallas and Fort Worth newspapers will tell how you didn't do what I told you to do and the next time I call someone and tell them what to do they will do it. Now listen, I want you to answer me in "No sir" and "Yes sir." I don't want you to write anything. I don't want you to act worried, just pretend this is a business telephone call. Now if anyone tries to make a telephone call, trip a burglar alarm, anything like that, any phone calls coming out of the bank, we'll know. We have got the phones tapped. You go along and do exactly what I tell you, do you understand?

P: Yes sir.

C: what we are going to do is a professional manner. You are a professional business man in your business and we are professionals in ours. You stick to your word and we will stick to our word. If you do exactly what I tell you nobody gets hurt. Do you understand?

P: Yes sir.

C: Okay. Now this is exactly what I want you to do. I want you to make an excuse to whoever you need to make an excuse to tell them you have to leave the bank for about half an hour, tell them you will be back before closing time. Now I want you to take a briefcase and I want you to go into the vault and grab the money, all 20s, 100s, 50s and 10s, all the money that is banded or that has rubber bands around it, put it into the briefcase, no ones or fives. If you are stopped by a guard or anyone who says, 'Where are you going?' or anything like that just relax. I can tell you are nervous, just relax, nothing is going to happen. If anyone stops you or tries to call the police while you're gone I guarantee you we will set that micro switch off and there are going to be a lot of f-u-c-k-i-n-g people hurt and just imagine what is going to happen to Mary. I want you, you have a Cadillac, right? Answer me.

P: Yes sir.

C: I want you to go out to your car right now, this very very important and listen and listen very good. I want you to go out to you Cadillac, get in it and before you start it flash the lights three times, on and off, on and off, on and off. Do you understand that it's very important?

P: You are giving a lot. There is no way I can remember all this.

C: You can remember it all now you just keep your mouth shut. I'm not going to stay on the telephone all day. I'm trying to be a gentleman about this and do this in a business like manner. Now if you don't want to do it that way we can make an example of you and the next time they will do what we are telling them to do. Do you understand?

P: Yes sir.

C: Now if you want to go down to the fucking morgue and take a look at your wife and not go to the football game and all that shit then you just keep fucking up and play the hero.

P: I don't plan to, I'm just worried.

C: Listen to me. You don't have to remember. You are a professional business man, it is your job to remember things.

The caller then tells him again to go out to his Cadillac and blink the lights three times. If he doesn't the whole thing goes boom and Mary

Lou will be dead. He tells Pond where to leave his car and names the street.

C: Leave the keys in the car, that is very important, and I want you to turn the parking lights on, just the parking lights, not the headlights. Do you understand?

P: Yes sir.

C: Okay, now you park the car there, you leave the parking lights on and the briefcase with the money on the front seat.

Caller then tells Pond to walk back to the bank and is specific about what side of the street to walk on. When he gets back to the bank he is to wait 45 minutes and then he can call the police department. He will get a call from his wife at 6:15 pm. For some reason in this case the money was never taken from the Cadillac.

After Burl and I listened to the tape we played it for the banker, Paul Calame, who identified the voice as being the same as the unknown extortionist who called him at the bank the day before. He said, "He (Nein) sounded like a TV announcer." We learned later Nein actually was a former radio announcer.

Since the tape had arrived in the U.S. Mail the Dallas office didn't know of our identification and arrest of Nein when it was mailed. But with the information from the Teletype the Dallas office authorized a complaint and warrant to be issued the previous day charging Nein with the attempt to extort funds from Douglas Pond on December 29, 1972. In less than 10 hours Nein had been charged in two bank extortion attempts and more were to come.

Investigators in Nashville and Louisville developed background information on Leonard Jerome Petersimes. Toll records revealed Nein's wife, Brenda, received a telephone call from Petersimes on December 12, 1973, between 5 and 6 p.m. Later that night she met him in Elizabethtown, Kentucky and he was driving a 1973 yellow Cadillac.

The wife's sister told investigators that Petersimes told Brenda Nein that her husband "was in a big jam in Memphis."

We found that Nein and Petersimes usually registered in a motel in the vicinity of the victim bank using their true names and license numbers. Both suspects had Cadillacs equipped with sophisticated police scanners. They monitored police frequencies and if they heard any broadcast indicating police activity in the area of the victim bank they would abandon picking up the extortion money.

A complaint and warrant was issued in Chicago on December 20, 1973 charging Nein and Petersimes with robbery by intimidation of $100,000 from Leroy Michael Corradino of Oak Lawn Trust and Savings Bank on June 15, 1973. Petersimes was arrested in Memphis two days later on these charges. Nein was already in custody on a $50,000 bond.

Since it was the first office to experience a similar bank extortion, the Chicago office coordinated a master list charting the movements of Nein and Petersimes developed through an exhaustive and thorough review of telephone toll records and credit card purchases made by the subjects.

This investigation disclosed that after almost every successful extortion in which they were suspects, Nein and Petersimes immediately went to Las Vegas. They were frequent gamblers and often heavy losers.

One day I was thinking about the information we had and the multiple jurisdictions involved. I listened to the "Pond Tape" again and tried to think of a way we could use this tape in the other cases. We often did what we called "six pack" photo line-ups. We would assemble five photos of persons similar in appearance, age and race of the subject along with the subject's photo. Then we would take the "six pack" to an eyewitness to a crime and ask him or her to look over the photos to see if they had recognized anyone, with the caution that the subject may or may not be included in the group of photos.

I thought, "Why couldn't a similar technique be used to identify voices?" I talked to AUSA Dan Clancy about obtaining voice exemplars from Nein and Petersimes to be played to victim bankers and their wives for possible voice identification and corroboration of the caller. This would require a court order. Dan liked the idea and got a court order requiring the suspects to furnish voice exemplars.

The subjects' voices were then recorded using a script prepared from the "Pond Tape." We recorded the voices of five agents with speech similar to Nein and Petersimes reading the same script for elimination purposes.

The FBI Lab made copies of the recordings for the various offices involved in similar extortion or extortion attempts. I sent these two recordings to these offices and asked them to play them for their victims and witnesses. They were told that six voices would repeat the same conversation on the 11 minute tape. The listener would sit in a chair facing away from the tape recorder. As each voice was played it was numbered 1-6. If the listener recognized a voice he/she was to write the number of that voice on a piece of paper. The tape could be played as many times as needed.

This innovation worked and numerous positive voice identifications were made of the two extortionists.

In a recently published FBI history of the Memphis office, prepared by FBI headquarters, the Nein and Petersimes case was cited. Not all the facts are correct but it is an acknowledgement of what we did:

"In the 1970s, Memphis also worked a case that would be significant for its innovations in voice identification and corroboration---and the first use of these techniques in federal court. The investigation centered on professional bank extortionists Larry Nein and Leonard Pertersimes who had extorted over $500,000 in 20 schemes across the nation. Their luck ran out in Memphis in 1976 (sic) when they threatened to bring harm to a banker's family and bomb his bank. Quick-acting agents caught the pair retrieving a $100,000 payoff from the banker.

"Voice identification nailed the extortionists by identifying them as the source of the threats." FBI Headquarters noted that the techniques applied would promptly solve 30 similar pending cases and countless more in the future."

One of the telephone numbers Nein and Petersimes frequently called was a Nashville number of a popular country and western star. At a later date Burl and I drove to Nashville, unannounced, to interview the star and his wife.

The husband was on the road but the wife was home and agreed to talk to us. She admitted knowing the suspects but denied knowing anything about their criminal acts. We told her the FBI had charged them with extorting hundreds of thousands dollars from banks across the country.

She told us that once when Nein and Petersimes were visiting she was cleaning their bedroom and opened a closet door. She saw a large canvas bag, which was open at the top, containing cash. She left the room and never let her husband know what she found. She admitted she was reluctant to tell us this. She didn't want to be a witness against Nein and Petersimes. We never did figure out how the star and his wife became acquainted with the criminals.

Only Nein was initially charged in Memphis although Petersimes was indicted later. Over my objections the U. S. Attorney chose to try Nein alone first. I wanted them tried together so we could charge them with conspiracy and more evidence could be introduced. I was outvoted by the prosecutors since there was a chance once Nein was convicted he would roll over on Petersimes who would then enter a guilty plea. There was no discussion about the possibility of Nein being acquitted since the prosecutors believed it was a "slam dunk" case.

So the trial began. Both Burl and I testified as to the events related in this story, as did Calame. I wish we had had a tape recording of the extortion threats but we didn't.

Nein took the stand and told the jury of eight women and four men a new story. He said in December 1973 he was a tourist in Memphis, came upon this car with its lights on, got in to turn off the lights and the next thing he knew this guy accosted him, pulled him out of the car and arrested him. This was not the Jack Carter story he told Burl and me.

As much as I would like to predict with certainty what a jury will do, I can't. When this jury came back with a verdict of "not guilty" you could have knocked me over with a feather. I believe AUSA Dan Clancy and the judge felt the same.

But Nein was not set free after the verdict. The U. S. Marshal took him to federal court in Chicago to be tried with his co-defendant Petersimes on the Chicago Oak Lawn Bank charges. The jury found them both guilty of bank robbery and bank larceny on September 18, 1974 but acquitted them on Hobbs Act extortion. Nein almost got away with this crime. Like the other extortions there was little if any physical evidence to speak of and no eyewitnesses of the pickup of the car. Except at the trial a 13-year old boy named Michael Gilhooley came forward and testified. He said he saw a man he identified as Nein driving away from what turned out to be the pickup spot. A ball bounced toward Nein's car who then got out and threw the ball back to the boy. Michael identified Nein. The voice exemplars of Nein and Petersimes also figured prominently in these convictions. Nein, then age 29, received a 12-year sentence and Petersimes, age 38, got 10 years.

After the Chicago sentences both subjects, through their attorneys, offered to waive any appeal rights on the Chicago convictions if allowed to plead guilty under provisions of Rule 20 (a rule that allows negotiated pleas on crimes in other federal jurisdictions) to outstanding indictments against Petersimes in Memphis and Nein in Richardson, Texas, and four other indictments in which they were jointly charged. All the prosecutors involved agreed to the plea bargain.

When I was researching these criminals for this story I found Nein was incarcerated in the Terre Haute (Indiana) Federal Correctional Complex for an unknown offense in 2010. He would have been released from his sentence in Chicago long before then and the plea deal he made would have taken care of five other extortion charges. It could be that convictions in other trials on bank extortions caused him to remain in prison continuously since 1974 but I doubt it.

Nein was the victim of a stabbing at the Indiana prison. The offender, Adam Orr, told prison officials that Nein had called him "a snitch and a liar" and "a rat." Orr said that all he had in prison was his name. When asked how many times he stabbed Nein he replied, "Apparently not enough." Nein suffered over 20 lacerations and stab wounds, a collapsed lung, rib and face fractures, and a possible kidney laceration but survived the attack.

Chapter 5
The Bank Robber & His Sleazy, Crooked Attorneys

Two white males went into a branch of the Memphis Bank & Trust mid-afternoon on February 11, 1974 with handkerchiefs taped to their faces with Band-Aids of all things, brandished pistols and announced, "This is a robbery." One of the robbers went behind the tellers' windows and emptied all the cash from the drawers while the customers and bank employees huddled on the floor, having been threatened with their lives if they moved. Burl Smith and I sped over there when we got the call that a bank robbery was in progress but the excitement was over. No witness saw a getaway car and the robbers escaped in an unknown direction.

Later that afternoon back at the office we studied the photos from the bank surveillance cameras. There were good shots of the robbers, both in their mid-20s, no facial hair, dressed in blue jeans and blue work shirts. In one photo, a face was clearly visible. His handkerchief had blown up revealing his features from the nose down. After a couple of minutes I said,

"Damn it, Burl, I think I know this guy, look at his Adam's apple."

"I do too. Burl said, It's James Douglas Gardner."

We both were well acquainted with Gardner having interviewed him on several previous occasions. He had a large distinctive Adam's apple just like the person in the surveillance photograph. He also generally fit the description we had. But we thought Gardner was in state custody on several robbery charges.

Gardner had been arrested and held in the Shelby County jail on several state charges of armed robbery and related offenses in July, 1973. He posted $7500 bond and was released from custody. Then he failed to appear in the Criminal Court to answer to the armed robbery charges. A fugitive warrant was issued and on November 19, 1973 Gardner was arrested and returned to the jail. He had ten indictments pending against him including armed robbery, his specialty.

Unknown to us, a few weeks before the current robbery, Harry U. Scruggs Sr. and Harry U. Scruggs Jr., Memphis attorney father-son combo, contacted Gardner in the Shelby County Jail to make arrangements to represent him on the state charges he faced.

The Scruggs, Senior and Junior, didn't know Gardner but his mother was a hostess at a restaurant they frequented and she insisted they contact him. Scruggs Jr., on Gardner's behalf, contacted the Shelby County Pretrial Release Program, and on January 31,1974, Gardner's original $7500 bond was reinstated and Gardner was released from jail on posting $1 additional bond.

Now that we knew the robber was no doubt Gardner, I got an arrest warrant charging him with violation of United States bank robbery statutes. Warrant in hand, Burl and I began looking for Gardner at his mother's house and other family and friends' residences. The people we talked to said they had not seen Gardner since his release from jail. We made spot checks at his mother's home when we had the time.

Four days after the bank robbery, on the late afternoon of February 15 we watched his mother's house and saw a vehicle turn into the driveway. Gardner got out of the car and walked into the house. We waited a few minutes and knocked on the door and Mrs. Gardner opened it. She knew who we were since we had talked to her several times in the last few days. Immediately she said, "He's not here and I haven't seen him since the last time you were here." I then explained the federal harboring laws that could put her in prison for lying to protect her son.

In a few minutes Gardner came into the living room from some other part of the house and told us to come on in. "Well, you know we have an arrest warrant charging you with federal bank robbery," I said. "I know I have the right to have an attorney but I don't know anything about a robbery." "Mrs. Gardner, will you sign a "consent to search" allowing us to search your house?" I asked. "Absolutely no!" she said. Gardner spoke up, "Mom, we got nothing to hide and if you refuse to sign the consent form they will just go and get a search warrant." She then signed the form.

I had already let the MPD robbery section know we hoped to search the house so two officers arrived shortly. One was Detective Ralph Roby who had been working with us on the bank robbery since it occurred. Burl watched the prisoner while the three of us searched. Ralph and his partner searched the attic and I went over the downstairs. I knew the attic would be covered with blown-in fiberglass insulation so had no argument with their going up there.

After about 30 minutes I heard a shout "Eureka!" Both officers hurried down the attic stairs, one carrying a cheap vinyl briefcase he had found hidden in the loose insulation. The briefcase was full of a large amount of US currency, some banded with Memphis Bank & Trust labels. Gardner's jaw dropped and he had a scared look on his face. We placed him under arrest and took him to the FBI office. By this time it was nearly 6 pm.

We told Gardner that with the evidence we had he would surely be convicted for the bank robbery. He denied any part in the robbery and asked to speak with his attorney Scruggs Jr. I called Scruggs Jr. and told him that we had James Douglas Gardner under arrest for robbing the

Memphis Bank and Trust on February 11, 1974. I put Gardner on the phone to talk to Scruggs. When he hung up he said, "My attorney says I shouldn't talk to you guys." We took him to the Shelby County Jail and booked him on federal bank robbery charges with a hold for the FBI.

On February 19 Gardner had an initial hearing on the bank robbery charges before a Federal magistrate. Scruggs Sr. appeared with Gardner but only to tell the court that he wouldn't be representing Gardner on the federal charges. The magistrate appointed a local attorney, Bruce Kramer, as Gardner's attorney.

On February 22 Bruce Kramer, with his client's permission, called the office and said he wanted to talk with Burl and me. Gardner had admitted his role in the robbery to Kramer and described in detail what had taken place.

When Kramer pressed Gardner about what had become of the cash, Gardner told him he paid the Scruggs their fees in cash from the robbery on February 11. In the late afternoon of the day of the robbery, he called the Scruggs at their law office and said he had some money for them. Gardner owed the attorneys about $6000 to represent him on the pending state charges. He went to their office around 5:30 with his brown briefcase containing the robbery proceeds. He was ushered into their law library where, in the presence of both attorneys, he counted out $5000 in cash from the briefcase. Needless to say Gardner didn't tell them the money was from a bank robbery earlier that day.

After counting the money Scruggs Jr. wrote Gardner a receipt in the amount of $6000 from one of the standard receipt books the attorneys used in their law practice. Gardner then left the office with the receipt.

The next day, February 12, one of the attorneys called Gardner and told him that when they had counted the money after he left they found that he had given them only $5000. I don't know for sure but I suspect Gardner just made an honest mistake. Gardner returned to the attorneys' office where he gave Senior ten $100 bills to make up the discrepancy. Senior gave him another receipt in the amount of $1000 from the same standard receipt book.

On Friday morning February 15, the same day we arrested Gardner, Senior appeared in the Shelby County Criminal Court with Gardner to obtain a continuance of the pending matters. Neither Scruggs was willing to tell the court that he was officially representing Gardner (called "signing the jacket") until he was paid the full $10,000, a common practice in criminal cases. Later that morning Gardner went by the Scruggs' law office. As he was leaving the office Senior approached him and asked him to return the receipts they had given him on February 11 and 12, and he did.

Attorney Bruce Kramer told us that Gardner's account of the payments to the Scruggs deeply disturbed him. Unsure whether to believe Gardner and uncertain about what to do with the information he had concerning the proceeds of the bank robbery, he had consulted a senior member of his law firm. Based on that discussion, Kramer called Scruggs Junior on February 21, and told him what Gardner had said about the two cash payments to them totaling $6000. "That story is bullshit. There's nothing to it," Junior said.

Kramer met again with Gardner and told him Junior had denied receiving any money from him. Gardner insisted he was telling the truth. He said that Jerry Harris, an attorney who had represented Gardner on the state charges before Team Scruggs took over the case, could verify his story. Harris told Kramer that Gardner had told him the same thing: Gardner had used the bank robbery proceeds to pay his account with Scruggs.

It was after his conversation with Harris that Kramer decided to talk with his client and obtain his permission to meet with us.

After Kramer left I went to my supervisor, Assistant Special Agent in Charge (ASAC) Dick Blay. and told him about my conversation with Kramer. I said I was going to investigate the Scruggs in an attempt to charge them for knowingly possessing and concealing money that had been stolen from a federally insured bank. He said he didn't believe I would be able to make the charge stick. He bet me a steak dinner that I couldn't get them indicted. This was a challenge I didn't intend to lose.

With the ASAC's tacit permission I made an appointment to talk to both Scruggs, that same day, February 22. Later that afternoon Burl and I interviewed them at their law office. I had never met either of them before. Junior was around 50 years old, a short man, somewhat overweight with his belly hanging over his belt. He was clean-shaven with thinning wavy hair in a strange unnatural shade of red. He made an attempt at dressing well but the overall impression was "sloppy." His father was an older version of Junior although better dressed and with white hair. Junior seemed somewhat "oily" to me; Senior was the gentleman of the two.

As if on cue both of them denied having any knowledge that Gardner was involved in a bank robbery until reading about it in the Commercial Appeal on February 16. I reminded Junior that on the 15th I had told him we had arrested Gardner for robbery of the Memphis Bank & Trust, also that he had talked to Gardner in my presence, and told him he'd been arrested for bank robbery. Junior made no reply to my comment. We told them that we had information that Gardner had made two large cash payments to them on the 11th and 12th of February right after the bank robbery. They both denied this without blinking an eye. They said that just this very morning Gardner had secured the payment of their $10,000 fee by signing a promissory note with his mother as co-signer.

When we asked to see their receipt books, Junior produced a book containing the carbon copies of all the receipts written during the course of their practice for part of 1973 and all of 1974 to date. It was a large bound book with three receipts per page. A permanent yellow carbon of each receipt page remained in the book after the receipts were torn out. I turned the pages in the book to the month of February 1974. The last receipt on one page was dated February 10, 1974 and the first receipt on the next page was dated February 16, 1974. The carbon copies for February 11 and 12 were missing. I took the book in my hands and turned the spine up so I could see the section between February 11 and February 16. It was obvious to me that two pages of the carbon copies had been cut or torn out of the book in the gap between the 11th and 16th of February, leaving only the ends of the pages where they had been bound into the book. I brought this to their attention and Junior explained that his wife had been taking telephone calls at the office on the evening of February 11 and had torn some pages out of the receipt book to take down telephone messages. Likely story.

On Monday, February 25 Gardner's attorney, Bruce Kramer met with Senior at his office. He again confronted him with Gardner's allegations that the Scruggs team had received cash from the proceeds of the February 11 bank robbery. Senior again denied that he had ever received any money from Gardner and insisted that nothing Gardner said could be believed.

No doubt realizing the feds were on their trail. Scruggs requested a meeting with the United States Attorney Tom Turley, an old school, no nonsense, maverick of mavericks attorney. Turley didn't go to law school but "read the law" almost like Abe Lincoln. At Turley's request I was there when Scruggs Junior admitted Gardner gave him cash but on Saturday, February 23,1974, he said, he took his half of the cash, $3000, to his home in a brown manila folder. After a sleepless night "wondering what was going on" he called his father who lived next door and asked his father to give him the other half of the money. He then met his father in the yard between their houses and Senior gave Junior his $3000. Junior then returned to his house. "I took the money and it was chilly that day and I threw the money into the fireplace and burned it up, every bit of it." He said he burned it because he didn't know where that money came from since Gardner had told him "so many tales."

I could have sought a search warrant for the contents of Junior's fireplace. However I thought a search wouldn't be productive. Harry Jr didn't seem to be the type of man who would dispose of money and anyway even if he had burned some bills they might not have been the ones we were after.

On March 12, 1974 I testified before the federal grand jury in Memphis about my investigation of Scruggs father and son. The grand jury indicted them both. The critical count charged them with knowingly possessing, concealing and disposing of money that had been stolen from a federally insured bank.

It was no surprise that Scruggs Junior and Senior pled not guilty to the charges. They were facing not only the possibility of jail time but also the loss of their licenses to practice law. The case went to trial in federal court in Memphis on June 9, 1975. I spent about 1½ days on the stand. Gardner had already made a plea agreement with the government and testified for the prosecution. He did a good job of relating to the jury his interaction with both Scruggs. On cross-examination he never wavered from the story he had told his attorney Bruce Kramer and us. Scruggs Junior took the stand and related his cockeyed story that made no sense at all.

Four days later the jury found both guilty. Senior was sentenced to pay a fine of $500 on each count of his conviction. Junior was sentenced to two concurrent terms of one year and one day in prison. I believe that Senior only received a fine because he was 78 years old; Junior was 52.

Both later appealed their convictions. One of their contentions was that they had not possessed the money "knowingly." The appellate court said, "Taking the Scruggs story at face value….they both knew when they disposed of the cash that (1) their client Gardner had been arrested and charged with the February 11 bank robbery; (2) they had seen the newspaper article with bank camera photos of a person who looked like their client caught in the act of robbing a bank; (3) that less than three hours after the robbery Gardner had appeared at their office with a briefcase full of cash in small denominations; (4) their client had told the FBI and two different attorneys that he had paid the Scruggs account a large amount of cash out of the proceeds of the alleged bank robbery; and (5) both Scruggs knew they were under suspicion by the FBI in connection with Gardner, the fee payments and the bank robbery proceeds since agents interviewed them at their office on February 22. "

The appellate court concluded that both Scruggs were put on notice as to the nature of the funds received from Gardner during the time they possessed the money based on "overwhelming evidence." Both convictions were upheld on February 22, 1977. It's ironic that that is the same day, February 22, that we interviewed them three years earlier in 1974. I must say I got some joy out of convicting two crooked defense attorneys and having the convictions upheld on appeal.

For his cooperation with the government Gardner received a reduced sentence on the federal bank robbery charges.

ASAC Blay never did buy me that steak dinner. When I would ask him about it he would just laugh.

Scruggs Jr. lost his law license on November 29, 1977 following the Court of Appeals decision and the U.S. Supreme Court's denial to hear his further appeal. He began serving his prison sentence the following month. On June 1, 1978, he went to a halfway house and began working as a welder.

On March 20, 1979, Scruggs Jr. filed a petition for reinstatement of his law license. His petition was denied. After several appeals the Tennessee Supreme Court found in July 1981 that Scruggs Jr. was fit to resume the practice of law. Scruggs had made restitution to the Memphis Bank & Trust of the money he admitted had been paid to him by Gardner. Since his release from prison he had been studying in his father's law office to prepare himself to resume law practice. He testified he had no desire to practice criminal law and planned to concentrate on domestic relations and probate cases. He admitted, "I did wrong....that was very stupid on my part. It was a mistake, I made it and I paid for it."

Finally, an admission! Probably only because he wanted his law practice back.

My now wife Barbara, who was then practicing law in Memphis, had a domestic relations case with Harry Scruggs Jr. on the opposing side about 15 years after his conviction. Outside court one day she told Harry that she knew me, knew me well. He came unglued, telling her how despicable I was, underhanded etc. etc.

Author doing the necessary paper work

Chapter 6
The Unlucky Bank Robber

"Sometimes it is better to be lucky than good" is a saying I've heard all my life. For those who are uninitiated "good" doesn't mean "good" in the moral sense but as in ability. So, sometimes you're in a lucky situation that pays off that has nothing to do with your skill. Supposedly Napoleon preferred lucky generals over good ones. This story is a great example of luck prevailing over skill.

In June of 1974 Burl Smith and I worked a bank robbery of the Union Planters Bank branch in Whitehaven in South Memphis. The robber got money from several different tellers and escaped with a total of $3000 to $4000. He was described as a male black about 35 years old, 5'9" with a slender build. Like most banks a surveillance camera was mounted near the front door that is activated by a bank employee during a robbery. The tellers at UP tripped the silent alarm and started the cameras rolling.

We did the usual investigation, interviewing the bank employees and customers who witnessed the robbery, and did a neighborhood canvas to see if anyone saw the robber or a vehicle. This yielded nothing of substance except a description of the subject.

Another agent took the reel of tape from the bank camera to a business that could immediately develop the film for us. He brought back one of the clearest bank robbery photos I had ever seen. I got copies to the local television stations and newspapers in time to have it shown on the evening news and in the late afternoon newspaper.

The next day I received an anonymous phone call. The caller didn't know the robber's name but knew he worked at a local carpet company. We took the photo to the business. The owner and several employees identified the person as Albert Franklin Hale.. The owner told me Hale had not reported for work the previous day nor had he shown up today.

Burl and I went to the address the owner gave us and interviewed several of his relatives who lived there. They all denied knowing the man in the photo. But several neighbors identified the man in the photo as Albert Franklin Hale.

Based on the information we had the US Attorney's office approved the filing of an affidavit for an arrest warrant for Albert Franklin Hale for federal bank robbery. The judge issued a warrant and Burl and I started tracking down the subject. We went to his home address and the carpet store but didn't find him. People said they hadn't seen him in days.

Hale was now a fugitive from justice. I entered his name, date of birth and description into the National Crime Information Center (NCIC), an enormous database operated by the FBI. If any law enforcement agency checked him in NCIC I would be notified immediately and he would be detained until the matter was cleared up.

Every bank maintains what is called "bait money." This is a packet of bills the bank has recorded the denominations, series and serial numbers of in its permanent records. Each teller has a packet assigned to her and keeps it in her cash drawer; the permanent record also identifies which teller has which bills. There are also two or three packets of "bait money" strategically placed in the bank vault in case a robber demands money from the vault.

Some banks have a sophisticated system in which the "bait money" is kept under a spring clip. When the money is removed the clip closes a switch, which sounds the silent alarm and turns on the bank robbery camera.

Another system some banks have is an "incendiary smoke bomb." This is a small thin metal case containing a smoke bomb. The case is inserted in a stack of banded bills and cannot be seen unless the stack of money is taken apart. The victim teller is instructed that in the event of a robbery to be certain that the bills containing the device are given to the robber. Every door of the bank has an electric eye that automatically activates the bomb device when it passes through the door. The smoke bomb is set to explode 30 seconds to a minute later. This bomb also contains a packet of red dye that is dispersed in a 6' to 10' wide circle.

I have seen cases where the robber wrecked his car when the bomb explodes and covers the interior with smoke and red dye. Also sometimes the robber will tuck the money into his shirt or a pocket. When the bomb explodes a considerable amount of heat is generated and the robber can end up with a painful burn. Most robbers have the teller put the money in a container of some kind. The dye is created from a chemical that is permanent. Some robbers attempt to bleach the bills but some residue always remains and the bills are discolored and can easily be detected as bait money. I have more than once recovered money that has been treated in this manner and knew it was obviously from a bank robbery.

In this case the bank didn't use the smoke bomb/dye pack. If it had, the robber, who took the money away in a paper bag, would have been in a mess. The bag would have exploded, scattered the dyed money everywhere and given the robber a nasty burn as well as covered him in the permanent red dye.

Each of the two victim tellers at Union Planters Bank had a stack of bait money containing ten $10 bills they gave the robber. The bank furnished me with a list of the bait money. When I returned to the office I entered the denomination, series and serial numbers of each bill into the NCIC. Every law enforcement agency in the United States submits data to the system such as serial numbers of stolen property, bait money, names of fugitives etc. When officers encounter suspicious property, such as currency, they check the property serial numbers through NCIC. If the system finds a match, called a "hit," the computer will spit out the name of the agency that originally put the information into the system and the particulars of the crime connected to it.

About two months later I received a telephone call from a Metro detective in Washington D.C. He had arrested a black male who gave his name as Robert Wilson. This man had $40 and change on him. The officer entered the money into NCIC and one of the $10 bills was a hit. The computerized record gave the officer the robber's true name, race, date of birth and description and that he was wanted by the FBI for a bank robbery in Memphis.

The D.C. officer went back to the prisoner and confronted him with this information. The suspect denied any knowledge of a robbery in Memphis and insisted that he was Robert Wilson, not Albert Franklin Hale. The officer locked him up with a hold for the FBI.

Subsequently, the subject was interviewed by FBI agents from the Washington field office. He continued to deny he was Albert Franklin Hale, and knew nothing about a bank robbery in Memphis.

Since the subject wouldn't admit to his true identity, I had to travel to D.C. to testify at a removal hearing held before a federal judge to establish if the person named in the arrest warrant is the same as the person appearing as the defendant in court. I testified as to the evidence linking Hale to the robbery. I also introduced the surveillance photograph. Comparing Hale, who was sitting in the courtroom, to the photo it was undeniably the same person. The judge determined that the subject was Albert Franklin Hale and ordered him removed to Memphis for trial.

Bank surveillance photo of robber

Hale never wavered in his story and elected to go to trial. Even with all the evidence against him including the bank robbery photo. He testified that he was not the person in the picture. He stated he didn't know how he had acquired the bait bill in his possession when he was arrested in D.C..

The jury deliberated for about an hour and a half and came back with guilty on all counts. He was sentenced to 12 years in federal prison.

At that time, and in retrospect, I wonder, "What are the chances of one $10 bill, out of the 20 bait bills hidden in thousands of dollars, showing up in $40 in the pocket of a man arrested in Washington?"

He was unlucky in that he hung onto this one bill all that time. I was the lucky one. After the trial and appeals, I traded one of my personal $10 bills for the bait bill which I still have today… along with the tellers' list of bait money.

Chapter 7
Danny Owens: Infamous Memphis Legend

In 1974 Arthur Wayne Baldwin arrived in Memphis, Tennessee on a Braniff airline flight from Seattle and brought with him 40 topless nightclub dancers (fully clothed for the airplane trip). After a month or two he opened the first topless nightclub in Memphis. The club was a smashing success and before long Baldwin had four local clubs and was making money hand over fist.

Danny Owens was born in 1950 in Northeast Arkansas. His family moved to Northern Mississippi where he graduated from Horn Lake High School. He dabbled in small time gambling, bought and sold cars wholesale and operated more than one lounge in Southaven and Memphis. He bought one bar when he was only 18 or 19. By this time Danny was 6' feet tall, 200 lbs. With his muscular build and naturally blonde hair some considered him handsome.

In 1974 Owens, who was to become Baldwin's archrival in the topless business, became known to law enforcement in northern Mississippi as a witness and possible murderer in a case related to a crooked sheriff in Desoto County. The FBI agent working the case said Danny was, "A big, handsome business-looking guy built like a linebacker with blond hair and blue eyes wearing an expensive blue blazer with brass buttons. There was something cold and crazy in his eyes. They had no feeling." The AUSA who interviewed Danny said, "When Owens stepped into my office, the look in his eyes gave me a physical chill, unusual for me. He was maybe the scariest guy I ever encountered. The coldness in his eyes and voice were unlike anything I had seen outside a movie. I lost my macho. No way I could intimidate this guy."

And in 1974 Danny and a Memphis thug, William James, got into a fight at the Hitching Post Lounge in Southaven. They began slugging it out and then both armed themselves with knives. James received several cuts and was pushed or fell through the plate glass front window of the lounge. He died of his wounds and Owens was indicted on a murder charge.

Owens' attorney was Bob Gilder, a noted North Mississippi trial attorney who basically only represented thugs in criminal cases. He wasn't a large man, sort of short and dumpy and disheveled in appearance. He had his office in Southaven abutting a topless nightclub. He allegedly had a peephole behind a framed law certificate where he could watch what was going on in the private rooms next door.

To observers it seemed that the prosecution had a winnable case against Danny. Partway into the trial Owens' girlfriend made calls to the prospective jury pool of 60 people. When the judge learned this he dismissed the existing jury panel and more jurors were called. Owens took the stand and testified he was trying to cut James but didn't know if he cut him or not. Gilder called an eyewitness who was in a restaurant across the street. He testified he saw James fall through the window and that he was hanging by one arm on the glass. This was the fatal wound. This witness said he ran across the street to help James and heard him say, "That glass did me in." In his closing argument Gilder said James's death was an accident. The jury's verdict was not guilty. Owens was released from custody and went back to operating, buying and selling lounges in the Southaven and Memphis area.

Two years later Art Baldwin hired David McNamee to manage one of his clubs. McNamee was a white male in his early 30's, and had stylish, medium length brown hair. He had been in and out of trouble with the law since his teenage years. Baldwin saw potential in McNamee and he soon became Baldwin's top lieutenant. In addition to the topless nightclub business Baldwin and McNamee owned a large liquor store near the Memphis airport.

In November 1976 Baldwin and McNamee had a parting of the ways. They filed lawsuits against each other over claims to some property. McNamee soon opened his own club on Winchester Road called " The Playhouse." In less than two years McNamee owned six topless nightclubs and he and Baldwin were major competitors.

In May 1978 Baldwin and one of his girlfriends were visiting The Playhouse. Before long Baldwin and McNamee got into an argument. Baldwin accused McNamee of underhanded tricks and of turning on him after he had hired and promoted him to his top management spot. The argument grew heated and McNamee began making nasty remarks about Baldwin's lady friend. The two almost came to blows but friends on both sides intervened and Baldwin and his girlfriend left the club. As he left Baldwin said to McNamee, "You haven't heard the last of this."

Two months later McNamee was found dead in the bathtub of his girlfriend's apartment. The Memphis Police Department homicide squad investigated and thought it looked like a professional hit. McNamee was shot three times; the third round fired into his right temple at point blank range. The investigators found a pillow in another room with three powder burn holes in it, obviously used to silence the shots that killed McNamee. Early on one of the persons of interest was Danny Owens who was then working for Baldwin.

As if by coincidence, in the fall of 1978 Baldwin sold Owens a one-half interest in one of his clubs located in South Memphis called The Library Club. As a result the Memphis Police Department increased its interest in Owens in connection with McNamee's murder. To this day this murder has not been solved.

After Baldwin opened his topless nightclubs in Memphis Owens had realized how much money Baldwin was making. While he might make $300 to $400 per night on one of his joints, Baldwin would make $2000 or $3000 per night from one of his topless clubs. Eventually we in law enforcement suspected that Baldwin and Owens had become partners in the topless nightclub business. In media interviews they both denied this.

The local governments didn't have any specific ordinances to regulate the topless clubs until several years later when they got busy trying to exert some control. For the most part the clubs were located at the southern edge of Memphis proper with many near the airport. At the height of the topless craze there were probably 15-20 in Memphis.

Most of the clubs were laid out the same: tables and chairs and perhaps booths around the perimeter and a raised stage more or less in the middle of the room with a rail around it and chairs near the rail. Most of them had from two to four brass poles running from the stage floor to the ceiling. The dancers would twine themselves around the poles as they began to strip and dance close to the rail so customers could tuck money into their G-strings.

Private booths in the rear of the buildings were fully enclosed except for a beaded curtain across the front. These were used for private dances at a hefty fee. An ordinance forbade customers from touching the dancers but this was largely ignored. For a fee a man (customers were 99% male, both white and black) could hire the dancer of his choice to do a "table dance" on top of his table for a few tunes.

Many of the dancers were young girls who had just turned 18; others, single mothers trying to earn some good money that usually averaged between $400 and $500 per night. Some were college students, which I found unusual but made sense given how much money they could make quickly.

The clubs made money primarily from a cut of the dancers' take, cover charges and sale of alcoholic drinks which were usually watered down and very expensive. Between dances the girls came out and sat with the customers who bought drinks for them. The customer could also "pay a girl out" for a few hours for the night and she could leave the club with him, at a cost well into the hundreds of dollars. Club owners denied any prostitution, claiming the woman was only an escort.

Club customers came from all walks of life, from the blue-collar laborer to company executives and in-between. Big companies would take their out of town customers to one of the clubs and sometimes spend one or two thousand dollars or more in a night.

As competition increased among the topless nightclub owners, incidents of violence became more frequent and more serious. Although McNamee was no longer a problem for Baldwin, Owens was becoming an even greater problem than McNamee ever was. It seemed that Baldwin had created his most serious rival again. Other topless nightclub operators were springing up but Owens and Baldwin were the key players in the business.

Between 1977 and through mid-1980 rumors of drug dealing and prostitution at the clubs were rampant. There were also incidents of suspicious deaths, armed robbery and several bombings. In December 1977 Vicky Dryer, a topless dancer for one of Baldwin's rivals, was run over by a car. It appeared she had car trouble and began walking for help when she was hit. Investigating officers could never prove it but suspected this incident was a deliberate murder in connection with the clubs. This case was never solved.

In February 1979, one of Baldwin's topless nightclubs businesses was the victim of three armed robberies. The Library Club, co-owned by Baldwin and Owens, was the scene of an attempted robbery shortly after closing time. A Texas prison escapee was shot and killed by a club security guard. In September 1979, burglars broke into Baldwin's residence and stole $20,000 according to what he reported to the police. The Memphis Police Department robbery squad developed information from a reliable informant that the burglars actually took over $100,000 from Baldwin's home. They were never able to prove this allegation and this crime was never solved.

In August 1979 Owens bought the remaining 50% of The Library from Baldwin and renamed it The Follies. In the next two years, Owens opened two more clubs of his own and appeared to be moving in the direction of opening even more. The next month, The Follies was firebombed. This case also was never solved.

In April 1980 the manager of The Follies, James Brothers, was found in the club parking lot after closing, beaten bloody and near death. It was first reported that Brothers had received the beating from unknown subjects. MPD homicide investigated this incident and got conflicting accounts from the various witnesses. In the end the story they got was that Brothers had left his car keys locked in his office and didn't have a key to the club. He reportedly placed a ladder on the hood of a security guard's car and was attempting to go through the window to his office when he fell and suffered the injury. He later died at the hospital. The coroner, after an investigation, ruled the death an accident. Brothers' family was very suspicious but the coroner's decision stood.

On July 20, 1980 Baldwin and Owens had an encounter outside a restaurant in South Memphis. Words were exchanged and a fight began. Baldwin was beaten so badly he had to be hospitalized but he refused to press charges against Owens.

In early 1981 Hickman "Hick" Ewing, the US Attorney for the Western District of Tennessee, held a meeting with his assistants to discuss the growing problem of organized crime and drug dealing in

Memphis. Hick was only in his mid-thirties but sported a head of thick premature gray, nearly white hair. He was a smart, perceptive lawyer, well suited for the role of prosecutor. He attended Vanderbilt University on a Navy ROTC scholarship and then served on active duty for five years, three in Vietnam.

The prosecutors came up with the idea of forming a task force made up of members of the state, local and federal law enforcement agencies in the West Tennessee area. Hickman then called a meeting with representatives from each agency and proposed a combined task force. All parties agreed and said they would contribute whatever manpower they could spare. I was selected to head it up. I chose officers from the agencies involved, subject to final approval of their command staff. It took some weeks to get the officers on board and locate an offsite building for an office which we found on Elvis Presley Blvd., just south of Graceland.

Walter Hoback, an ATF (Alcohol, Tobacco and Firearms) agent was my right-hand man. Walter, despite the surname of Hoback, could not deny his Italian heritage with his stocky build, dark hair and complexion. He also had a fiery temperament and didn't take any guff from anyone, including supervisors. Walter was one of the best investigators I ever worked with.

AUSA Tim DiScenza was designated the coordinator and prosecutor for our group. Tim and I had been working together for years. He was another one of Italian heritage, very obvious to the eye. Tim had been a combat helicopter pilot in Vietnam and still flew a small, single-engine Piper airplane regularly. Sometimes when we needed to interview a witness in a city, too far to drive but too close to fly commercially, Tim would fly us there. Once I got into the passenger seat while Tim did his pre-flight check. When he turned the key to start the plane nothing happened. He got a maintenance person to come out and jump the battery. I said, "I'm ready to get out. I don't want to go in a plane that had to be jumped." Tim assured me it would be all right and we went on our way with no further problems.

Our locally created task force morphed into the Organized Crime Drug Enforcement Task Force (OCDETF) in 1982 when this program was established by the Justice Department to mount a comprehensive attack against organized drug trafficking and related crimes such as money laundering, tax and weapons violations and violent crime. It was a national program combining the resources and unique expertise of numerous federal agencies and state and local law enforcement officers in each of the 94 federal judicial districts. Since it was created OCDETF operations nationwide have led to more than 44,000 drug-related convictions and the seizure of over $3.0 billion in cash and property assets.

The various news media in Memphis were publishing stories and accounts of the escalating violence connected with the topless nightclub business observing that almost none of the crimes had been solved. They also noted that there were two or three major drug distribution networks reportedly operating in Memphis with impunity.

The first target the task force selected was the topless nightclub business. This business fit within the organized crime definition since it was a criminal enterprise dealing in drugs, prostitution and violence. Baldwin and Owens were the topless nightclub kingpins and the dirty tricks between them continued. We opened a file on Owens and with Baldwin as my informant, and other officers contacting their informants and reviewing public records we began to take a close look at Danny.

Art Baldwin had become my informant in April 1978. He was already a convicted federal felon and was facing a major indictment on cocaine charges. Baldwin came to Hick Ewing and offered to help the FBI in any way in exchange for help in the drug charges. Hick called me to come meet Baldwin who I already knew. I explained to Art that to stay in our good graces he couldn't engage in any criminal activity unless Hick and I approved. This was the same time as the investigation of Governor Ray Blanton, and Baldwin became a vital source for not only that case but also as an informant against Danny Owens.

In thinking about Danny Owens I recalled a home invasion robbery on April 2, 1979 in Poinsett County, Arkansas not far from my hometown. The victims were Frank Hyneman, his wife Marzee and their housekeeper. The Hynemans were in their mid-60s, down to earth, quiet people, the typical grandmother-grandfather types. Hyneman was a wealthy farmer and businessman and chairman of the board of the First National Bank of Trumann. I knew the Bureau had recently investigated the embezzlement of over $400,000 from Hyneman's bank. Former state representative Jim Brewer, chief executive of the bank, was identified as the embezzler and was serving a prison sentence. Later I learned he was Danny's cousin.

The Hyneman robbery was particularly brutal. Two men dressed in suits and ties appeared at the front door at about 6:30 in the evening. They knocked and when the housekeeper opened the door they told her they were from the FBI and needed to talk to Mr. Hyneman again. They were admitted without question since agents had been to the home several times in the past to interview Mr. Hyneman about the embezzlement. They pulled out handguns and stole jewelry worth $400,000 and $2300 in cash. The robbers used chains and padlocks to chain the Hynemans and their housekeeper to a refrigerator and left.

I obtained the police report along with photos of the jewelry taken and called the chief investigator and we discussed my theory that Owens might be involved. I reminded him that Owens grew up not far from the Hynemans' and his father was still in the area. "That's why I think Danny may have been part of the robbery, plus our CIs are telling us he set it up and is fencing the jewelry."

The Arkansas investigator told me they had developed four suspects, members of the "Dixie or Hillbilly Mafia," a loosely knit group of professional criminals. They were committing armed robbery, home invasions and other crimes in Northeast Arkansas, Western Tennessee, and Southwest Missouri. Three months after the Hyneman robbery four gang members, Leonard Spears, William Cassel, Joseph Bumgarner and Bill Caplinger were arrested.

Shortly after the arrests Art Baldwin showed me a ring he had bought from Danny Owens. When I looked at it, I thought, "Bingo! I remember that ring from somewhere." It looked almost exactly like the most valuable ring taken in the Hyneman armed robbery. I told Art I needed to take it for now as possible evidence in a robbery. I later compared it to photos of the ring stolen and decided they were identical. Sgt. Dennis King, an officer with the Memphis Police Department and a member of the task force, took the ring and showed it to Mrs. Hyneman. She immediately identified it as the most expensive one taken. I told the Arkansas investigator and he said they were getting the same information as us: Danny Owens was involved in setting up the robbery and was fencing the jewelry.

Before the case went to trial in Arkansas state court, Patti Bumgarner, wife of Joseph Bumgarner who was called the "Godfather of the Dixie Mafia," worked out a deal with the prosecutor to testify for the state in exchange for dropping any charges against her. Danny wasn't charged in state court either.

At the trial on July 16 1982, Patti Bumgarner testified that Danny Owens came up with the initial idea to get the Hyneman's jewelry. His contact was Caplinger who enlisted Spears, Cassell and her husband to carry it out. Patti admitted she bought the chains and padlocks for them. Another conspirator Michael Anderson provided guns and handcuffs although he withdrew from the plan before it took place.

Patti said the robbers had two-way portable radios, including a police radio to monitor police broadcasts.

Patti testified that on April 2, at about 6:30 pm the four robbers left her home for the Hynemans. They returned about an hour later with a bag full of jewelry they gave to her and that she hid for them.

About a week later, she said, the four men discussed in front of her the jewelry and how much they would get from Danny Owens. They ultimately decided to sell the jewelry themselves and give Owens ten percent "off the top." Patti got the jewelry from the hiding place, and gave it to her husband and Caplinger, who went to Memphis to meet Owens. Her husband came home with $7000 as his "first cut." There were more trips to Memphis, she said, and more sales and money.

Michael Anderson testified that he and Caplinger later went to Memphis and picked up a sack of cash from Danny Owens, $36,000 in $100 bills, the proceeds from the sale of an 8-carat solitaire diamond ring.

The Arkansas prosecutor decided not to seek an indictment against Owens. I suppose that one of his reasons was that his witnesses were criminals themselves who had made a deal with the state. Later Owens said that all the prosecution witnesses had been coerced into testifying against him. He said the person who actually set up the robbery was his cousin, Brewer the embezzler. But the threat of prosecution for his part hung over Danny's head for several years.

On more than one occasion Owens told the press how he felt about law enforcement officers. He respected the local police; said they were only trying to do a good job and make a living. He didn't have any respect for prosecutors, state or federal, who he believed were trying to get ahead politically regardless of whether the people they were "harassing" were guilty or innocent. One was AUSA Tim DiScenza.

He believed that Tim had a personal vendetta against him. Owens also said he knew about the task force investigation of him since the summer of 1981.

We believed that the Arkansas state trial witness testimony about Owens' involvement was true. We put pressure on other people who we believed knew Danny's role in the robbery. Even though Danny wasn't charged in Arkansas we had a case against him for interstate transportation of stolen property. There are several ways to penetrate a criminal organization such as Owens'. One way is to develop an informant who can introduce an undercover agent into the organization. A second is to concentrate on lesser players and obtain a prosecutable case on one of them and then offer them a deal to inform on the organization from the inside.

One man close to Owens was Forrest Pope. Walter Hoback and I decided to put as much pressure on Pope as we could. Pope had a cocky attitude that he carried on a slender, short frame. He was only in his late 20s but already well into a life of crime.

Walter and I began surveilling Pope two or three days a week hoping to catch him "dirty." We approached him in public since he refused to come to the office for an interview. Each time, he became very angry cussing us up one side and down the other. We kept hoping to push him over the edge and he would do something foolish. Then we might be able to convince him to cooperate and help us build our case against Danny.

In the spring of 1982 Walter and I approached Forrest outside the Circle Café in East Memphis and found he was carrying a small vial of cocaine. We didn't arrest him but told him we were going to report this to the MPD narcotics squad. We decided to give him some time to think and he then might possibly talk to us about Owens.

The next afternoon I was in the office at my desk when the

switchboard operator called and said she had a man named Forrest Pope on hold who wanted to talk to me. I asked her to tell him I was on the other line and would be with him in a couple of minutes.

I hooked the recorder I kept in my desk drawer to the phone and checked to make sure it was working. I put a header on the tape with my name, the date and time, then told the operator to put Pope through to me. Pope started the conversation with a string of profanity directed at Walter and me. He then got specific and accused us of continually harassing him. He said he was "fixing to get it done and he didn't care if he did die but he was going to take somebody with him. You all have pushed me too far." He said that there was going to be another Shannon Street deal because he was going to take three or four with him. Pope was referring to an incident where a Memphis policeman was killed in a home on Shannon Street the previous month and the police killed at least seven occupants of the house in a subsequent siege.

I immediately went downstairs to the US Attorney's office and played the tape for Tim DiScenza. He authorized the filing of an arrest warrant charging Pope with possession of cocaine and threatening to kill a federal officer.

The next morning Walter and I arrested Pope and put him in the Shelby County Jail on the charges. His attorney, Bob Gilder, told the judge that Pope had made threats against individuals in the past but had no intention of carrying them out. He said Pope was a traveling jewelry salesman who lived a flamboyant lifestyle and enjoyed the idea that some people thought he was a big time operator. FBI and ATF agents, he said, were continually questioning Pope about Danny Owens. Gilder claimed there was no association business-wise between Pope and Owens. US Atty. Hickman Ewing contended, however, that Pope's mental and drinking problems made him a danger to others in the community and Pope shouldn't be out on the streets. He then played the profanity-filled tape for the judge. "We are dealing here with an individual who is very unstable," Ewing said. The judge agreed and ordered Pope to be held without bond until his trial.

I learned about a colorful character, John C. Johnson/ GI John, from an informant. Johnson worked for Danny as a doorman/bouncer at one of his clubs and was fired. My informant thought Danny hadn't treated him right.

I met GI John in late December. He didn't look like a bouncer to me. He was a slight young man with long brown hair, not muscular at all and only suited for the job of "doorman," the one who collected the cover charge and hollered for the bouncer if there was trouble. He had once been the dogcatcher in Southaven. John said Owens had threatened him with bodily harm because Owens suspected he was making silencers for other people. John explained that his father owned a large machine shop. When John was 16 he started working for his father and had become a good machinist One of his specialties was making silencers for pistols. He had made a silencer for a 9 mm semi-automatic pistol for Danny when he was still working for him. I asked if he thought he could get back up with Owens and offer to continue to get him pistols and silencers. He said he would try and get back with me.

I gave him a telephone recorder to record his telephone conversations with Owens. John called me in the next few days and said he had a tape for me. He had Danny Owens on tape putting in an order for two silencers. John told him it would take a few days to make them.

I told him to go ahead and make the silencers and let me know when they were ready. Four days later John had the silencers finished. I told him that I would get back to him. The mere possession of a silencer is a felony under federal statutes.

I got the task force together and we discussed how to proceed. We knew that Owens would be very careful. It was entirely likely he would send someone else to pick them up from John. We had no idea where the exchange would take place and when it would happen. I rented four nondescript vehicles to cover the exchange when it did take place. We didn't dare use our regular cars since Owens knew we were investigating him. For all we knew he had his people surveilling us and had a description of the vehicles right down to the license plate numbers.

John called Danny and told him he had the merchandise ready. Owens told him he would see him in a couple of days. After a week Danny hadn't called the CI so I told him to make the call.

On a tape dated June 27, 1982 John asked Owens to help him "get something done" with two silencers he was holding for him. Owens replied, "You know, you put them in a hole in the ground. They ain't going nowhere." We already knew that Owens had a waterproof container buried in the backyard of his home in Southaven where he stored weapons. We were sure he was referring to that. Danny's house was modest, worth less than $100,000 in the mid-1980s; the only evidence of its ownership was that it sat on nearly three acres and was surrounded by a seven-foot rock wall equipped with surveillance cameras.

By mid-1982 Danny was beginning to feel the heat. His attorney James Gordon told me he wanted me to set up a meeting with him, Owens, US Attorney Hick Ewing, AUSA Tim DiScenza and me. After talking to Tim I set the meeting to take place in his office. Danny hoped to trade information in exchange for the FBI easing up on the investigation. Owens offered to provide information on a possible contract killing, a drug deal and a man dealing in illegal weapons if the FBI would end a tax probe and the investigation into any role he might have had in the 1979 armed invasion and jewelry heist at the Hynemans.

The prosecutors refused to make a deal. Danny said, "I guess the contract killing will have to go through. I can tell you about illegal firearms later if you change your mind." We knew he meant GI John

Johnson. I was convinced Owens had no idea Johnson was working for me as a CI. Danny wasn't as smart as he thought he was.

We continued to build our case against Owens but by August 1982 we decided we had gone as far as we could and Tim DiScenza began preparing a grand jury indictment.

On August 25,1982 I presented the case to the Grand Jury. Later in the afternoon they returned a three-count indictment charging Owens with illegally possessing and manufacturing firearms and silencers; planning the 1979 Hyneman robbery and selling the stolen loot; and attempting to recruit someone in August 1980 to kill Art Baldwin. In anticipation of the indictment the task force was covering Danny's known locations. We had no luck in finding him and began hearing that he had left the country.

No one who might know Owens' whereabouts would give us anything except that he was in South America. We believed Owens had left with his new wife Gayla, a stunning young blonde former topless dancer, and had probably taken a large sum of money with him, perhaps a million dollars, or had the ability to get the money from wherever he was. We later learned they had left the country about ten days before the indictment was returned. Judge Harry Wellford issued a fugitive warrant for him.

I now had an international fugitive case on my hands. Any lead we developed had to be worked through the US State Department. We finally got some feedback he had been in South America, then in Switzerland and might now be in Morocco.

A Memphis police officer and excellent investigator, Lieut. Larry Goodwin was assigned to the task force. He heard from a source that a couple of months before Owens had purchased a steamer trunk from him and had paid for it with a credit card. Larry's source gave him the original signed slip. I had a good friend in the security department of

Union Planters Bank, which had issued the credit card. He agreed to monitor the account and let us know as soon as any charges were made to it and where and what was purchased.

A few days later the security officer called and said the credit card had been used to rent a car in Casablanca, Morocco. The State Department has jurisdiction and moves slowly in these matters. I didn't hear from them for about four days. The local authorities in Casablanca had gotten the name of the hotel where Owens was staying with his wife Gayla. When officers searched the hotel room, it appeared whoever had stayed there had left in a hurry. A lot of clothing and other personal items were left behind. The Casablanca police put out an all points bulletin on the rented automobile; it was located the next day abandoned near the airport.

Two days later Gayla was back in Memphis trying to arrange a meeting with Tim DiScenza to plead with him to speak to Judge Harry Wellford about reducing the $4 million bond he had set for Owens. Tim refused to talk to her.

Interpol put out a notice to all airports that were logical destinations for flights from Casablanca. Next I learned Owens had passed through Gibraltar en route to Gatwick Airport in London, England. I contacted our legal attaché there instead of waiting for the slow process of the State Department and advised him that Owens was on the run. Working with Scotland Yard they determined that Owens had recently arrived at Gatwick. They also found that he had contacted the airline and told them he had left a valuable ring in the washroom at the Gibraltar airport. He wanted to know if anyone had turned the ring in. As luck would have it Gibraltar airport officials advised that a ring fitting the description had been found and turned in. They said they would put the ring on a flight to Gatwick the next day.

We could hardly believe our good fortune. If Owens came to the airport requesting his ring, Scotland Yard would give it to him and arrest him. This is exactly what happened on October 22, 1982. Danny Owens was carrying false identification, $59,000 in cash and a list of countries that don't have extradition treaties with the United States.

Upon getting official notice of Owens' arrest, the US Attorney in Memphis began preparing documents to have Owens extradited to the US. Under the United States treaty with Great Britain, authorities had 45 days to start the extradition process. If they didn't, Owens would be released from custody. AUSA DiScenza told a local newspaper that the documents necessary for Owens extradition had been sent to the State Department and the matter was now in the hands of its diplomats.

The State Department continued to work with their counterpart in Great Britain to perfect Owens extradition. One of the sticking points was that Owens had several tax evasion charges against him. The agreement between the US and Great Britain excluded extradition for these. Eventually the tax charges were dropped and after four months of haggling the extradition process was completed.

The Memphis US Attorney's office arranged for two US Marshals to fly to London and bring Danny back. Tim DiScenza convinced the Bureau that three task force officers should accompany the marshals and attempt to interview Owens. Walter Hoback, Sgt. Dennis King and I made the trip.

The two Scotland Yard officers who arrested Danny met us at the airport. Later that afternoon we talked to Owens in an interview room at the jail. He was cordial but only asked for news from Memphis. When we tried mentioning the charges against him he said, "That's all smoke and mirrors you got nothing on me." We never got him to talk.

Upon returning to Memphis, Owens went before Judge Wellford. His attorney Bob Gilder attempted to get the judge to lower Owens' bail from $4 million dollars to "a more reasonable bond." The judge refused and ordered Owens held in custody until after his trial or the bond was posted. If convicted on all counts, Owens could receive a maximum penalty of 52 years in prison and a fine of $52,000.

Next Gilder argued there had been so much excessive pretrial media coverage his client couldn't get a fair trial in Memphis. The judge granted his motion to move the trial to Nashville.

Danny Owens' trial began in the US District Court on June 30, 1983, presided over by USDC Judge Tom Wiseman, in Nashville.

Our case against Owens was broken down into three parts:

1. Setting up the plan to rob the Hynemans in April 1979 and fencing more than $100,000 of the stolen jewelry.
2. The attempt to recruit someone in August 1980 to take a $10,000 contract to kill Arthur Wayne Baldwin, his rival in the topless nightclub business and supplying a silencer-equipped 22-caliber pistol for the murder.
3. Possession of firearms by a convicted felon in late 1981.

Before G I John Johnson, our first witness, took the stand I introduced the tapes of telephone conversations and face-to-face meetings between Owens and him. With Johnson on the stand Tim DiScenza took him through the various transfers of firearms and silencers, at least six of each, to Owens. In each instance Tim played one of the pertinent tapes. Johnson tended to elaborate beyond the questions that Tim asked. He was enjoying himself on the stand and wanted to describe to the jury how to make a bazooka, hand grenade, pipe bombs and other explosive devices. You could tell the jurors were rolling their eyes. Some of the jurors were obviously tired of him. Some witnesses need to be reined in and he was one of those.

After four days of testimony the trial was delayed due to an emergency the judge had to take care of.

When the trial resumed nine days later, Art Baldwin testified that Owens sold him a ring in July 1979 that was stolen in the Hyneman robbery. Although he made a good witness it didn't help our case that he was then serving federal prison time for attempting to firebomb one of the topless clubs Danny owned.

William Caplinger, Leonard Spears and Bill Cassell testified that Owens was involved in planning the Hyneman robbery and fencing the stolen loot. They were then all serving time in state prison for the crime.

Cassell testified Danny offered him, Caplinger and Spears $10,000 to kill Art Baldwin. Danny gave Caplinger a red toolbox containing a 22-caliber pistol equipped with a silencer for the hit. Danny said Baldwin needed to die "because he snitched on Ray Blanton (former governor of Tennessee) and was no good in general." According to Cassell they considered the killing for a few days, then decided it would be risky and told Owens that and returned the tool box and pistol to him.

ATF agents Walter Hoback and Randy Little, along with SA James Hoberg and I, testified at length about the case against Owens. The news media reported that our testimony provided support for that of the less reputable convicts and informant government witnesses. In other words, we were the good guys, ones without shady backgrounds and convictions.

The government attorneys maintained Owens fled the country in August 1982, 10 days before the indictment was returned, knowing he was about to be indicted. Judge Wiseman told the jury flight to avoid prosecution can be interpreted as evidence of guilt unless rebutted by the defense.

In his cross-examination of the prosecution witnesses, attorney Bob Gilder suggested that Cassell, Spears and Caplinger were trying to win reductions in their Arkansas state sentences. And he inferred

Baldwin was still hoping to retake control of the topless nightclubs in Memphis by sending Owens to jail. He said all four were lying to better themselves.

Danny's father Buddy Owens testified for the defense. He said he, not his son, bought the firearms from Johnson but never any silencers. Buddy was about 50 years old then. He wasn't a muscle builder like his son but looked like a complete typical redneck.

Next Gilder called Joe Bumgarner as a defense witness. He was also serving time for plotting and carrying out the Hyneman robbery. He testified that federal prosecutors and FBI agents tried to get him to frame Owens. Under cross-examination Bumgarner admitted he had told a different story to federal prosecutors the year before.

Owens' wife Gayla and his mother testified that the August trip to Europe was a delayed honeymoon for the couple who were married in May.

Danny Owens took the stand as the last witness for the defense. He made a good witness and mostly blamed this whole case on overzealous FBI agents and assistant US Attorneys. He named Tim DiScenza and me specifically as the ones trying to frame him. Owens admitted during his direct testimony that he had bought firearms in the past for his father and even test fired one of them.

On cross-examination Tim and Assistant District Atty. Dan Newsom, who was on loan to the US Attorney's office for this case, questioned Owens extensively but could not shake his story. Dan was another Vietnam veteran.

Ever the showman, defense attorney Bob Gilder said in his closing the government's case was built by "an 'overzealous' prosecutor, Asst. US Atty. Tim DiScenza, and an FBI agent, Corbett Hart Jr., "who would make J. Edgar Hoover turn cartwheels in his grave." He called the Hyneman robbers who testified for us a "parade of thieves, riffraff, scum and the lowest form of life." GI Johnson was a "kook" in Gilder's words, who should have been prosecuted for making silencers and a bazooka and instead was "walking around loose today."

Tim DiScenza retorted that Gilder was trying to focus the jury's attention away from Owens by "assassinating the character of an FBI agent." And, Owens "knew he was guilty when he fled the country with a list of 'honeymoon countries,' Morocco, the Ivory Coast, Tunisia and Cameroon, none of which has an extradition treaty with the United States."

The judge gave the jury their instructions and they retired to the jury room to deliberate. On July 14, after deliberating for 11 hours, the jury came back with not guilty on all counts in the indictment. Those of us on the prosecution side were stunned and all we could do was shake our heads in disbelief, and in some cases hang our heads. But the jury had spoken and Owens was now a free man. Some of the jurors went to the back of the courtroom and embraced Owens' wife and mother.

After the trial, one female juror said, "We just didn't believe the government witnesses. We thought Owens was the most convincing witness." My friend SA Ellis Young's sister Anita had a friend on the jury. She told Anita, "That agent Corbett Hart had 'shifty eyes.'" Great.

Atty. Gilder had apparently raised suspicion in some jurors' minds about my relationship with Baldwin. Gilder in his cross-examination and closing statement had convinced the jury that the witnesses were making up the charges against Owens in order to hopefully reduce the prison sentences they were serving. One juror said, "Maybe now he can go home and be with his son because a little boy needs his father." Several months earlier Gayla had given birth to a baby boy.

Most of the agents, officers and prosecutors returned to the Nashville FBI office to discuss how we went wrong in this case. None of us blamed the jury, a cornerstone of the American judicial system. I got my luggage and went to my car, which was parked, on the street next to the Federal Building. Reporters had been lying in wait for me and began asking questions while I put my things in the trunk. Normally I would have had something to say but I only gave them a "No comment." As I stood at the back of my car while the cameras were whirling and reporters shouting, I suddenly thought about the only other not guilty verdict where I was the case agent, the bank extortionist Neim. Like this case, the government had more than enough evidence but the jury didn't think so. I didn't take the Owens verdict as hard as I did the Nein case realizing that no matter how hard we worked or what the evidence some cases don't end the way they should.

Back in Memphis we wondered how could it be that our task force spent more than two years investigating and building this case, only to lose at trial? We were at an all time low in morale and badly discouraged about the verdict.

After a few days, however, we decided not to give up on Owens because we knew without a doubt that he would cross the line again. We kept a watchful eye on Danny and continued to contact his known associates in hopes of developing some crime we could charge him with. Danny had to be a multi-millionaire so he really didn't need money but he surely was up to something that would eventually come to our attention.

One of Owens' associates that we were interested in was Thomas Tiller. He had previously worked for Danny in his clubs but the two had had a falling out a couple years before. Tiller was from a large family in Memphis that over the years became a household name due to the barroom brawls they were involved in and usually won. On one occasion when four of the Tiller brothers were running a bar six or eight bikers came in. Before long there was an argument between the bikers and the Tillers. When the fight was over all the bikers were laid out on the floor and the Tillers were still standing.

In September 1983 Thomas Tiller had just finished a five-year state prison sentence after he copped a plea on a murder charge. He came to Owens looking for a job and Danny hired him to manage one of his topless clubs. On November 22, 1983 Owens and Tiller were sitting at a table in the club. In through the door came eight Iron Horsemen motorcycle gang members carrying ball bats, pistols and motorcycle chains. Owens had several of their "Old Ladies" (a biker term for their girlfriends who were certainly not old) working as dancers at his topless clubs. Owens and the Iron Horsemen had been feuding for some time. Some of the gang members felt Danny wasn't treating their Old Ladies properly.

In his account of the encounter Owens said he got up and moved quickly to confront the gang members. He assumed that Tiller was right behind him and would back him up. When he looked back Tiller was running out the back door. The gang members began beating Danny with ball bats and chains. They quickly had him on the floor and continued to beat and kick him. Paramedics took Owens to the hospital where he remained for a couple months. Five days after the Owens beating Tiller had the good sense to go to work for Art Baldwin.

While it was never proven, it was common knowledge that the Iron Horsemen were also retaliating for a 1981 beating Owens and Jimmy Whitten had given eight club members. Danny and Whitten used baseball bats and put the Horsemen in the hospital. We tried to talk to Thomas Tiller about Owens after he went to work for Baldwin but he wouldn't tell us anything.

About a month after Tiller entered Baldwin's employment, an informant told me Tiller was driving a stolen Cadillac. We started surveilling Tiller during daylight hours and two days later saw him driving a white Cadillac with Texas license plates. With the license plate number we got a hit from Texas that it was stolen and wanted in a murder investigation of a topless dancer in Houston.

I told the surveilling officers to keep an eye on Tiller while I got an arrest warrant. The officers kept watching him at a local motel. When Tiller left the room and walked up to the Cadillac the officers placed him under arrest for interstate transport of a stolen vehicle.

The US Magistrate found probable cause to hold Tiller and set his bond at $500,000. While his trial was in progress one of his brothers approached me in the hallway outside the courtroom during a break. He stood very close to me and with witnesses all-around said, "The Tillers will not forget this. You better watch your back."

I told the Assistant US Attorney handling the prosecution about my encounter and he felt that the threat was not specific enough to charge threatening a federal agent. I also told my SAC about the veiled threat. He wanted to assign a couple of agents to babysit me for a while. I said, "It was just one of the young Tillers running his mouth. I'm convinced nothing will come of it." The SAC finally agreed with me.

The jury came back with a verdict of guilty. We tried to talk to Thomas Tiller again. If he would cooperate with us, I said, and tell us what he knew about Owens, we would try to get his sentence reduced. He declined our offer. That's the last contact I ever had with any of the Tillers.

There is an old adage, "The wheels of justice grind slowly but exceedingly fine." Nearly 10 years after his acquittal the OCDETF obtained an indictment in 1992 naming Danny Owens, his son Blake Owens and six others with charges of gambling, prostitution, money laundering and drug trafficking.

At the ensuing trial a witness testified that in May 1991, Blake Owens handcuffed an employee, John Howard, and forced him to bend face first over a desk. They pulled his pants down and while Blake restrained him Danny beat him with a large wooden paddle. Howard suffered searing and severe bruising. The Owenses suspected Howard of having stolen money out of electronic gambling machines Danny owned.

After three months of testimony all the defendants were found guilty as charged. On one count Danny was found guilty of laundering in excess of one million dollars.

I felt vindicated that Danny was finally brought to justice but was sorry that I wasn't on the task force that finally nailed him.

After serving 21 years, Danny Owens was released from prison shortly before his 66th birthday in 2016. I learned from a reliable source that Danny's mother is operating three topless nightclubs in Jackson, MS. Maybe Danny is working for her.

Chapter 8
The Mountain Man: Billy Dean Anderson

In January 1975, after nearly 25 years of crime, some petty, some major, and five prison escapes, Billy Dean Anderson was placed on the FBI's Ten Most Wanted Fugitive list. The case was assigned to my former partner and good friend Burl Smith. Burl had been investigating Billy off and on since 1974 when he was charged with federal Unlawful Flight to Avoid Prosecution (UFAP). I had a part in the investigation later.

Burl had transferred to the Cookeville, Tennessee, RA, a part of the Memphis Division. In Director J. Edgar Hoover's rebuilding of the FBI he wanted to assure the American people that if the FBI's help was needed in a certain location, an agent could be there within two hours. Hence he created these smaller offices called Resident Agencies (RA).

Billy Dean Anderson's home was in the Wolf River Valley of Fentress County in the mountains of north-central Middle Tennessee, close to the Kentucky state line. The Wolf River rises at the base of the Cumberland Plateau in a rugged hollow about three miles southeast of the small community of Pall Mall where Billy was born July 12, 1934. The county seat of Fentress County is Jamestown, about five miles south of Pall Mall.

Front porch of home of Ina Hughes Billy's Mother

The terrain is full of hills and hollows with roads that twist and turn. A stranger could get lost in a heartbeat. Archaeological digs have revealed the area was inhabited 12,000 years ago by nomadic tribes. Hardscrabble agriculture, saltpeter mining and moonshining were the only means of income for early homesteaders. A major source of naturally occurring saltpeter, the main ingredient in gunpowder, was mined from the caves of the county.

Pall Mall is famous as the birthplace and home of World War I hero Sergeant Alvin C. York. York was awarded the Congressional Medal of Honor for his acts of bravery in the war. Sgt. York belonged to a fundamentalist church and unsuccessfully tried to avoid the WWI draft by claiming to be a conscientious objector. He ended up a hero using his marksman skills, honed in Tennessee, to silence German machine guns and along with eight other men capture 132 enemy prisoners.

The people in these mountains live by a different code than most in the United States. Since the days after the Civil War, many have made their living making moonshine whiskey and bootlegging. These folks are resentful of authority and extremely suspicious of any strangers in their community and very religious.

Billy Dean was the illegitimate son of Ina Anderson (pronounced "Iner" by the local people) and Owen Wood, his acknowledged father. Billy was somewhat of a loner, spending a lot of time roaming the mountains, which led to his becoming very knowledgeable of the area. This knowledge would become valuable to him later as he hid from the law.

In May 1958 Billy became a fugitive from justice on a warrant issued for the burglary of a liquor store in Nashville. A month later he was taken in for questioning on this crime. He gave his name as William David Upchurch. Somehow he managed to get away from the officers and walked all the way home to Pall Mall from Carthage, Tennessee, a distance of 50 miles.

On June 15, 1959 Billy picked up some friends to go to the movies at a drive-in in Jamestown. There was a long line of cars waiting to pay, so Billy decided to go in through the exit. The owner caught him and made them leave even when Billy offered to pay. "Just get the hell out of here. I don't want your money." Billy felt humiliated in front of his friends and decided to get revenge. He dropped off one friend and then with Elam Crabtree and a borrowed shotgun headed back to the drive-in. On the way he told Elam, "We'll raise some hell down here to get the law away from us then we'll get him (the drive-in owner.)" So they drove around in the country and shot out some signs as a diversion.

Around nine-thirty that night Fentress County Sheriff Irvin Jones got a call that wasn't unusual, someone was shooting road signs. While he was checking out the shooting, Billy and Elam were back at the drive-in and assaulted the owner and shot but missed hitting him. The dispatcher called Jones about the shooting at the drive-in so he headed back to town. Jones had his blue lights flashing when Billy and Elam met him going the other way. "See I told you it would work," Billy told Crabtree.

The drive-in owner was still conscious when Jones got to him. He said someone had tried to kill him and described the vehicle they were in. Jones knew who it was and found Billy and Elam at Crabtree's house. He arrested them and searched the car. He found two shotguns, a pistol and some unfired cartridges. They were charged with assault and battery and attempted murder. Billy, then 24 years old, got a four-month sentence.

On September 10, 1959, Billy wrecked a car, was arrested and charged with DUI and reckless driving. He was found guilty and fined $150 plus court costs. Unable to pay, he remained in jail.

On Monday, January 4, 1960, Billy was waiting in jail to go to court for another DUI. Sheriff Irvin Jones unlocked the door of the cold, damp cell and said, "Let's go, boy, you're going across the street, but you'll be back." Billy knew he wouldn't.

In the courthouse the sheriff locked Billy in a room on the second floor. The room was cold and moisture had formed on the window. He wiped it off and looked out to see if he could spot his friend, William Dotson Jennings, known to everyone as Dottie. Dottie was supposed to be circling the courthouse ready to pick Billy up. "I might kill myself in the jump," he thought, "but I'm going to do it if Dottie shows up." The familiar car turned the corner, Dottie waved and Billy jumped, breaking his fall in a bunch of bushes under the window. He reached Dottie's car and they took off.

Meanwhile back in the courtroom, someone whispered in the sheriff's ear, " Did you know one of those fellows you put back in that room jumped out of the window?" The sheriff rushed to the room. Billy wasn't there.

Dottie drove Billy to Muncie, Indiana, the home of many people from the Fentress County area who went there for jobs.

In August 1960, Billy Dean got into an argument with a bartender in Muncie, and was charged with carrying a concealed weapon (brass knuckles) and contributing to the delinquency of a minor. He didn't go anywhere without a knife, brass knuckles or a pistol. He was locked up in the Muncie city jail and promptly tried to escape by taking out a ceiling grate and concealing himself between two walls. A jailer missed him and, after a search, Billy was found in his hiding place. He ended up serving nearly a year in an Indiana penal farm.

Billy Dean surfaced in early 1962, again in Muncie. A favorite hang out there for Billy and others was the Cozy Lodge Bar. Billy decided to rob this bar and enlisted an old friend, Finley Barnett, as an accomplice. Since he was well known at the bar Billy wore a shirt with a hood to conceal his identity. The two robbed the bar at gunpoint and got away. A customer later identified Billy since his hood fell off revealing his face. He was arrested and placed in the county jail awaiting trial.

Billy hadn't been in jail long when he hatched an escape plan, but he had to lose weight to carry it out. For five months he nearly starved himself, only eating enough to keep his strength up. When he thought he was thin enough he found his escape opportunity on Saturday, May 5, 1962, at around two in the afternoon.

The jailer herded Billy and nine other prisoners into the bullpen while their cells were being cleaned. He didn't tell the others about his plan (they couldn't have succeeded without losing weight first and it was better to be alone) but when the time came, he tricked them into helping him. "I bet we can get out of here," Billy said and handed a push broom to another inmate and showed him how easy it was to raise the metal corrugated ceiling panel that lay on a steel joist. The prisoners all looked up and saw a narrow black hole not more than 10-13 inches in diameter. None was brave enough or thin enough to try but the bored prisoners were eager to help Billy escape.

The nine men formed a human pyramid and boosted Billy up to the ceiling. He forced his way up two stories through a metal galvanized vent and air duct. He even had to go around a curve to reach the roof of the jail.

The prisoners who helped Billy kept quiet and he wasn't missed until the 9:00 p.m. roll call. The jailers figured the only way Billy could have escaped was through the air duct since once before some juveniles had tried the same thing.

Billy was wanted for jail breaking in Tennessee and Indiana so he headed to Kentucky. He knew a friend, Delmer "Bigun" Fitzgerald, had recently moved from Indiana to Park City, Kentucky, a small town near Bowling Green. Bigun and his wife, Betty, were trying to grow tobacco. Billy offered to stay and help them for room and board since he knew about growing tobacco from hiring out back home.

Billy had been at the Fitzgerald's for nearly five months when he started getting restless. He needed to move on but didn't have much money. He went to the Park City State Bank to cash his last paycheck from Bigun, $3 a day, and inspect the inside of the bank. He had to wait in line for a few minutes and couldn't believe what he was hearing. Two old men were talking about a gang who had robbed several banks in the area the last year.

One of the men said, "You'd have to be a fool to rob a bank across the alley from the police station."

"The bank has been in business since 1908 and has never been robbed," said the other, "and I'll bet it never will be."

"You never know, old-timer," Billy said. "There are a lot of fools in the world." Billy loved a challenge and craved excitement like cool water when thirsty.

On October 8, 1962, Billy and a partner carried out the robbery of the Park City State Bank. They parked their car close to city hall, just in time to see Police Chief Pete Wright get in his car and leave.

Shortly after the bank opened that day a teller looked up and saw a man (later identified by authorities as Billy Dean Anderson) standing in front of her and the other cashier. In her words "he looked like he was going to a Halloween party." He actually was a white man in black face trying to hide his identity. The robber got the money from the cashiers and then demanded the cash from the vault. He ordered the two cashiers and three other adults and a child into the bank vault. He warned the hostages to stay in the vault for ten minutes or he would kill them all.

As the robber was leaving the bank he met another customer entering. He ordered him into the vault with the others. This customer didn't do as told and saw the robber get into a vehicle with another man driving. When local police officers arrived the customer gave them a description of the getaway car and the direction it went. The robbers got away with over $13,000.

FBI agents from the Bowling Green RA arrived promptly and investigated the robbery. Two months later Billy Dean was charged with robbing the Park City State Bank.

On Saturday night October 27, 1962, less than a month after Billy robbed the Park City Bank he wanted to go to Jamestown and show off his car. Just before he got there he saw a teenage boy standing beside the road hitching a ride to town. He recognized him as a long time friend, 16 year-old George Long. Billy stopped and George got in. To show off in front of George, Billy gunned the motor, popped the clutch, and spun a little as he pulled out onto Highway 127 in Jamestown.

Unluckily for Billy, two young state troopers behind him stopped at a red light and saw the Ford weaving. Steve Webb, age 31, was from Jackson County Tennessee and had been patrolling the streets of Jamestown for four years, The other trooper J. C. Elmore, was from

Crossville, Tennessee and had only been working in Fentress County for eight months.

Trooper Webb turned on the patrol car's lights and spotlight and pulled Billy over. He walked up to the driver's side of Billy's car,

"I need to see your driver's license."

What fer ?I didn't do nothing wrong."

The trooper looked around inside the car, could smell beer and saw empty cans in the car. Webb told Billy to step out of the car as he reached inside to grab the keys from the ignition. Trooper Elmore went to the passenger side to talk to young George Long.

When Webb reached for Billy to take him out of the car, Billy pulled out a .38 caliber police revolver and shot Webb in the right shoulder. The bullet came out his back between his shoulder blades. Webb fired back six times before he dropped his gun. Most of the bullets hit Billy's car not him. When Billy saw the gun fall, he turned and shot through the car at Trooper Elmore on the passenger side. The shot missed Elmore and probably was the one that struck George Long and put him in a wheelchair for the rest of his life.

Elmore shot three times at Billy. Two bullets hit him, one in his stomach. After Elmore had fired two shots from the front of the car, he went around the patrol car, and came up upon Billy from behind, and struck him over the head with the barrel of his pistol.

Sheriff Irving Jones wasn't far away when a passing motorist stopped him and told him about the bloodshed. When he got to the scene Webb was begging Elmore to give him his gun so he could shoot Billy and George. Jones said, "I seen enough blood already," and kicked the gun under the car.

Billy was taken to the Fentress County Hospital in Jamestown. Sheriff Jones had a deputy guard the door to Billy's room.

Billy eventually pled guilty to the charges of shooting with intent to kill Trooper Elmore and wounding Trooper Webb. He had to be carried into the courtroom since he couldn't walk. While in the state prison system he was fitted with braces for his lower legs and could walk after a fashion.

After serving three years, two months of his three to five year sentence Billy was released from prison on March 9, 1965. But his feet didn't hit free ground since there was still an outstanding warrant for him for his escape from the jail in Muncie, Indiana.

U.S. Marshals took Billy to Muncie to answer the charge of robbing the Cozy Lodge Bar the previous year. He pled guilty and was sentenced to 10-25 years. The judge suspended the sentence with the condition that Billy never return to Indiana.

In October 1966, Billy was driving near Jamestown with two friends when he met Sheriff Irvin Jones and Deputy Shirley Hays coming from the other direction. Billy pulled into the middle of the road in an attempt to run the Sheriff off the road. Jones maintained control,

Billy stopped and Sheriff Jones walked toward him. Billy fired a shot at Jones and a shoot out commenced. When the firing stopped Billy had emptied his gun. Jones, thinking Billy was out of ammunition, went near him to arrest him. Billy stuck his pistol into Jones' stomach and pulled the trigger three times but it didn't fire. A later check of the pistol found one round had misfired. The two officers fired a total of 17 shots with none hitting Billy or his passengers.

In January 1967 Billy was tried by a jury on charges of assault with a deadly weapon and attempt to commit murder. He was found guilty and sentenced to two consecutive seven-year terms in state prison. He was paroled in November 1969.

Two months later Billy was back in Indiana despite the judge's order. Billy was working at a service station and got into a dispute with a customer who called the police. Billy's criminal past caught up with him and he was arrested for parole violation, carrying a pistol without a permit, resisting arrest and public intoxication. The same Indiana judge revoked his suspended sentence and gave him 10 years in the state prison. He only served 16 months and was released on parole.

When Billy returned to Tennessee he married a local girl Betty Koger. On Saturday December 29, 1973 Betty was drinking with some friends at the Candlelight Club near Jamestown. At closing time she saw the owner stuff a large amount of cash, from the night's receipts and a poker game, in the corner pocket of a pool table. She heard him say he would take the money to the bank on Monday. She told Billy about what she had seen when she got home. She wanted to break into the club and steal the money. Billy told her he'd been out of jail for only six months and didn't want to go back.

As soon as Billy got out of bed the next morning she started in on him again. "It will be easy to break in and get the money….we're broke and you don't get your (Social Security) check for three more days." He finally agreed to do the burglary.

At two in the morning they gathered the tools to knock a hole in the cinderblock wall near the back door of the Candlelight Club. By five Billy had made a hole big enough for Betty to reach in and unlock the door. Billy said, "We gotta hurry up and git out of here, what time is it?" "It's almost 5:30," said Betty as she looked at the shiny gold-plated watch Billy had bought her for Christmas.

Someone heard the racket and called the Fentress County Sheriff. The dispatcher sent Deputy Webb (Junior) Hatfield to check the building. As Deputy Hatfield turned into the driveway at the club he saw two vehicles on the parking lot, one he knew belonged to the owner of the club. He didn't recognize the other car but he could tell it hadn't been there long since the windows had no frost on them on this cold winter night.

Betty was fumbling to unlock the door when Billy heard the tires crunching on the gravel, "Somebody's coming, douse the light. Hurry up, get around the corner." As Billy peeked around the corner he saw Junior get out of the car and check the front door. Billy grabbed his tools in one hand and picked up his rifle with his other. After checking the door Junior circled around the parking lot so he could see the back door and saw a large hole in the wall near the door. Billy recognized Junior immediately. Billy threw the crowbar to make noise and frighten Junior away. Junior heard and decided whoever was breaking in was still there. He left the parking lot as fast as he could thinking, "I have to get to the nearest telephone and call for back up." Billy walked around the other corner and hunkered down beside Betty's car. He could see a passing semi-truck was keeping Junior from leaving the parking lot. "Hah, I'm going to have some fun with him," Billy told Betty. He rested his 30.06 Springfield bolt-action high-powered rifle on Betty's car and shot at the police car hitting the rear passenger door. Betty begged him to stop but he fired a second shot that went through the rear door window, the protective cage and the seat below the headrest. The bullet cut the zipper on the deputy's jacket and hit his left arm. By instinct Hatfield's foot pushed down on the accelerator and the patrol car took off spinning gravel just as Billy fired again and the third shot missed the car.

Deputy Hatfield drove toward Jamestown steering the car with his right arm and trying to press his left arm against the car door to stop the bleeding. He knew he would bleed to death if he didn't get help soon. He got to a service station about a mile and a half south of the Candlelight. The owner saw Junior's condition, pushed him over to the middle of the seat and drove him to the hospital. The doctors saved Junior's life but he was never able to work again.

As soon as the deputy's car left the parking lot Billy and Betty headed for home, down the mountain toward Pall Mall, his safe zone in the valley. He told Betty to turn off the highway and go down Angel

Mountain Road. Betty pulled over at at a secluded stretch of road. Billy walked into the woods a short distance and buried the rifle and a 12 gauge single barrel shotgun under the frozen leaves. He planned to return the next morning after the heat was off and move the weapons to a safer place.

They then drove to Betty's mother's house where they had left her three small kids. They felt it would be safer there than going home to their trailer. Billy limped up the rickety stairs to a bedroom to sleep. He took a .22 caliber pistol from his pocket and put it in one of his boots by the bed.

Early the next morning Billy heard a commotion downstairs. "He's in the bed upstairs passed out drunk," Betty said. He knew it was the law. "We got arrest warrants for both of you." "I ain't done a damn thing, and ain't going with you," Betty told the three lawmen standing at the door.

Billy knew Betty was putting up a wildcat fight. He then heard footsteps coming up the stairs. He might have run but decided to stick to his plan thinking they had no evidence since he had hidden the gun. A deputy said, "Get up and put your boots on, we got arrest warrants for you and your wife for shooting Junior Hatfield." The officers handcuffed Betty and Billy and drove them to the Jamestown jail. Knowing Billy was an escape risk jailer Buster Stockton tied Billy to the cell bars for three days.

At a hearing on Friday, January 4, 1974, the judge set Billy's bond at $50,000 and Betty's at $10,000. Betty made bond and went home to her children. When Billy found out that the charges against her had been dropped, he knew that she had turned against him. He was charged with attempted burglary at the Candlelight Club, assault with intent to murder Deputy Hatfield, and the use of a deadly weapon in the commission of a felony. Because of his long history of criminal offenses he was also charged with violation of the habitual criminal statute. Billy's propensity to escape was well known so he was transferred to a more secure jail in Wartenburg, Tennessee.

After Billy had been in jail for a while he sent word by his mother that he wanted Betty to visit him. She agreed but only if his mother came along. Betty went into the jail with a frightened look on her face and blurted out, "I done what I done for the kids. They needed their mother." She had snitched him out.

"Looka here," said Billy. " I shouldn't of listened to you, and I shouldn't have married you, but that's over and done with. You're the reason I'm in this mess, now you can help me get out. Here's what I want you to do. Buy a box of cheap cigars and hide a small saw blade between the layers of cardboard on the inside of the box. And don't tell nobody about this, especially mother." Betty brought the hidden saw blade the next time she visited.

Billy shared a cell with Glen Hicks, who had been in jail for two years awaiting trial for murder. They began the arduous process of making a hole in the thick steel wall under Hicks' bed. One watched and listened while the other chipped away. The saw didn't work as well as Billy hoped and Hicks became discouraged. Billy took one of the industrial diamond pins out of his leg brace and attached it to the saw blade. This worked better but the work was still slow. It took them more than a month to get the hole big enough to crawl to freedom.

Billy talked his half-sister Jenell into helping with the escape. On Sunday, August 4, 1974, the two escaped through the hole. Jenell was parked around the corner from the jail and had with her what Billy wanted: a sheet of paper in a stamped envelope, a change of clothes, a knife and a pistol. Jenell drove them out of Wartburg to a secluded spot near the edge of a large wooded area. Billy told Hicks, "I'm going home----you're on your own" and he disappeared into the woods and from the law enforcement radar.

The jailer didn't realize Billy and Hicks were missing until the next morning at 7:30. They had been gone nearly 12 hours by then. Local officers located and arrested Hicks a few days later. He never gave up Billy.

In the meantime Billy walked to a bridge at the west end of the Morgan/Fentress county line. On the crumpled paper Jenell had given him he wrote a short, obscure note to his friend Glen (Squirrel) Evans in Pall Mall. He told him to come to the bridge as soon as he could and wait. Billy put the letter into the closest mailbox.

Thirteen days after the escape Squirrel picked up Billy as planned. They headed to Marrowbone, Kentucky. Since Billy needed money he decided to rob the Marrowbone Bank. He stole a car that was parked with the keys in it. In the back seat he found a woman's overnight case that contained a blonde shag wig, a pair of dark silk stockings, a green sweater and a pair of gloves. He parked in front of the bank, right next to a new looking Cadillac. A small black man (later identified as Elzie Kirk, nicknamed Bean) was cleaning the glass front door of the bank. Billy put on his newly found disguise and walked toward the bank. "This is a stick up, get inside." Bean grabbed Billy's arm, the one with a gun in it, and both men fell backwards. Billy fired two shots into the front of the bank. Bean got up and once Billy was out of sight he ran to the beauty shop next door to call the police.

Billy went in the bank, held his gun to a bank officer's face and said "Fill it up." He got away with $13,418. Billy drove the stolen car to Metcalfe County where Squirrel was waiting for him. They abandoned the car and headed to Muncie in Squirrel's truck.

The FBI investigated the bank robbery and identified Billy as a suspect. Agents in Muncie threatened his relatives with prosecution if they withheld or provided false information. They said he hadn't been in touch with them and they wouldn't tell even if they knew where he was.

Billy realized he had to leave Indiana but he also knew he wouldn't be safe in Tennessee. Squirrel and Billy headed south.

Shortly after the jail escape, the FBI obtained a federal fugitive warrant charging Billy with attempted murder of a law enforcement officer. This is when FBI agents Burl Smith and Jim Harcum began their search for Billy in the hills and hollows of Fentress County and beyond where he had family and friends.

Burl had information Billy was living with "Bigun" Fitzgerald and his wife Betty who now lived near Bald Rock, Kentucky. Early one morning Burl gathered a team of agents near Bald Rock. They entered Fitzgerald's house without any problem but found only Bigun, his wife and two children. Like everyone else they didn't know Billy's whereabouts. The agents noticed breakfast dishes on the table with five place settings. The Fitzgeralds could not, or perhaps would not, explain the extra place setting. Burl believes there was a good likelihood Billy had been there and escaped before they got in the house.

The agents searching for Billy Dean soon found that a normal fugitive investigation was not going to work. Interviews with friends, family members etc. produced no information of value. His mother, who was apparently the only person Billy was close to, was hostile to law enforcement. However, she and her husband, Omer Hughes, allowed Burl Smith and Jim Harcum into their home many times and were courteous to them. Ina never relented in her assertion that Billy was dead. The agents also watched the Hughes in the grocery store, trying to determine whether they bought more groceries than would be logical for them. Efforts to surveil them while driving, even with Bureau aircraft overhead to help the ground units, were frustrated by the fact that Omer drove his 1948 Jeep at about 15 miles per hour.

On January 3, 1975 the Bureau sent a notice to all law enforcement, local, state and federal, seeking their help in locating Billy Dean Anderson. It consisted of several photos, his fingerprints, and crimes he was wanted for. A few weeks later, on January 21, 1975, Billy was placed on the FBI Ten Most Wanted Fugitives list.

An intensified investigation began with more interviews of all known family members and associates in the Jamestown and Pall Mall area. The results were no different: no one knew anything.

Burl was frustrated spending so much time and effort searching for Billy while the government was supporting him with Social Security disability checks. Perhaps, he thought, he could find out where the checks were being cashed. Burl learned the checks were mailed to his mother's address, payable to Billy and endorsed in what appeared to be his name, all handwriting the same. An officer at the Union Bank in Jamestown told Burl Ina cashed the checks at his bank. Four of the checks were sent to the Bureau lab for latent fingerprint examination. The lab found three prints, none belonging to Billy. Ultimately the Bureau was able to get the checks stopped because Billy didn't have a current medical review of his continuing disability.

Burl and Jim suspected Billy's friend Squirrel knew his whereabouts and watched him constantly and talked to him often. They also tried to interview Betty Koger but she was so hostile they gave up on her. The agents continued to be persistent, however, showing up without warning to keep the pressure on the locals.

An FBI status report in April 1975 read in part, "The subject is possibly staying at various locations in very remote sections of Fentress and Pickett Counties of Tennessee and Wayne and Pickett Counties of Kentucky. He is likely being supplied with food and other necessities by moon shiners and general outlaws.

"Consideration has been given to the saturation of this area by numerous agent personnel; however, the conclusion has been reached that the area is too large and there are too many locations in which subject could possibly be staying, noting that he has in the past lived in the woods practically like an animal."

Another contemporaneous FBI report stated that the Fentress County Sheriff "has advised that most of the residents are either related in some fashion to the fugitive or are associated with him. The fugitive is reportedly somewhat of a 'folk hero' in the area."

Agents from the four field divisions most actively involved in the effort had a conference in July 1975. The group recommended 30 agents (10 each from Memphis, Louisville and Knoxville) go into the rugged area to conduct simultaneous interviews and an intensive effort to either locate Billy or flush him out. It was estimated that over 1000 interviews of residents and relatives had already been conducted in the Pall Mall area alone in the previous six months.

The saturation began August 11, 1975 and continued for five days. The agents crisscrossed four counties in Tennessee and Kentucky talking to anyone who would talk to them. They also searched every abandoned building spotted either from their vehicles or the airplane that buzzed overhead. Some of the agents concentrated on the caves in the area of Ina's house.

I was part of one terrain search in the rough and wild area. We lined up with about five yards between each other and moved in a line. We knew if anyone left an established road and went less than a mile into the wilderness, unless a local and knew the country, he could quickly become lost. It's all ridges and hollows (referred to exclusively as "hollars" by the mountain people) and they all look the same. The area is also heavily forested with mostly hardwoods and a generous sprinkling of pine. In some places there are thickets where the growth is so close together that it is impenetrable. The day I was there it was hot and the chiggers were biting.

The Wolf River Cave, known locally as Blowing Cave, has seven miles of passages and is 160 feet deep. Footprints preserved in the cave prove that Indians explored it over 500 years ago in their bare feet. The agents reported the searches of the caves revealed conclusively that none had been used for human habitation.

Despite interviewing 732 people during the special investigation the Bureau was no closer to learning the whereabouts of Billy Dean. A subsequent report stated once again, "Subject's relatives and associates are extremely hostile and it is believed that any effort to cultivate these individuals would be fruitless at this time. The consensus of interviewing agents was that any information furnished by most of the local people is mostly if not all, suspicion, and unfounded gossip, such as is very common in this area."

The only new lead came from a review of Billy's medical records in the fall of 1975. Agents learned his leg braces needed continuous repair or refitting. The Bureau printed 3,500 circulars showing Billy's picture and description that were distributed to orthopedic and prosthetics practitioners hoping Billy would have repairs made and they would notify the Bureau if he did. Nothing came of this effort.

In June 1976 FBI agents along with ATF (Alcohol, Tobacco and Firearms) agents and Kentucky state police followed what turned out to be another dead end. They had information that Billy might be engaged in moonshining and a big still was supposed to be in Bald Rock, Kentucky. Only six abandoned stills were found.

One bright point in the investigation occurred in early fall 1976 when an anonymous woman called and stated Billy Anderson and two of his friends had carried out the September 1, 1973 robbery of the Mooreland Bank in Indiana. All three were indicted and the two friends apprehended on September 29, 1976 in Muncie. Both men refused to furnish any information about Billy but one said, "I think he is in

Jamestown, Tennessee and not Muncie----he would be crazy to be here with all the heat and TV coverage in Muncie."

In the winter of 1976-77 an FBI source told the Bureau: "I hear stories when I go back to the Wolf Creek (River) area about him living in caves and having food for the next six months, and I believe that he could possibly do this, as he is a loner. He is a killer who everyone is afraid of, and he is very proud of his reputation and would not be arrested without a fight of some type... I believe he is in Tennessee, probably living in the mountains, and is probably receiving help from people in the area."

The Bureau believed from this source that Billy would soon sneak in to visit his mother. With this idea in mind the FBI lab installed a low light camera near the mother's house with a view of her front door. The signal from the camera was transmitted by microwave to a camper concealed nearby. The photo surveillance lasted about a month as the agents watched Billy's mother and stepfather going about their daily business. One night Omer turned on the porch light and every night thereafter. The light kept the low light camera from seeing anything but the bright light. Even when the camera did work the agents saw nothing helpful.

The search went on, still with no results, when another approach was tried. In August of 1977 the FBI used a cooperating individual to deliver a cigarette lighter to Billy's mother, intended to be a gift for Billy. A small transmitter was located in the lighter tuned to a certain frequency and was to periodically issue a "beep." This sound could be picked up by a receiver in an aircraft flying over the area where Billy was believed to be and his location pinpointed. Some signals were heard and recorded but could not be located nor could they be verified as coming from the concealed transmitter.

In September 1977 Supervising Special Agent Cecil Moses was

transferred to the Memphis division and became the boss of the squad that handled fugitives. Cecil had made a rather fast move from street agent into the administrative tier of the Bureau. He was very popular with the agents who worked for him since he had lots of experience on the street and had the reputation of "an agent's agent." He could "walk the walk and talk the talk."

Upon arriving in Memphis Cecil began a thorough review of Billy's extensive file. As Cecil read the file and thought about it he became convinced Billy was alive and hiding in the mountains of Fentress or Pickett County not far from his family who were probably providing him with necessities.

Cecil was born in the mountains of Whitley County, Kentucky, an area much like the Pall Mall country, and as a matter of fact, as the crow flies, fairly close. He was about the same age as Billy and grew up with the same sort of people as Billy did. Cecil believed Billy felt the same as he would: he would rather live in a cave in the mountains than go to prison.

Late in the fall of 1977 Cecil called a conference of agents from Memphis, Knoxville, Indianapolis and Louisville who had been working the case. We all knew that there was considerable resistance and hostility toward us from the mountain people. It was either give up or move forward. Cecil said, "We don't do that, the case stays open until he is caught or we verify he is dead." We thought, "Here we go again!"

Cecil then approached the SAC with a new game plan. Cecil wanted more assets. He wanted authority to install a PIN register on Ina Hughes' telephone to record the telephone numbers for all incoming and outgoing calls. Agents couldn't listen to conversations but use the telephone numbers from the PIN register to locate names and addresses of the callers and numbers called. Further Cecil proposed that each division make more agents available to work the case and put boots on the ground for searches of places where Billy likely could be hiding. And he wanted frequent air surveillance. Headquarters agreed to just about everything Cecil proposed including permission to increase the $2000 reward to $10,000 for information leading to Billy's location.

Before Cecil's plan was put into action he went to Billy's mother and begged her. "I don't care, just have him surrender, all we want is for him to have his day in court. I don't care what the outcome is. We've got $10,000 cash. I don't care if you take the money and hire a lawyer. Our job is to bring him in." She screamed at Cecil, "You know my son is dead, you are just harassing this old woman." He knew she was lying and it turned out that she was. Before he left Cecil told her, "We will find him someday and when we do, we will probably have to kill him and his blood will be on your hands."

At the next all-agents meeting we began discussing the possibility of an undercover operation in Jamestown. A plan was developed to send two agents posing as burglars and stick-up men from Nashville. Their story would be that they were being hotly pursued by the law in Nashville and had to leave for a while to let things cool off. My friend and cohort Special Agent Gene Stevens and I quickly agreed to take the assignment. Only one or two high-ranking law enforcement officers who covered Fentress County would know our true identity.

During Director Hoover's regime Bureau agents did little if any undercover work. Shortly after his death in 1972 headquarters started an undercover program and sent a communication to all offices asking for volunteers. I was accepted into the program in 1976 and given a full set of identification in the name of Joe Ray Stewart, an actual high school friend whose name I could easily remember. The Billy Dean Anderson case was my first significant and extensive undercover assignment.

When Gene and I got to Jamestown we rented a mobile home and began visiting the town's two bars, one on each end of town out in the county, Maw's Place and the Candlelight Club. Beer drinking was illegal in the city limits. We began laying down our cover story to people we talked to. We had previously purchased some used auto parts, some home electronics including a couple small TVs and other appliances. Word got around very quickly that we had stuff for sale at a good price.

Of the two bars we liked Maw's the best. Our routine was to go there around 4 p.m. every day and stay until 10, sometimes till the 2 a.m. closing. Gene and I each had grown a beard and let our hair grow out some, not the normal 1978 FBI style. We wore jeans, cowboy boots and a hat almost always. Gene was a big, tall likeable Texan who could talk to anybody he met without hesitation. We both had Southern accents and were able to use the local grammar without any problem. Basically we were country boys at heart and in reality, who just happened to have the greatest career possible: FBI agents.

Since the bars could only sell beer we could nurse a drink all night and not become drunk. From time to time we would ask about a famous outlaw from the area we had heard about in Nashville. Often we could get someone to talk about Billy Dean and some even said they believed he was hiding from the FBI somewhere in Fentress or Pickett County.

We got into some interesting situations while hanging out at the bars. One night a man came in who had just returned from Muncie, Indiana. He was telling his friends he had become a member of the mob up there. Most of his friends didn't believe him since he was a notorious liar.

After this mob member had been back in town for about a week he got into an argument in Maw's with another customer. The argument escalated with threats from the mob man to kill the other. The other man pulled a knife from his waist and put it on the bar in front of him. The bar owner, whom everyone called Maw, convinced him to go home. The man went out the front door and turned right, alongside a series of floor to ceiling windows. All at once shots rang out from inside the bar. The mob man was seated at a table near the rear. He had pulled out a 9 mm semi-automatic pistol and was shooting at the windows. He wasn't much of a shot, the first two or three rounds passed through the top of the windows. He continued to fire rapidly and gradually brought his shots lower. Just as the other man neared the end of the building one round hit him in the hip.

Most of the customers, including Gene and me, ran out the back of the bar and left before the sheriff arrived. The shooter was arrested and made bail the next day.

George Long, the young man believed to have been shot and paralyzed by Billy, frequented the same bars. I got to know him quite well as he liked to play pool and so did I. We played together often and he finally told me why he was in a wheelchair. He said it was not proven conclusively that Billy fired the shot and even if Billy had shot him accidentally he had long ago forgiven him. He still looked up to Billy as a hero in the Wolf River valley. He didn't know if Billy was still alive and hadn't seen him since he started running from the law.

One night after we had been in Jamestown about two months, we were at Maw's and stayed until closing time. There was a good crowd and everyone was having a good time. The man who had done the shooting earlier was playing the fiddle. I'm not a great judge of music but to me he seemed to be good. There were often impromptu performances at the bar. People brought fiddles, guitars and banjos. There wasn't a stage, they just played and sang from where they happened to be.

A group of about 20 people decided to go to the home of a bootlegger in an area known as "Billy Goat Ridge" after the bar closed. Gene and I were invited so we joined them. We arrived there at about 2 a.m. Twenty to 25 men and women were sitting around a wood heating stove drinking and talking. It was obvious this was a bootlegger's house since there were two large garbage cans filled with empty beer cans. We soon discovered he only sold beer, no whiskey. We joined the others and it wasn't long before the marijuana came out and joints were passed around the circle. Gene and I faked taking a toke when they came to us.

We had been there about an hour when I left the room and went into the kitchen for a drink of water. A rough looking guy came in and started talking to me

"Who are you two guys anyway?"

I gave him our undercover story.

"Bull shit! We know you have been all over Fentress and Pickett County buying from bootleggers and moonshiners. We think you are ABC agents."

"I've been called a lot of things in my life but never the law. I don't know whether to be offended or flattered."

"I tell you what. If we decide you are ABC agents you will never get off Billy Goat Ridge alive tonight."

I said I was not worried since we weren't ABC agents and if they were thinking straight, they would figure that out.

I went back to the main room and whispered to Gene what had been said in the kitchen. We decided to stay a while longer since if we left in a hurry they might really think we were ABC and the undercover investigation would be over.

We stayed at the party but both of us watched everyone carefully. If someone left the room we paid close attention when they returned. By then the whiskey was gone and someone suggested to take up a collection to go to a bootlegger who sold hard liquor.

Gene and I put in $10.00 each. Two men left with the money and returned shortly with three or four fifths. We didn't stay much longer, and left without incident. We considered that a close call but also thought the guy could have just been a loud mouth. We were thinking that probably at least half the people there were armed, including some of the women.

We didn't change our routine after the incident on Billy Goat Ridge. We continued to visit both bars every night. One night we were at the Candlelight Club when a guy at the bar was running a "Hide the Pea" game. He had three walnut shell halves and a glass ball about the size of a large pea. A player would put up money then turn his back while the operator moved the shells around. Then he would say "Okay" and the player would try to guess which shell had the pea under it.

We watched the game for a while and then Gene and I had a private discussion. We decided I would become a player while Gene smoked and watched the operator move the shells around. When the operator said okay I turned around and spent a little time deciding which shell to select. Gene had his cigarette in the left, right or middle of his mouth indicating where the pea was. I purposefully picked the wrong shell some of the time but in the end we made about $50 and quit.

After another drink we left the bar and headed down the snowy driveway. We were about half way to our car when I heard a noise, looked behind me and saw a truck bearing down on us. I grabbed Gene and we tumbled to one side as the truck roared past us. We suspected someone at the bar had told the operator about our scam and had come after us. We didn't return to the Candlelight for about a week after that night.

During the time in Jamestown I met Betty Koger Anderson who frequented both bars and talked to her every chance I got. Eventually she asked me to visit her home for drinks. I tried to talk to her about Billy using the same line, having heard of a famous outlaw and wondering who he was. She said, "You are talking about Billy Dean Anderson. I married him and he is a no good son of a bitch who once got me into trouble with the law. But I got out of it by saying Billy forced me to help him commit a crime. I told them all about it and they let me off." She claimed to know nothing about where he was and hadn't talked to him for years.

This undercover assignment was an education for me about these mountain people and I knew for certain what a task faced us in locating Billy. I was familiar with all the years of interviews of family and friends, and from spending time with the local people I knew firsthand their uncooperative and hostile attitude.

These were always a clannish people who took care of things themselves and never trusted any type of government authority. I remember an incident that occurred while we were there. A young man was accused of assault by a 13 year-old girl. No report was made to the sheriff. About four or five days later the accused man's house was burned to the ground. No one made an arson report.

After Gene and I had been in Jamestown for over three months we met in Cookeville with our supervisor Cecil Moses and other agents who had worked the case and reviewed what we had learned. We agreed that we had all the information we were going to get so the undercover operation was closed down. We spent a few more days in Jamestown, we told everyone we had gotten a call from one of our buddies who had a big job lined up in Knoxville and wanted us to help him.

Gene and I prepared a joint report outlining what we had established. Based on our observations and discussions with the locals, in our opinion there was a 95% chance that Billy was hiding somewhere in the mountains of Fentress or Pickett County, supplied by friends and family members. Those who would venture to say something about Billy's whereabouts believed the same.

Despite Gene's and my efforts and all the years other agents had spent on this case we were no closer to knowing Billy Dean's exact location than when we started the investigation.

From late 1978 to mid-1979 Burl Smith, Jim Harcum and other

agents from Memphis, Knoxville and Indianapolis continued to press individuals and law enforcement officers who might have information regarding Billy. We kept hoping that someone who knew something would talk to us but that never happened.

Over the years agents had consistently heard that Billy was extremely close to his mother, Ina Hughes. He would frequently visit her under cover of darkness, stay for several hours and leave before daylight. An agent from Indianapolis learned there was a great likelihood Billy would visit his mother's home the latter part of June or early July 1979. His half-brother Jerry Hughes was expected to visit over the July 4th holiday. The brothers hadn't seen each other in years. Once Cecil Moses said there were three holidays when a man would go home: Christmas, Mother's Day and the Fourth of July.

In early June there was another meeting of the agents working the case. We developed a plan to capture Billy Dean in late June to early July. One team of three agents would maintain a command post in a van about five miles from the mother's home. Five agents would be on the ground in the wooded area adjacent to Ina's house. An airplane with a pilot, co-pilot and observer would surveil from the air and maintain radio contact. Cecil presented the plan to our new SAC Bill Beavers who had recently transferred to Memphis and he approved it.

In order to have secure radio communications the Anderson family members were given code names: Ina Hughes-Mama Chicken, Omar Hughes-Papa Chicken and Billy Dean Anderson-Chicken Little.

We began carrying out the plan on the evening of June 29, 1979. Ed Young, who was the SWAT team commander, reminded us who we were dealing with. It was almost for sure Billy Dean wouldn't surrender without a fight. He said, "If you shoot, shoot to kill." We repeated the same procedure for three nights and saw no one enter the house through the field. Beavers discontinued the operation on July 2. Information indicated local residents were questioning the increase in vehicle traffic.

At 9 p.m. on Friday, July 6 we began the surveillance again. We were a little later that night because of traffic on the highway and clear skies that made dark come later. The command post van dropped off SAs Ed Young, Burl Smith, Richard O'Rear, Ron Risner and me on US 127 (an east-west road) about 300 yards west of Ina Hughes residence near a large pasture west of the house. We crossed a shallow dry ditch and through a fencerow that was mostly grown over with trees and brush. We had night viewing goggles, handi-talkies with earpieces, base stations and repeaters, and SWAT weapons including a M79 gas gun, .9 mm Sigsauer semi-automatic pistols, semi- and automatic rifles and .12 gauge shotguns.

WANTED BY THE FBI

INTERSTATE FLIGHT - ASSAULT TO MURDER, ATTEMPTED BURGLARY

BILLY DEAN ANDERSON
DESCRIPTION

Born July 12, 1934, Fentress County, Tennessee; Height, 5'8"; Weight, 160 to 170 pounds; Build, stocky; Hair, brown; Eyes, blue or green; Complexion, fair; Race, white; Nationality, American; Occupations, artist, mechanic, laborer, tree surgeon, farmer; Scars and Marks, scar across nose, scar left side of forehead, surgical scar right side of stomach, surgical scar lower spine; Remarks, reportedly wears braces on both legs and suffers from atrophy of legs; Social Security Number used, 314–36–7484.

CRIMINAL RECORD

Anderson has been convicted of robbery, carrying a concealed weapon and assault with intent to commit murder.

CAUTION

ANDERSON, WHO IS BEING SOUGHT AS AN ESCAPEE FROM A TENNESSEE JAIL, HAS BEEN CONVICTED OF ASSAULT TO MURDER LAW ENFORCEMENT OFFICERS. ON AT LEAST THREE OCCASIONS HIS SHOOTING AT INVESTIGATING LAW ENFORCEMENT PERSONNEL INCLUDED FIRING AT POINT-BLANK RANGE WHILE EXITING STOPPED VEHICLE AND WITH RIFLE FROM AMBUSH. CONSIDER ARMED, EXTREMELY DANGEROUS AND AN ESCAPE RISK.

The front door faced the highway and the back door was about 12 yards east of a grown-in fencerow running mostly north and south. We worked our way north and east toward a large pine tree where Smith, O'Rear and Risner took up their position. Ed and I continued east and a little north to a large oak tree in the north-south fencerow.

A Bureau plane surveilled the area before we were dropped off and continued each night of the operation. They could see us and the area and communicate with everyone on the ground in case of radio problems due to transmission limitation in the rugged mountain area. Jim Harcum and SAC Bill Beavers were in the command post van concealed across the road and south of Ina's house.

We did a radio check to make sure everyone could communicate. Agents Smith, Risner and O'Rear, were located at the pine tree, with night vision goggles, their weapons and a high intensity searchlight. Ed and I had night vision goggles, shotguns and pistols and he carried a M79 grenade launcher that was capable of firing flares into the air. When fired the flares burn and hang suspended below a small parachute keeping them in the air to illuminate a large area for several minutes.

We could see and smell the Hughes outhouse that was eight yards away, across the fencerow. At approximately 11:30 pm we heard two female voices outside the rear of the house and could tell they were walking in our direction. They also had a small dog with them who began barking. As they got closer to our position we could tell it was Ina Hughes and a younger woman who we believed was Jerry Hughes' wife. Ina said, "I wonder what that dog is barking about out here." The other woman said, "Oh, he always barks when he's outside. It's probably a squirrel or possum." We thought for sure we were going to be discovered.

One or two minutes after midnight I heard male voices coming from the direction of the Hughes residence. I could make out a word or two from time to time. It was obvious that the people were outside. I reported this information over the radio and indicated that Billy might be visiting his mother.

A few minutes later I heard a female voice from the same direction say, "Goodbye. I love you." I reported this on the radio and my belief that Billy was here and would probably be leaving the house shortly. I next heard someone moving from the residence. Then Burl reported on the radio he saw a man walk from the porch of the house, along the side and rear and then stopped at the fence. Burl had a light-amplifying telescope and saw the man had a rifle in his hand.

I heard the fence squeak as it moved as if someone pushed down on it. I then moved approximately six steps south, under the shadow of a tree about eight inches in diameter in the fencerow. Within seconds I could see the man with the gun walking from the fencerow in the general direction of the pine tree where Smith, O'Rear and Risner were located. After taking about ten steps in that direction the man turned at an angle to the right and began moving in the general direction of Ed Young and me. I could clearly see the man was carrying a shoulder weapon in his right hand and a long stick in his left. I could also see he had some kind of pack over his shoulder. There was no doubt in my mind that the man in the field was the fugitive Billy Dean Anderson.

He was about 50 feet from us when he started in our direction. I shouted in a loud voice "You there in the field. FBI. Stop or you are a dead man." I saw the man look directly towards me. I yelled again, "Move and you are a dead man." The man never said anything or stopped his movement. He raised the shoulder weapon and pointed it at me.

I fired two successive rounds from my shotgun believing he was going to shoot me. He went down and was moving around making sounds. No other shots were fired. Ed fired a flare in the air and we could clearly see the man was on the ground.

After the two shotgun blasts all hell broke loose. Jim Harcum later told me that when he and the SAC heard those shots they left the command post on a dead run. Jim went to the back of the house where Ina was hysterical and screaming for Billy. Since Ina knew him, Jim was able to calm her down some and got her to sit down on the front porch with the rest of the family. Jim later went with her to the hospital when it appeared she might have had a heart attack.

I could hear both male and female voices from the direction of the Hughes residence. A female said, "Oh Billy, Billy, They've shot Billy." A second female said, "Jerry, don't go out there." A male said, "Nothing's happened. Everything is okay." A second male said, "I heard someone say 'stop or you are a dead man' and I saw a flare."

Richard O'Rear, from his position under the pine tree, turned on a searchlight and aimed it in the direction of the house. I shouted for the agents at the pine tree not to approach since I wasn't sure of the condition of the man down and didn't know if the people approaching from the residence were armed. Ed Young continued to fire another flare as soon as each burned out.

Ron and Burl moved toward two men who had climbed the fence and were walking toward them. After reaching these two men, later identified as Omer Hughes and Jerry Hughes, Ron and Burl had them lay down and checked them for weapons. Neither was armed.

The man on the ground was recognizable as Billy Dean Anderson and it appeared that he was dead, having been hit both in the face and upper body by the shotgun pellets. According to the subsequent autopsy 23 out of 24 lead pellets from my shotgun entered Billy's body.

SAC Beavers directed Ron Risner to examine the rifle lying by the body. It was a bolt action .22 rifle. The safety was in the "fire" position. Ron slowly slid the bolt back to expose a live round in the chamber. Ron found a .25 automatic pistol in a pouch on Billy's gun belt and a chrome plated .22 Ruger automatic in a homemade holster attached to Billy's belt. There was live ammunition in the chamber of both pistols and each magazine was fully loaded. The leather gun belt must have been made by the famous Alvin York for Billy because tooled into it were the words "York" and below it "Bill Anderson."

Holster made by Billy

Billy's gunbelt and contents

Once all of the hubbub had settled down and the body removed, Ed Young came up to me and said in a low voice, "What in the hell happened to 'Chicken Little'?" "Hell, I didn't have time to say Chicken

Little. I was too busy."

The first agent who saw Billy was supposed to say over the radio; "I have Chicken Little in my sight." None of us ever said Chicken Little.

Burl and Ron escorted Omer and Jerry back to the house and made everyone sit on the porch. Two small children and Ina Hughes and Jerry's wife Rita came out onto the porch from inside. Burl went in the house and found no one else inside. He saw a .410 gauge single-shot shotgun on the sofa. It was unloaded. Two other shoulder weapons were leaning against the living room wall.

SAC Bill Beavers reported the shooting incident to Bureau headquarters:

"It is felt that extenuating circumstances make this case different than other shooting situations involving Bureau fugitives. As the Bureau is aware, Billy Dean Anderson has been a fugitive for almost five years. During most of this time there have been persistent rumors that he was residing in a cave in the mountainous area in the general vicinity of this mother's home. The information was pervasive that Billy had a great love for his mother and visited her on numerous occasions although not only the family but also residents of the area have never verified this information due to lack of cooperation. As a result of this and the fact that subject Anderson was able to evade the authorities for this extensive period of time, he became somewhat of a folk hero in this rural community.

"With this background and the lack of impartial witnesses it can be anticipated that allegations of execution of the subject will be generated in the community. An analysis of the circumstances of the shooting would tend to refute this. The deployment plan as analyzed clearly indicates that at the location where the subject was struck there was no possibility of any of the apprehending team to be caught in crossfire. The only Agent to fire exhibited tremendous restraint and professionalism in only firing two rounds and neutralizing his adversary and then only after he announced his presence to an obviously armed and dangerous fugitive. The subject did not heed the order rather his actions revealed his intentions to resist.

"In view of the subject's history and propensity for violence, especially directed toward law enforcement, the fact that only one Agent, who felt his life was threatened, was the only Agent to utilize fire power, exhibits the restraint displayed. It is felt the circumstance could have justified additional fire power by other members of the team."

As SAC Beavers predicted there was an outpouring of support for Billy after his death. A newspaper article in Clinton County, Kentucky reported a version of the shooting according to Billy's half-brother Wallace Hughes. He said Billy was gunned down by FBI agents and left to die in the field. One local resident sought signatures for a petition to ask for a Congressional inquiry into the shooting. The locals believed "thirteen super intelligent federal agents" had caused the wrongful death of a crippled man.

But where was Billy Dean all those years since he escaped from the Morgan County jail?

There had been rumors, but no hard evidence, that Billy had been hiding in a cave near his mother's house. Agents conducted extensive searches of caves in the area without any success. Nearly two months after Billy's death Sheriff Tommy Williams, TBI agent Ed Ashburn, Pickett County Sheriff Edward "Hawkeye" Dowdy and officers Ralph Browning and Steve Cooper found his hideout with the help of Gib Long, George Long's father. Billy had been living a meager existence in a cave with an opening three feet in diameter. The access was only visible within a few feet of it since big rocks and brush surrounded it. The opening led to a 20-foot drop to a chamber below. A 30-foot corridor led to another chamber. Billy had set up a water collection system here; they found 53 jugs of water. Billy had constructed a bed out of 1 ½ to 2-inch saplings that were covered with two quilts and a homemade sleeping bag. The cave temperature remained in a tolerable range of mid-60s but it was damp.

Brushes and paint were also in the cave. We learned later that Billy had artistic talent. He began painting while in prison and produced about 300 full sized paintings, mostly religious in nature. He also was an accomplished woodcarver. Today many of his paintings are in churches and homes in Fentress County.

Billy's cousin Hag Wood had led Billy to this particular cave in 1974 when Billy fled from Indiana with Squirrel and returned to the area of his birth. Billy had recalled a cave his grandfather had shown him many years before. They had put rocks over the entrance so their hunting dogs wouldn't fall in.

When Billy asked Hag if he knew this cave Hag replied, "Yeah, I know where it's at. I dug a big bunch of sang (ginseng) right above the cave not long ago." The two searched for the cave entrance but at first all the limestone outcroppings looked the same. Hag finally found it by following the signs he made the day he dug the ginseng.

In over 30 years the big limestone rocks had wedged in tightly. "It'll be a good place if you can git those big rocks out," Hag said. With the help of a crowbar Billy and Hag cleared the entrance, working for a week. Hag wanted to make a ladder but Billy said, "No, someone would see it." Billy threw a long knotted rope across a large limb of a tree near the cave entrance so he could use it to climb the 20' out and back into the cave. When he left he would hide the rope nearby.

For the more than four years Billy lived in the cave Hag Wood and his family and Ina Hughes supplied Billy with his necessities. However the Woods didn't find out about the killing until the next morning when a neighbor telephoned them. That night, after dark, Hag and his father

Charlie went to the cave to see if there was anything left that would link them to Billy and to get Billy's belongings before the authorities found the cave. They carried out his Bible, diary and a few other things. These family members were some of the hundreds who had been interviewed again and again during the investigation but they never gave Billy up.

Later Burl Smith told me he, other agents and local law enforcement, once searched the area where Billy's cave turned out to be, which was on property adjacent to the Woods family land. For this search they approached not near the Woods' residence but from another access. Burl believes it is possible they could have walked by the cave entrance without seeing it since it was camouflaged by rock and brush. He figured Billy never used one particular path to come and go since they didn't see any spot with a noticeable trail.

Billy was always the aggressor in the shootings with law enforcement. He provoked the officers, not the other way around. I believe he hated the law so much that when he encountered officers something snapped in his mind and he did something that he knew would result in a confrontation.

In the shoot out with Troopers Webb and Elmore Billy purposely committed a traffic offense knowing the troopers were behind him and would make a traffic stop. Without provocation he surprised Trooper Webb and fired the first shot.

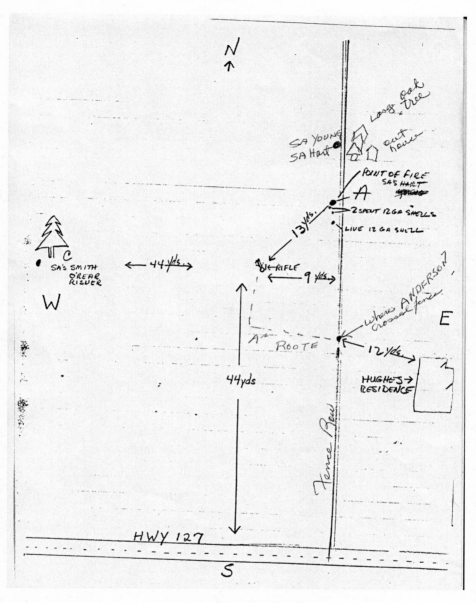

Diagram of Shootout Location

Rifle of Billy Dean Anderson

Billy tried to run Sheriff Jones off the road and when Jones turned around and approached Billy's car Billy started shooting first, after deliberately provoking the officer. In the Candlelight Club burglary attempt Billy shot at Deputy Hatfield, a man he had known all his life, saying, "I'm gonna have some fun with him."

The Bureau dubbed Billy Dean Anderson "the Mountain Man." The official report said the investigation "was unique in that this fugitive lived the life of a backwoodsman and utilized methods of wilderness deception. The investigation was further hampered by the unwillingness of the local rural population to assist the FBI in its effort to capture this dangerous fugitive."

To this day Billy continues to be a folk hero to the locals and legends abound about his death. Ironically he is buried in Wolf River Cemetery just a few yards from the grave of the World War I hero Sgt. Alvin C. York.

Billy Dean Anderson where he fell

Swat Team after shooting L to R RonRisner, Burl Smith, Corbett Hart, Ed Young and Richard O'Rear.

Chapter 9
Where is the Jigsaw Man?

It seems like bizarre cases had a way of finding me or perhaps it's just the wide scope of investigations we do at the FBI. I wound up with a case involving a local radio talk show host, a kind of program I would never listen to, in 1975. The man was Jim Fields someone I knew nothing about.

On August 13, 1975 I got a call from the chief of security at Union Planters National Bank. He told me the assistant branch manager, Carl Allen Hall at their Union Avenue bank, had been called by a person demanding he be loaned $15,000 or he would reveal an extramarital affair Hall was having with one of the tellers.

When I went to the bank and interviewed Hall he told me a man who identified himself as Bob Lewis, a private investigator, had called him. Lewis said his client Ann Townsend owed $20,000 in gambling debts to a Chicago mobster and wanted to take out a loan to "take the heat off." Lewis went on to say, "If she doesn't pay up, a contract will be put out on her." Lewis then alluded to the affair Hall was having with one of the bank tellers and that this information would be kept secret if Hall cooperated and made the loan. Hall said he couldn't make a loan without some type of security so Lewis offered the titles to two 1975 Cadillac automobiles that his client owned.

Hall had managed to end the call with Lewis without making any firm commitment and went to his manager. The manager went up the chain of command at the bank to the security chief who then called me.

It was clearly a violation of the Hobbs Act, since one of the elements the law covers is extortion by fear, in other words blackmail.

I hooked up a recording device on Hall's telephone and showed him how to use it. I then called a friend of mine, Sergeant Ralph Roby in the Memphis Police Department robbery squad, and asked him to meet me at the Bell South telephone company security office. I let the Bell South security chief know Roby and I were on the way to his office to discuss an extortion case.

Ralph Roby was a veteran police officer I had met shortly after I arrived at the Memphis FBI office. He was a tall, strongly built man who had an affable personality and was soft spoken normally but could get tough if necessary.

I explained to the security chief what I had learned from the banker and what we needed: recordings of Lewis's calls to Hall and a way to trace the caller's location. The phone company has a device called an electronic Bulldog that if connected to the banker's phone, any incoming calls to his phone would be locked onto the "Bulldog" and would not let go after the caller hung up. The line would remain "live" until Hall hung up. This would allow the phone company to immediately trace the call to the originating phone and give its location.

There were no more calls from Lewis that day except for one at Hall's home at about 10 p.m. Hall told him his wife was present and he couldn't talk business.

The next morning at 9:30 Lewis called Hall at the bank and the conversation was recorded. Lewis wanted to know how the loan was coming along and Hall told him he was working on it and to call back that afternoon. Unfortunately Bell South had not completed the Bulldog hook up so we couldn't trace the caller. I was assured it would be finished within the hour.

Lewis called again at 2:15 p.m. Hall told him again he needed collateral and Lewis said he would bring two car titles, one in the name of James Townsend and the other in the name of Ann Townsend. Hall said, "It is going to be extremely hard to make this loan but under the circumstances I guess I have no choice." This time the tracer worked and the originating phone was a pay phone in the Memphis Medical Arts building, which was only five or six blocks from the Union Planters Bank branch.

A security officer from the phone company went to secure the phone booth while I called two fellow agents to go there and process it for fingerprints.

At 3:40 p.m. the extortionist called again. Hall told him the Townsends would have to come in and sign the titles in person. Lewis said he would send someone else and suggested that they meet at a nearby motel but Hall said he couldn't do that. Hall told Lewis he would have a check ready at the bank. During this conversation Sgt. Roby and I were standing alongside Hall passing him notes of what to say. Lewis said "his people" would not accept a check; the funds had to be in cash. He said he would send a runner to come by the bank to deliver the car titles and pick up the money.

Lewis said, "Put the money in a package. The messenger is a runner, more or less, and I don't want him to know how much money is involved." "When will he be here?" Hall asked. "He'll be there by four o'clock with the titles," Lewis replied. About five minutes later a slender young man with a brown envelope in hand walked into the bank. He asked for and was directed to the assistant manager.

This last phone call had been traced to a pay phone in the lobby of the nearby Methodist Hospital. A Bell South security officer secured the booth and two agents went to process the booth. In both incidents the security officer took the receiver in a gloved hand and used wire cutters to cut the cord. He handed the receivers to the agents, which allowed us to send them to the FBI lab to be processed for fingerprints.

When the runner opened the envelope at the bank to show the titles to Hall, Sgt. Roby and I stepped out of an adjacent office and confronted him. We identified ourselves and told him he was under arrest. He gave his name as Gregory Simmons. We didn't interview him on the spot but handcuffed him and handed him over to another Memphis police officer who was out in the bank parking lot. I put on gloves and opened the brown envelope. Inside were two titles, each for a 1975 Cadillac, one in the name of James Townsend, and the other titled to Ann Townsend.

We next listened to the recording of the last phone call to the banker's phone. Roby said, "I know that voice. It's Jim Fields." I asked, "Who's that?" He told me Fields had a talk show on local radio station WWEE that Roby often listened to. I had never heard of the guy but I was soon to know all about him.

Roby took Simmons to the MPD robbery bureau and explained the seriousness of the situation. Simmons insisted he was only a runner but refused to say who had hired him.

Apparently Simmons called Jim Fields since at 5:30 p.m. he showed up at the police station and asked why Simmons had been arrested. This was my first look at Jim Fields. He appeared to be about 30 years old, dark hair and neatly trimmed beard and moustache. He was shorter than me, perhaps six feet and outweighed me by 15 or 20 pounds. I told Fields that Simmons had been arrested as part of an investigation into bank extortion. Fields denied knowing anything about it. When I asked him if he would sign a consent to search his residence, Fields replied he had nothing to hide and signed the form.

Roby and I, along with two other Memphis police officers, searched Fields' home, which was in Midtown Memphis not far from the bank. We found a piece of paper with the name "Bob Lewis" written on it, the same name the extortionist had given to the banker Hall. We learned later that this was the name of the production manager of Memphis radio station WHBQ where Fields recorded commercials. Roby also found a note pad with a series of numbers on it which turned out to be the VIN numbers on the two titles Simmons brought to the bank.

In Fields' bedroom I located a rectangular shaped box with the words "Little Leroy Lettering Set" stamped on the top. I had never seen or heard tell of this item. When we opened it we found several plastic templates of all shape and kinds of letters and numbers and several different colors of ink pens. Upon reading the instructions we came to the conclusion that a person could color in a number or word using a template and the resulting document would like it had been typed. Fields, we surmised, had used this set to fill out two blank titles for the Cadillac cars.

We returned to the police station and confronted Fields with this evidence but he continued to deny any knowledge of the titles or that he had sent Simmons to the bank with them.

We went back to Simmons and told him what Fields had said and that it looked like Fields had set him up to be the fall guy in this extortion attempt. Simmons eventually told us what, according to him, was the absolute truth. His true name was George Mitchell Sea. He said he had studied radio broadcasting under Fields and looked up to him as his mentor. Fields had hired him to be a combination chauffeur, companion and errand boy.

Sea said that the previous day Fields told him he had a deal cooking and would need Sea to run some errands. Today Fields told him to deliver the envelope to the bank and pick up a package from the banker. He was not to open the package but to call Fields from a pay phone as soon as he had it and then he would give him instructions as to where to deliver it. He claimed that Fields told him if he got stopped at the bank or arrested he should say he was an errand boy for Mr. Lewis of the FBI.

Fields promised Sea that if he got locked up he would get him out of jail. You have to wonder at this point what Sea was thinking, almost being forewarned that he might be getting into something illegal.

We returned to questioning Fields about the two car titles, not telling him what Sea had said. Fields continued to deny any knowledge of the titles and claimed he had never seen them before. In the meantime several Memphis police officers who were faithful listeners to Fields' radio show listened to the tapes and were ready to swear under oath the voice on the calls was Jim Fields. We told Fields about the voice identification by the officers but he still insisted he had nothing to do with the attempted extortion. He claimed he was with his girlfriend Debbie Socha when the calls were made to banker Hall.

At about 10 p.m. I told Fields he was under arrest for federal crimes: attempted extortion and bank larceny, and took him to the Shelby County Jail.

The next day I filed an affidavit for arrest warrants which a federal judge approved and I served them on Fields and Sea in jail. They subsequently had a preliminary hearing, were bound over for trial and released on a $5000 bond each.

One of the first persons I interviewed was Debbie Socha, the girlfriend who was Fields' alibi. She worked for an optometrist, Dr. Steven Shum, so I went to his office. Debbie was a tall, slender blonde probably 22-24 years old and very attractive. She maintained that Fields was with her on the day in question. I told her she would no doubt be called as a defense witness at Fields' trial and if she told this story in court I believed she would be committing perjury. Dr. Shum sat in on the interview and when I said this he told me the interview was over and not to bother Debbie again.

Not long after Fields' arrest we received a tip that a local firm, Letter Graphics, had printed the Cadillac titles. We interviewed the employee who had waited on the customer and had him describe the person. His description fit Jim Fields. We asked him if he thought he could recognize him again and he replied, "Yes." I told Sergeant Roby about this development and we decided to hold a line-up to see if the Letter Graphics employee could identify Fields in it. This was an important step to take since at this point in the investigation we could not link Fields to the car titles except for speculation that he prepared them. Actually we didn't have any witness who could put Fields' physical presence in the scheme.

Roby rounded up four police officers and Joe Dailey, a lawyer and legal advisor to the MPD who later became a Criminal Court judge for the line-up. All five were close in size and appearance to Fields. Since Fields was out on bond I called his attorney and asked him to bring in his client the next day at 2 p.m. for the line-up. Fields could have refused but his enormous ego and his story of innocence must have compelled him to agree to it.

I went to Letter Graphics the next day and gave the employee a ride downtown. Promptly at 2 p.m. Ralph began the line-up. The process only took about 10 to15 minutes. The witness positively identified Fields in the presence of Fields' attorney as the man who came to the business and had the titles printed. For Joe Dailey it was quite an experience, one with the remote possibility of being identified as a criminal.

It wasn't long before the FBI lab report came back on the latent fingerprints from both telephone receivers and the car titles. Some of the latent prints from the car titles matched prints of both Sea and Fields. Only Fields' prints were on the telephone receivers. The monumental surprise was Fields' true name was Billy Max Coleman who had a prior federal felony conviction in Arkansas for interstate transportation of stolen money orders. He served 13 months of a three-year sentence.

When I did a background check on Fields/Coleman. I found he

141

had applied for a FCC (Federal Communications Commission) radio broadcast license three years before in Little Rock, Arkansas, after he had been released from prison. One of the questions on the form was "Have you ever been convicted of a felony?" to which Fields answered, "No." I went to AUSA Dan Clancy who had been assigned the Fields and Sea case to see what we could do with this information. He authorized an arrest warrant for the false answer on the application. I obtained a warrant and arrested Fields again, who was quickly out on bond, again. Some of the news media and Fields' supporters thought this was overkill but it wasn't. At trial he could possibly be acquitted on the extortion and bank larceny charges but the FCC charge would almost surely result in a conviction.

I also learned that Fields had been commissioned a "Special Deputy" by then Shelby County Sheriff Roy Nixon and allowed to carry a gun "for security." Since convicted felons can't carry firearms he was also indicted for carrying the gun.

The public reaction to Fields' arrests was incredulity. He had never been on television so his face was not familiar but for radio listeners his name was a household word. On the radio he came across as urbane, well educated, intelligent and highly articulate. It was hard for his faithful audience to believe that such a man would plan and try to carry out such a clumsy shakedown and why would he do it?

Fields/Coleman was born March 23, 1944 in Browns Church, Tennessee, an unincorporated area outside of Jackson in West Tennessee. He served in Vietnam, married and divorced and once was a Baptist minister.

Fields' radio career was in part the creation of Bill Thomas, the former general manager of WWEE-AM, a weak-signal station in Memphis that needed, according to Thomas, "something unique and off the wall for people to get to know we were on the air." The program

Thomas had in mind was a call-in sex show "Feminine Forum" and he chose Jim Fields to be the host. Fields' resonant voice was familiar because of commercials he made for the former William B. Tanner Company in Memphis some of which were aired locally.

(The Tanner Company was in the business of making radio commercials and used an elaborate barter system to exchange airtime on radio stations all over the country for its professional commercials that often included musical jingles. In 1983 my colleague and close friend SA Chuck Allison was heading the investigation, a white-collar crime case with the Tanner Company and its higher-ups as subjects accused of extortion and pay-offs. I went with Chuck and a dozen or more agents in a "raid" pursuant to a broad search warrant on the corporate headquarters that occupied an entire seven-floor building in Memphis. My job was to secure the legal office and detain the ten attorneys who worked there. This is where and how I met the lawyer who would become my wife.)

At some point the former Billy Coleman changed his name to Jim Fields. "I needed a one-syllable last name…like Rick Dees and George Klein," he said. When Thomas called Fields to offer him a job, according to Thomas, "…some of the first words out of Fields' mouth were that he was concerned about security and would require a uniformed guard during the time he was on the air." He never got the armed guard he wanted.

The show was broadcast live from a glass booth in the Mid-City Building. Thomas said, "Jim fancied himself such a ladies man he was convinced he would be shot by some jealous husband. He was vain, self-centered and had an ego the size of a room. But all of these things, handled properly, were an asset in this business."

Response to this show was good but ratings weren't. Callers bared their souls to Fields about anything from philandering to incest. Thomas felt the listeners didn't want to admit being fans of a call-in sex show so he changed the format to a general call-in talk show. Ratings were still modest but some advertisers asked Fields to do their commercials and even let him change the copy.

Fields told his audience outrageous stories like he was Jewish and had served in the Israeli Army. But he would also, Thomas said, "Do things on the air like assemble volunteers to paint an elderly person's house. In a lot of ways he was a very giving person."

Marge Thrasher, a former colleague at WWEE, said about Fields, "He told me he owned land in Belize in Central America. I think he just heard where the country was and thought. 'I believe I own 10,000 acres down there.' If he uttered something it became the truth."

Fields taught broadcasting part-time at the Elkins Institute in Memphis. One of his students was George Mitchell Sea. Sea learned of his teacher's growing notoriety and suggested he "might need a bodyguard." WWEE had refused to provide one so Fields hired Sea. As talk-show host he made less than $20,000 a year but paid Sea $50 a day plus expenses in cash. Sea lived in Fields' rented house in Midtown Memphis and drove him to and from work most days in Fields' old Cadillac.

In August 1975 Fields learned about the affair the banker was having with the teller when Fields met her at a party and she, like those who called his radio show, "bared her soul to him." She was a good-looking young woman carrying on with a 40-year old married man. Fields seized on the opportunity to concoct the extortion scheme using this casually acquired knowledge.

When the December trial began Sgt. Ralph Roby sat next to AUSA Dan Clancy and me at the prosecution table. Ralph worked the case right along with me from the beginning and deserved to be there. In many movies, television series and books the relationship between FBI agents and local officers is contentious. The writers portray the FBI as the big gun who comes into a situation and claims credit for solving the crime when the locals did most if not all of the work. This always rankles me since I know it's not true. It may have been the case in times past and perhaps happens infrequently now. Some agents feel that since they have a college degree and belong to the most prestigious law enforcement agency in the country as well as having jurisdiction in the entire United States they are better than local officers and don't really want to work with them. They are in the minority.

The first witness was the bank teller who told how she had revealed to Fields the affair she was having with her boss, a married man with a family and unwittingly gave Fields the ammunition to set his plan in motion. Bill Thomas and Marge Thrasher identified Fields' voice from the bank tape recordings, as did Roby and other police officers who had listened to the tapes. Hall, who by this time had been fired by the bank, testified to his telephone conversations with Fields.

The employee of Letter Graphics who nailed Fields in the line-up testified that he produced the two automobile titles for Fields. Dr. Jim Townsend testified that he had never met and did not know Fields, and did not own a Cadillac.

As I predicted the defense put on Fields' girl friend Deborah Socha who tried to alibi for him but it was flimsy and the jury didn't believe her.

One witness said Fields needed money and had mentioned bankruptcy. He liked to pick up the tab and spent wildly. He bought antiques and rented a billboard to ask a departed girlfriend to come back to him. Perhaps his shaky financial situation was the motivation behind the extortion.

Fields didn't take the stand but Sea did. When Fields' attorney was cross-examining him he badgered him, "That's really you on those tapes, isn't it? You imitated Jim's voice all the time, didn't you? You fooled your friends and family impersonating him didn't you? You were good at, weren't you?" Sea vehemently denied this and it appeared the jury believed him.

On December 15, 1975 the jury returned a verdict of guilty as to both counts against Fields and acquitted Sea. One juror later told the media that he believed Fields was behind it all and Sea was only his unwitting dupe. I had no argument with his acquittal.

Fields' attorney Ted Hansom requested that his client remain free on his $5000 bond pending sentencing. Dan Clancy argued strongly against this telling the court Fields was an extreme flight risk. He pointed out that Fields had used an alias for years, really didn't have any ties to the community and was facing up to 20 years in prison. The judge noted that it was almost Christmas and Fields would be able to spend the holidays with his family before going to prison and allowed him to remain free.

Sure enough Fields failed to appear at his sentencing hearing the second week of January 1976. His attorney, Hansom, appeared in court and told the judge he had not heard from his client since right after the trial and didn't know where he was. The judge issued a bench warrant for Fields' arrest and I began trying to run him down.

After interviewing several family members and friends I determined Fields had skipped town on Christmas Eve. One of his friends told me the last time she saw him he was driving a pick-up truck with an in-bed type camper. He told her he was going to Belize where he owned land. Others I talked to said they believed he had fled to Mexico.

In view of this development I put Fields'/Coleman's name and identifying information in the FBI NCIC (National Crime Information Center). If Fields were to be detained by any law enforcement agency in this country or many others, his fugitive status would be revealed. Even if he were to use an alias we had no knowledge of but was fingerprinted and these prints were submitted to the FBI and NCIC, the prints would be identified with his record and his true identity would be discovered. Further if he were in custody when his status was known he would be held in jail until the U.S. Marshal could pick him up and return him to Memphis. If he had been released we would have a place to start looking for him.

I also asked the Bureau for permission to advise our legal attaché (legate) in Mexico City and the U. S. State Department of Fields' fugitive status and ask for help in locating him. The Bureau has an agent known as a legate assigned in most major cities in the world. The agent cannot conduct any independent investigation in a foreign country but acts as a liaison between the FBI and law enforcement agencies abroad. My request was approved.

About a month later the legate advised me his sources determined that Fields was living in the camper he unloaded from the pick-up truck at a remote farm in Belize. I sent detailed information to the State Department asking that an attempt be made to confirm his location and to advise the U.S. Attorney's office in Memphis so they could begin extradition proceedings. This was assuming the United States had an extradition treaty with Belize. Unbeknownst to me the Memphis bonding company that had posted the bond had also obtained the same information and beat me to the punch.

But Allied Sentinel Bonding Company eventually lost the $5000 bond it posted for Fields. The former manager, Jack Whitlock, spent another $3000 searching for Fields in Belize and neighboring Honduras. He said that the company sent three investigators to Belize. "He had driven a pickup truck with a camper on it to Belize and took the camper off and set it up on a little farm there. He convinced the farmer he was his long-lost nephew. I still cry over the $8000," Whitlock said. "We've given up from the standpoint of getting our money back but we would still like to find him as a matter of principle."

Whitlock believed a translator he hired in Belize must have sold information to Fields and helped him escape. He thought the escape had been only hours or minutes before his investigator found the camper trailer with Fields' clothes, billfold and other belongings abandoned inside. I am convinced that if the bonding company had waited we would have had Fields in custody.

There have been reports through the years that Fields has lived in Sweden, Africa, Texas, California and occasionally Memphis. A year after he disappeared he, or someone claiming to be him, wrote to then U.S. Representative Robin Beard offering information about South American drug trafficking in exchange for Fields' freedom. Nothing came of it.

In 1985 the banker Carl Hall told a reporter who was writing a story about Fields, "I'd still like to see the guy brought to justice. I left (Union Planters who fired him) with my integrity intact. I was doing what I thought was my civic duty when I reported it to the FBI and I have a lot of resentment toward UP for the way they handled the situation." He was working for another bank and thought Fields was either dead or working as a government informant.

Fields' mother Lessie Coleman related to the reporter she had last talked to her son on Christmas Eve 1975. "He just said he was going to leave. 'Mom, I'm going to tell you beforehand so you'll know, and if you don't hear from me, don't worry.' I guess I just felt numb all over, like a part of my life was gone. I think it was just as hard for him." When she asked how to reach him, he told her she couldn't. Even in 1985 she still worried whether her phone was being tapped or her house watched. She said, "I know the FBI don't believe me when I tell them we don't hear from him. But if they're watching and listening I'm sure they've been as disappointed as I have."

Fields' sister Betty Mullins remembered her brother "as a God-called minister." She said she prayed for him every night since he disappeared and that perhaps "God will open a door that will make it possible for him to come back. I think God called him, because, without schooling, I don't think anybody would know the Bible like he did."

Broadcaster Marge Thrasher was on the air in the early 1980s when a guy in dark glasses held up a sign in front of her glass broadcast booth that said, "Fields is in town." She "went gulp." He didn't show up but she still continued to expect him. To her Fields was a "sociopath," a guiltless chameleon who was whatever he wanted to be at any time and at whatever costs to those around him.

His attorney Ted Hansom said, "If he were to shave his beard and comb his hair differently, I'm not sure I would recognize him on the street tomorrow."

Agents from the U.S. Marshal's office continued to check with Fields former girlfriend Debbie Socha. She told them, "You are wasting my time and yours." In 1985 she said, "I don't think he would call me now but I shouldn't assume anything. Trying to figure him out was like trying to work a massive puzzle. And he wouldn't give anybody all the pieces." What he did, she said, "was mesmerize people. He must have been crazy."

All these years later I believe Jim Fields became mixed up with a narcotics gang in Central America who learned he was willing to rat on them to law enforcement. They no doubt killed him and disposed of his body down in a deep isolated well. Otherwise in all these years he would have surfaced in the United States and the Bureau would have found him.

Jim Fields mug shot

Chapter 10
Elvis Presley and the Den of Thieves

W ith his humble beginnings and rags to riches story Elvis Presley was a natural target for con men. From living with his parents in public housing at $35 a month, at the time of his death, August 16, 1977 at age 42, he had $5 million in the bank. He told his manager Colonel Tom Parker, "You take care of the money coming in and me and my daddy will take care of it going out."

The FBI never investigated Elvis as a subject but as early as 1956 a person wrote to Director J. Edgar Hoover lamenting Elvis' performance at the city auditorium "...the filthiest and most harmful production that ever came to this town for teenagers...I would judge that he may possibly be both a drug addict and sexual pervert. In any case I am sure he bears close watch." The Director replied, "While I appreciate the interest prompting you to write, the matter to which you refer is not within the investigative jurisdiction of the FBI."

In late 1970 someone contacted the Bureau and said Elvis wanted to tour the FBI headquarters and meet with Hoover. Hoover was advised, "Presley's sincerity and good intentions notwithstanding he is certainly not the type of individual whom the Director would wish to meet. It is noted at the present time he is wearing his hair down to his shoulders and indulges in the wearing of all sorts of exotic dress." Hoover rejected his request. He did get the tour however.

I saw Elvis Presley perform in late 1954 and 1955 in my hometown, Trumann, Arkansas, when I was home on leave from the Army. He was booked into local joints that lined Highway 67, right on the county line between our "wet" Poinsett County and "dry" Craighead County. Little did I know then what a star he would become.

My only personal meeting with Elvis came in the early 1970s. One of his gang, called "The Memphis Mafia," gave him a .38 caliber semi-automatic pistol for his birthday knowing he loved guns. Elvis had one of them call the Memphis FBI office and check the pistol through NCIC. It probably entered his mind that it could have been bought on the street since his group included some rough characters although they were for the most part relatives and longtime friends. They provided companionship, security and protection, as well as being his confidantes.

The NCIC inquiry came up a "hit" as a stolen pistol. Every agent in the office wanted to go to Graceland and retrieve the pistol. I somehow wrangled my way to be one of the agents. When we arrived at the gates to Graceland we were met by Elvis's father Vernon driving a small jeep. He unlocked the gates and we followed him up the curving driveway to the mansion. Elvis welcomed us at the door. He was clearly impressed to be in the presence of real FBI agents and we were likewise almost giddy at meeting him and shaking his hand. He asked us what we did and how we liked it in a very down to earth manner. He was known to be sort of a "cop nut." Elvis went to another room and brought the gun to us, unloaded. "I'm glad I got this checked before I carried it around," he said. "Thanks for coming over here." We left with the pistol and memories of meeting The King in person.

In June of 1976 Glen Reid, one of the assistant US attorneys, called me. "Do you know attorney Beecher Smith," he asked. "I know him, but not well."

"He's in the Glankler firm that represents Elvis Presley and family. Beecher is concerned that Vernon Presley has gotten himself and Elvis into a bad deal, maybe a scam, and wants our help. It seems that some men, previously unknown to Vernon, contacted him with a plan to buy, refurbish and lease back to Elvis a Lockheed Jetstar he isn't using. Come down to my office so I can fill you in."

Glen told me Elvis, through his father who held his power of attorney, was attempting to sell the Jetstar (not the famous Lisa Marie) he owed $600,000 on. Beecher Smith was suspicious about a proposal made by five men who were ostensibly in the aircraft refurbishing and leasing business and suspected it was a scam to steal the Jetstar and several hundred thousand dollars from Elvis. Vernon Presley was negotiating a deal with these men representing four or five different corporations in Miami, New York City and Boston.

Glen said, "Will you give Beecher a call and see what you can find out?" "Yeah, sure." So I went to Smith's office and got the details.

The basic plan was for a corporation in Miami to borrow enough money to pay off the present indebtedness on the Jetstar plus about $350,000 for converting it into a cargo hauling aircraft. That corporation would then own the jet and oversee the conversion of the plane and when completed would lease it back to Elvis Presley for seven years at $16,755 per month. Presley would then lease the aircraft to another corporation involved for seven years at $17,755 a month which would net him approximately $1000 per month. If all parties performed as provided in the contract Presley would be rid of the aircraft that he was making payments on with no income being generated. Prior attempts to sell it had failed. It looked like a win-win situation. Considering the income Elvis had in 1976 netting $1000 a month seems paltry. But it would more importantly get him out from under servicing the loan at nearly $20,000 a year and there was a provision after seven years for Elvis to buy back the plane for a dollar or continue the lease agreement for $1000 less a month.

" I don't see anything amiss right now, Beecher," I said. "But keep me in the loop."

It was six months later in early January 1977 when Beecher Smith called with the news: Elvis Presley had lost about $350,000 to $400,000 on the Jetstar deal he now believed was fraudulent. When I met him at his office he explained the Jetstar deal in more detail from the beginning. I left Beecher's office with two boxes of documents, including his notes, to analyze. I spent three days reviewing the agreement Vernon made and all the parties to the transaction. In its bare bones form it was easy to understand. However there were so many players and convoluted transactions in the implementation of the scam I practically needed a scorecard to keep it straight.

I learned Memphis attorneys Charles H. Davis, a senior partner in the firm, and Beecher hosted a meeting at their office on June 24, 1976 with most of the players to discuss the proposed sale and lease back of the Jetstar.

The deal contemplated the sale of the Jetstar by Elvis Presley (through his father, Vernon acting under power of attorney) to WWP Leasing (actually a cover for Fredric Pro who led the scam.) WWP was to borrow enough money from the Chemical Bank of New York to cover both paying off the present indebtedness on the aircraft, which was over $600,000 and also upgrading it in order to qualify it to haul cargo. This upgrading had an estimated cost of $350,000.

The purchase money from WWP (Pro) to Presley would be released first to Presley's lending bank to pay off the outstanding indebtedness on the Jetstar, then certain funds would go to Fredric Pro's corporation for upgrading the plane, and the balance of the funds would be released to another corporation in Miami for supervising, directing and reporting on the upgrading of the aircraft as invoices were issued for work done.

Vernon Presley signed the lease agreement on June 25, 1976 and he prepared two checks to WWP, both in the amount of $16,755, representing the first and 84th monthly rental payments. At the same time Frederick Pro wrote three checks made out to Elvis Presley, two in the amount of $17,755 each, representing the first and 84th monthly payments, and a third check, as required under the sublease agreement, in the amount of $40,000. Fredric Pro, who was also a pilot, took the keys to the Jetstar and his copies of the documents and left for the airport to get the plane. Vernon Presley took the checks from Pro along with his copies of the documents and left for his bank.

Shortly thereafter Beecher learned all the checks Pro wrote to Presley were returned by his bank. Beecher called Pro who told him that the money was coming from Jamaica or some other place and that there had been an error in the transfer of funds. This had to have put Beecher on alert.

About three weeks after the original agreement was signed, Pro's attorney Sidney Zneimer came to Memphis with a new Chemical Bank agreement. While Zneimer was in the law office with Smith and Davis, another of the con men, Raymon Basner, arrived unannounced. Basner had with him invoices for payment for upgrading already done on the aircraft. Davis didn't want Vernon Presley to approve them because, under the lease, the release of funds for upgrading was the responsibility of WWP. Presley eventually, with the approval of his attorneys, signed these invoices allowing WWP to make the payments. His attorneys didn't want Presley to be placed in a position of supervising the upgrading and modification of the plane.

Unknown to the attorneys Vernon had been given a cashiers check in the approximate amount of $338,000 payable to Elvis Presley from the Chemical Bank of New York. Vernon deposited the check in Elvis' account at National Bank of Commerce. Presley told the attorneys that another player Gabriel Caggiano had called him and requested that instead of WWP disbursing the funds, as provided under the lease,

Presley himself should pay the upgrading invoices.

Caggiano had told Presley that Hans Achtman, another player, said he didn't know whether the work was done or not and didn't want the responsibility of disbursing the funds.

Beecher Smith said, "That's crazy. Achtman is in the aircraft leasing business and should have no problem understanding whether the work has been completed or not." Vernon said, "Well, Caggiano, Basner, and Pro came to Memphis and contacted me. We all went to the Whitehaven branch of the National Bank of Commerce and in the presence of my banker, I took their invoices and wrote out a personal check in the amount of $17,500 to pay one."

Beecher learned that at the same time Vernon Presley had the bank issue four cashiers checks for invoices for work done: $32,000 to Air Cargo Express Inc. (also a Fredric Pro company), $129,500 to Trans World Airlines and $45,000 to World Aircraft Exchange, Inc. At least Vernon had the sense to not pay in full a $117,500 invoice payable to WWP/Pro but deducted $78,510 for the bad checks Pro had given him.

Beecher Smith made numerous telephone calls to check up on the progress and upgrading of the plane. Pro told him that the delay in funding by the Chemical Bank had caused his company to be somewhat behind in the cargo hauling conversion.

Over the next few weeks Pro made various representations to Smith concerning the upgrades such as the wings of the Jetstar had been removed and x-rayed for any faults and tests had been done. Pro told him he had flown the plane on test flights with FAA officials and it would be just a matter of days before the plane would be ready.

The monthly lease payment of $17,755 to Presley was now past due. Beecher sent a notice of default to Pro demanding immediate payment or else Presley would repossess the plane as provided in the agreement. On October 11, 1976 the National Bank of Commerce in

Memphis received a Telex, addressed to Presley's banker Clarence Carter:

"With regards to the Elvis Presley transaction, by the request of Mr. Frederick Pro, Seven Oak Finance Limited has bank confirmation that his business Air Cargo Express has an account in excess of US $500,000. Signed A.C. Scott-Brown, Seven Oak Finance Ltd."

When Pro made no payments, Milo High, Elvis Presley's personal pilot, went to Miami to repossess the plane. Since Pro had been flying the Jetstar for a couple months and had apparently neglected routine maintenance, it was not airworthy when High arrived. It took several thousands of dollars of work before he could fly it back to Memphis.

Once Vernon repossessed the Jetstar he had some decisions to make. The plane was collateral for the Chemical Bank loan. No payments had been made and the bank had the right to foreclose and take the plane from Presley. The bank had appraised the plane at $950,000. Elvis would have to assume the loan if he wanted to keep the plane. Vernon opted to assume the loan and keep the Jetstar. Elvis was back where he started except he now owed $950,000. The total loss was over $400,000 since Vernon had written checks in excess of $100,000 to the con men.

After finishing my review of the records I had a good understanding of the subjects and corporations involved and how they had successfully executed their plan. While the plan was complicated with the number of subjects and corporations and the convoluted transactions, the net result was that these crooks stole Elvis Presley's aircraft temporarily and approximately $450,000 of his money.

I discussed the case at length with AUSA Glen Reid. "If you can obtain evidence to support the allegations in the records we will have a prosecutable case of fraud by wire, mail fraud, interstate transportation of stolen property, conspiracy and possibly other charges," he said.

I sent my first report on the case to Bureau headquarters on March

3, 1977 titled "Frederick Pro–subject, and Elvis A. Presley–victim."

When the Bureau receives any communication from a field office the names of the principals listed are checked against an index of persons presently under investigation or at any other time in the Bureau's files. Pro's name especially rang bells. He was one of a group of high-flying conmen called "The Fraternity." They were involved in operating several phony offshore banks that were nothing more than an office, telephone, Telex machine and high tech copying machines.

The bank scam went like this:

One of the members would issue a document like a letter of credit in the amount of one million or more dollars certifying that the borrower had an account with the bank more than large enough to cover a loan. He would present the document to a financial institution and use it to secure a large loan. Once the funds were disbursed the borrower would disappear and never make a single payment. The document appeared to be legitimate but in truth it was issued by an offshore bank that was essentially a shell. Attempts by the bank to contact the borrower would prove useless. Communications sent to the issuing bank were never answered. The lender bank then suffered a considerable loss.

Several FBI field offices had one or more cases under investigation resulting from the phony instruments generated by the bogus offshore banks. This group would open and close these banks on a regular basis to avoid detection by law enforcement agencies.

Within a couple days after my report arrived at the Bureau I received a teletype, also sent to several other offices working on cases connected to the Fraternity. This teletype directed the other offices to send me a summary of their work to date. Eventually 34 field offices worked on the combined investigation.

I learned the Indianapolis division had an undercover operation, titled OPFOPEN, an acronym for "Operation Fountain Pen," ongoing in an attempt to develop information about Pro and a person named Karl Kitzer as well as other associates who were operating bogus offshore banks. These basically nonexistent banks had flooded the United States with hundreds of millions of fraudulent financial documents, most of which were successfully used to obtain loans from American banks and other financial institutions in the amount of several hundred million dollars that were never repaid.

The Indianapolis division's undercover operation had been up and running for several months. Two undercover agents had gained Kitzer's confidence and were traveling around the country with him, learning more and more about his illegal activities.

On May 5, 1977 the two undercover agents and Kitzer flew to New York City and registered at the Mayflower Hotel. Kitzer telephoned Pro to set up a meeting for the next day at the Essex House hotel. When the agents and Kitzer arrived at the hotel Pro gave them a business card: Frederick P. Pro, Director Trident Consortium, 128 Central Park South, telephone 212 –757 –8037. The undercover agents described Pro as a white male, approximately 6'1" tall, weighing 190-200 pounds. He had graying hair and wore glasses, had a heavy build and was approximately 45 to 50 years of age.

Pro asked Kitzer if it was okay to talk in front of these guys (the agents.) Kitzer told him they were okay. Pro said he was handling approximately 150 telephone calls per day arranging deals initiated by 11 individuals working as brokers for him throughout the United States. Pro said he was operating Trident Consortium in New York City, a company operating worldwide, and he was the U. S. agent.

Pro bragged how he had conned Elvis Presley out of his Jetstar aircraft. Kitzer commented Pro had previously told him that he was going to steal Presley's aircraft and Kitzer had said "Mission Impossible." Pro reminded Kitzer that shortly after leaving the ground in Memphis with Presley's aircraft he had called Kitzer. "I used the airplane's air-to–ground telephone system to call you at your home in Minnesota and told you I was flying Presley's aircraft." Kitzer recalled the telephone call and was amazed Pro had pulled it off.

On May 26–27, 1977 I attended a status conference in the New York City FBI office, attended by agents from the Indianapolis, Memphis, and New York divisions to discuss the Pro/Kitzer matter. The two undercover agents from Indianapolis were there as well as two assistant United States attorneys from New York City and AUSA Mitchell Kerry, who was assigned exclusively to a New York strike force working this case. At the end of the conference a decision was made that the Memphis case would be the catalyst case to prosecute Kitzer and Pro. Hopefully this would lead to their cooperation with the government and most if not all the other offshore bank cases could be solved.

All the offices involved continued their investigations to strengthen the Memphis case. I did a complete review of the investigation to date to determine if I had missed anything in the heat of battle. Nothing popped up.

Elvis Presley died in Memphis on August 16, 1977. The Memphis U. S. attorney had anticipated bringing the case before a federal grand jury on or before August 15 but for some unknown reason he didn't. Elvis had no direct dealings in the matter so he was not to be a witness. From then on the FBI titled the matter "Elvis A. Presley (deceased) – Victim." Later, however, the timing sent some repercussions through the "Elvis death conspiracy " community who tried to make some link between the Jetstar deal and his death.

On September 4, 1977 I prepared a report bringing headquarters and other offices up to date. On October 6, 1977, Memphis AUSA Glen Reid said he expected to present the case to the federal grand jury on or about October 13. I sent an Airtel to the offices involved advising them and asked the offices where the subjects lived to make preparations to locate and arrest them once an indictment had been returned.

On October 13, 1977 I presented the case to the federal grand jury and late that afternoon they returned a 17-count indictment charging Frederick Peter Pro, Phillip Karl Kitzer, Laurence Wolfson, Raymond Baszner, Gabriel Robert Caggiano, and Roy Everett Smith (aka "Cowboy") with mail fraud, wire fraud, interstate transportation of stolen property and conspiracy.

When the sealed indictment was opened on October 18, 1977 the various field offices began making arrests. Subjects Pro, Kitzer, Wolfson and Caggiano were arrested that same day. On October 20 Baszner and Smith surrendered to FBI agents in Miami. All the subjects waived a removal hearing and were eventually returned to Memphis where they had bail hearings, posted bail and were released.

All the subjects appeared for their next court dates except for Pro who fled the country.

A fugitive warrant was issued for his arrest and now I had another fugitive investigation on my hands. With the help of other field offices we traced Pro to Ontario, Canada. I called the Royal Canadian Mounted Police and gave them the information I had for Pro's location. His name had been entered into the NCIC which would give the Mounties authority to make the arrest. They found him and held him until the U. S. Attorney's office provided the necessary documentation. Pro waived an extradition hearing and was returned to Memphis to remain in prison until trial.

Attorneys for Pro and Kitzer contacted the U. S. Attorney's office in Memphis and made arrangements to meet with the government lawyers to discuss a possible plea agreement. The attorneys eventually worked out a plea agreement. The agreement allowed them to plead guilty on the Memphis charges and serve a period of 10 years in federal prison. In return Kitzer and Pro would cooperate with the government and give a statement setting forth all the information they had about the fraudulent offshore banking scams. The government also agreed to not file any charges in connection with other ongoing investigations involving these two subjects in other jurisdictions.

FBI agents interviewed Kitzer and Pro over several days. They and their associates in The Fraternity procured many fraudulent loans across the country. Kitzer estimated that the total amounted to approximately 2.5 billion dollars. This number might have been a figment of his imagination but there were extensive losses to U.S. financial institutions. Subsequently more than 30 cases were solved and The Fraternity was demolished.

In October of 1980 Pro and Kitzer were admitted to the federal witness protection program at their request since each of them furnished information implicating members of the mob.

On August 21, 1978 the trial against the remaining defendants began in U. S. District Court in Memphis. Vernon Presley was in bad health and was allowed to give his testimony before a video camera so the tape could be shown to the jury. On September 11, 1978 Judge Harry Wellford ordered a mistrial and no new trial date was set. I cannot recall what incident precipitated the mistrial.

Vernon Presley died on May 26, 1979. Now both Elvis and Vernon were dead.

On May 17 1982 the second trial began. Approximately 20 witnesses testified for the government including me and several other agents from different divisions. The defense attorneys only called a few witnesses and in my opinion put on a poor defense. On June 14, 1982 the jury returned with a guilty verdict as to all defendants on each count of the indictment. They were subsequently sentenced and received substantial terms in the federal prison system.

This was a complicated financial case but I enjoyed working it. I recall one statement made by the banker from Chemical Bank during direct testimony at the trial. He said that "every morning when he arrived at work while the loan was being processed, Pro, Wolfson and Caggiano were already there, perched just like a flock of buzzards on a bench outside his office." Vernon Presley had once told Beecher Smith, when cautioned about what he might be getting into, "I would take a ride with the Devil if I was holding the reins." As it turned out he was taking a ride with several devils and he was NOT holding the reins.

We might not have completely put a stop to fraudulent offshore banking but this case put a very big dent in it.

Another Elvis FBI story involved the stealing of his body from Forest Hill Cemetery in Memphis. My good friend and FBI colleague Ed Young knew a criminal Ronnie Tyler, known as Bear. Two men Ed had an ironclad case on, a Shelby County deputy and an attorney, tried to get Bear to kill Ed for $50,000. Bear got cold feet and went to the FBI. When the contract killing case went to trial Bear was the star prosecution witness. One of the defense attorneys dropped a bombshell when he asked Bear if he had been part of a plot to steal Elvis's body from the cemetery where it was initially buried.

Bear had promised Vernon Presley never to tell this story and hesitated. The judge told him he was under oath and to answer the question and Bear did.

When Elvis died his family wanted to bury him at Graceland but state laws prevented this even though Vernon told the authorities the body wouldn't be safe at a public cemetery, someone would try to steal it. Bear approached Vernon with a plan. He would hire two unsuspecting men to rent a backhoe and dig the body up in the early morning. What he didn't tell them was that after they had been digging awhile he was going to call the police. They started digging, he called 911 and they were arrested at the scene.

Now Vernon Presley had ammunition for the authorities: Elvis's body had been stolen and recovered but would never be safe at the cemetery. They agreed and to this day Graceland is the resting place for Elvis and his parents Vernon and Gladys.

Chapter 11
The Window Washer

Petty thefts were rampant at two National Bank of Commerce branches, Cloverleaf and Nonconnah, in early 1976. Petty cash, personal property in desk drawers, small items like postage stamps started coming up missing. Some vending machines and tellers' drawers were tampered with. The bank's head of security, Jack O'Hearn, gave me a call.

ATF SA Walter Hoback and I talked to the branch managers. They said the thefts appeared to occur at night or over the weekend when the banks were closed.

This was when windows were washed and carpets cleaned by ITT Building Services.

The banks had surveillance cameras, but standard procedure was to have them in use only during operating hours in order to monitor employee transactions and to aid in the event of a robbery.

As one of our first steps, Walter and I visited the office of ITT and found that for the last several months, employee Larry Dailey had been cleaning both of the branches experiencing the petty thefts. Of course, our prime suspect quickly became Mr. Larry Dailey, aged 30.

We then decided to "bait" both branches. The coming weekend, we would put money in somewhat accessible locations with hopes of confirming our suspicions. We had recorded the serial numbers of these bills as well as sprinkled them with an invisible dye powder. The powder would transfer easily to anything that touched it and when that item was then placed under a black light, it would show a luminous purple color.

On that Friday, I was reading an article in *The Commercial Appeal* about two ITT employees washing the outside windows of NBC's skyscraper in downtown Memphis. They were at work on a scaffold 15 stories up the side of the building. The photo caption identified the men. One was none other than our suspect Larry Dailey. I thought, "What a coincidence."

Saturday morning, Walter and I again discussed our plan. We would drop bait money in an unlocked drawer in the bank manager's desk at the Cloverleaf branch, Mr. Dailey's first stop of the day. Once he was finished cleaning, Walter would remain there and continue our surveillance while I followed Larry to see if he might stop somewhere to stash any stolen property along his way to cleaning the second branch where we also stashed cash. He didn't make any stops so we didn't have an issue with a search warrant.

At nine, we photographed Larry Dailey entering the Cloverleaf branch. He stayed inside for about two hours and then left. Walter went in, with a key we had been given, to check to see if the money was missing and I kept an eye on Larry Dailey.

I followed Larry to the Nonconnah branch and photographed him entering the building. Walter joined me with the news the bait money was missing from the Cloverleaf location. We continued watching as Larry Dailey cleaned the second branch and when he exited to return to his work van, we approached and showed him our identification. We asked him to accompany us back inside the bank, which he agreed to willingly.

We told him we were interested in a number of thefts at the Cloverleaf and Nonconnah branch banks. We also explained that these thefts were a violation of the Federal Bank Larceny Statutes and carried a heavy federal prison sentence. Mr. Dailey said he didn't know what we were talking about. We took out the black light, hooked it up at one of the desks, and turned it on. Larry put his hands under the light. They were covered in purple powder.

We arrested him for bank larceny and, as is protocol, took all his property off him. The bait money from both locations was in his pockets. We handcuffed Larry and drove him downtown to the county jail for booking.

On Sunday morning, barely two days following *The Commercial Appeal*'s picture layout article on window washing, showing Larry Dailey doing an honest day's work, he was featured again, this time in "FBI Scrubs Bright View of Washer." There was another photo of Larry Dailey washing windows, but this time the story described his far from clean activities.

Chapter 12
TENNPAR: Cash-for-Clemency in Tennessee

In early September 1977 I was at my desk in the FBI office in Memphis, catching up on some paperwork when I got a call from an attorney I knew slightly. Sammye Lynn McGrory, the wife of his client Jerry Cook, was in his office and had told him a tale I needed to hear. He said if it was okay he was going to send her over to talk to me. I said, "Sure, I'll be waiting for her."

It wasn't long before my visitor was there. Sammye was in her mid-30s, nicely dressed and attractive with a worried look on her face. A few months ago Jerry Cook, while serving a 15-year prison sentence for armed robbery, had escaped from custody. She met him, an escaped convict, and fell in love practically at first sight. They had a short courtship and were married. Then Jerry was charged with first-degree murder and was back in jail. She sold her house to raise the money for an attorney to represent Cook on the murder charge. She was desperate to find a way to get him released.

Recently out of the blue she got a call from Bill Cole who had once been a cellmate of her husband's at Brushy Mountain prison (the one infamous James Earl Ray escaped from). He asked her if she wanted to get Jerry out of prison. "I would go anywhere anytime or do anything if that would help get him out," she said. He told her he knew someone in Governor Ray Blanton's administration who could get it done. Cole gave her directions to a trailer where he lived in middle Tennessee to meet this person.

The following morning, not knowing what might happen and what a dangerous situation she might be getting into, Sammye nonetheless drove from her home in Southaven MS to Cole's trailer where she met him and his wife Beulah. Two other men were there, one a large man with a swarthy complexion, later identified as Bill Thompson. Thompson took her to a back room of the trailer to talk. He knew about Jerry Cook and the murder charge hanging over him. He said that if Cook didn't get convicted on the pending murder charge he could get him out of prison for $25,000. "Can you get that kind of money?" She replied, "How can I be certain you can deliver?" The man looked her in the eye and said, "Lady, this comes straight from the governor's office." She told him she would try to get the money together. Not long after that Cook was convicted on the murder charge and the deal appeared to be dead. She kept trying to get back in touch with Cole but he wouldn't talk to her.

Now Sammye didn't know what she was going to do next. She had hired a private investigator to help in Jerry's defense. He knew a Tennessee Alcoholic Beverage Commission agent, Ernest Withers, who had connections in Nashville that might help her. Withers, a black man in his 50s, had a photography business in Memphis in addition to being an ABC agent.

Sammye met Withers but decided she didn't trust him so she checked with her attorney, and he suggested she talk to me. She told me she was so desperate to get Cook out of jail she would work with us against Withers, if it would help get her husband out.

I told her the FBI would do everything in its power to help but I couldn't promise her anything. She agreed to record her next telephone conversation with Withers with the recorder I gave her.

About five days later Sammye called to report on her progress with Withers. He told her he would see what he could do for her, but needed $2000 down and airfare to and from Nashville. He explained he had to meet the person he was working with face-to-face to discuss this matter.

I was aware that my good friend and colleague SA Hank Hillin was working a case with allegations that if someone had enough money they could get a prisoner released by paying a person in the Blanton administration. Hank was the Assistant Resident Agent in Nashville. He was tall, a good-looking man, "a poster boy for FBI recruitment." I had known him ever since I transferred to Memphis in 1972. Hank became an agent in 1955, about a year after I graduated from high school so he was a lot more experienced than I was.

The code name for the investigation was TENNPAR, for Tennessee pardons and paroles. A governor has the power to alter the terms of a convicted criminal's sentence by granting clemency which could moderate, lessen or mitigate in some form or fashion the harshness of the sentence. Included are probation, parole, commutation of a sentence to time served or a death sentence reduced to life in prison. A pardon is a forgiveness of a crime, wiping the slate clean as if the crime had never occurred.

As soon as Sammye McGrory left, I called Hank and related her story. He was very excited at and said, "Wow I've been working this case for a year and you hit a homerun the first time out." He said that Bill Cole, the person McGrory had mentioned, was presently cooperating with the government. He had told Hank about the woman coming to his trailer and talking to Bill Thompson but couldn't remember her name. He said they called her the "Toy Lady," because she had so many stuffed animals in her car. He said he would send me photographs of Bill Cole and Bill Thompson.

At my next meeting with Sammye I showed her the photographs and she recognized both as the men she met in the trailer.

Several days later Sammye recorded her second conversation with Withers. He told her he had seen "his people in Nashville" and that

Cook's release would cost between $12,000 and $15,000. They said:

Withers: The difference is that what it really takes---- now, I don't have no figure---but I would think that if they gave a figure, they would give a figure much more than what we have talked about, based on he----who he is.

McGrory: Are you talking about to get him on the street now?

Withers: Right

McGrory: You think it will take much more than six or seven thousand?

Withers: Well, I mean, I don't ----I would think that you-----you couldn't even expect to get him on the street for less than $12 to $15 thousand dollars.

We waited a few days before Sammye called Withers to confirm if she paid $12-$15,000 Jerry would be cut loose, using a script I gave her.

She posed the question and suddenly Withers became very evasive and said, "Maybe we had better table the idea. I mean maybe you have, I don't know, I get the feeling that maybe, maybe you should just deal with a lawyer and not with me. Because I don't want to get in no hassle about trying to do a favor."

The next evening I waited until about nine to pick up the tape from Sammye at her house. I didn't want to go there during daylight hours and possibly be seen by someone who knew me. I got the tape and headed home to listen to it.

I realized immediately that something had gone wrong. Withers was backing out of the deal and "cleaning his skirts" at the same time. He was downplaying the suggestion that there was anything illegal about his conversation with Sammye and he was successful. I felt terrible thinking I had asked Sammye to push Withers too hard and had blown the opportunity to go up the line.

About an hour later the Bureau switchboard operator called and said he had an irate man on the phone who wanted to talk to me. I recognized the caller, Renfro Hays, as the private investigator that Sammye had hired. I knew he knew me by sight since he was attorney Bob Gilder's PI. I told the operator to patch the call into my home telephone.

When I answered the caller lit into me with a string of profanity. I asked him what his problem was. He said he had seen me at Sammye's tonight and a couple nights ago. He accused me of trying to develop a romantic relationship with her (actually he used a crude term). He said Sammye was his girlfriend and he didn't want to see me around her. I told him he had it all wrong that I was covering a lead from another office who wanted her interviewed as a possible witness in a case in Little Rock. He said he didn't believe me and that the next time he saw me "He was going to kick my ass." I asked him what was wrong with right now and offered to meet him to discuss this matter. He said that's what he wanted to do. I suggested he come to the Southland Mall which was only a mile from my home. He agreed and I told him I'd be there in 45 minutes. I called two other agents and asked them to meet me at the mall and park out of sight of my car while still being able to see what was happening. We waited there for over an hour but the PI never showed up. He was all bluster.

When I had first listened to the tape that night I thought I had blown the case by having Sammye press Withers too far, but I now realized the PI had warned Withers that I was talking to Sammye and that is why Withers ended his relationship with her. I still blamed myself for not meeting Sammye at some location other than her home. If she had told me Hays was her boyfriend I would've picked up the tapes somewhere else.

I called Hank the next morning and broke the bad news and apologized for screwing things up. He told me not to worry that it had happened to him several times in this case. Someone would agree to cooperate and then something happened and they changed their mind.

I thought I needed to become more familiar with the Tennpar case and try to figure out who the players were. I talked at length with Hank and reviewed the active investigation file. I certainly had no idea then that over a year later I would provide, through my informant, evidence that ultimately led to the indictment of several high-ranking Blanton administration officials.

On January 18, 1975 Leonard Ray Blanton became the 44th governor of Tennessee. Blanton had dark hair and rough features. He grew up in Adamsville, Tennessee and lived with his family in a sharecropper's shack during the Depression. His "dirt-poor" upbringing in the cotton fields of West Tennessee imbued Blanton with a rough-hewn populist tendency that endeared him to the working classes and many state employees.

As he was assembling the members of his cabinet prior to his inauguration, Blantton delayed the appointment of his legal counsel as long as he could. The governor's brother Gene was pushing for his good friend Eddie Sisk to fill the position. Sisk, a lawyer in private practice, had been a mainstay on the governor's election committee. Gene told Ray, "You owe him (Sisk) that job, Ray. The boy worked like a dog for you." Blanton wasn't sure about Sisk and doubted he had the experience or was smart enough to do the job. He tried to put Sisk off, "Don't worry Eddie. There'll be other good jobs. I'll see that you get one." Sisk replied, "No sir, I will be your legal counsel or I won't be anything." After Blanton gave Sisk a long stare, he finally said, "Okay, you got the job".

Sisk was in his early 40s or late 30s, over 6 feet tall, heavy build, with brown hair worn long in the 1970s style. By virtue of his appointment he became the chief liaison between the governor and the Board of Pardons and Paroles, a board created to advise the governor on all clemency and pardon decisions and whether to sign extradition orders. While the Board advised on these decisions, its advice was not binding. The power to release prisoners, grant clemency or approve an extradition ultimately rested with the governor.

Soon after Sisk became legal counsel he hired Marie Ragghianti as Tennessee's extradition officer. They had met in 1974 at a political function at Vanderbilt University when Marie was a senior. Rumor was they were lovers.

From the beginning the relationship between Sisk's office and the Board was strained. Sisk told them right away that he represented the governor in matters pertaining to the Board, and they soon realized that talking to Sisk was as close as they would get to the governor. Sisk's approach was aggressive confrontation. He was authoritarian and wanted them to understand up front that the governor made the decisions: The Board was advisory only and they needed to keep that in mind when they sent over their recommendations. If he told them the governor wanted the application granted, they were to approve it.

After the retirement of Board member Dorothy Greer, on May 11, 1976 Gov. Blanton appointed Marie Ragghianti as the new member and chairman of the Board of Pardons and Paroles. It was obvious that Sisk believed he could control/manipulate Marie to accomplish his and the governor's wishes as to certain petitions for clemency whereas her predecessor wasn't subject to political influence.

Marie's promotion to the Board allowed Sisk to name a new extradition officer. Charles Benson, a pudgy, likeable young man with a sparkling smile and a disarming friendliness had gone to work in Sisk's office in late 1975 as Marie's assistant, so it was logical that he should take over her old job. He was married, a college graduate and was finishing his fourth year at the YMCA Night Law School in Nashville. Benson had been introduced to Sisk by Lt. Fred Taylor of the Highway Patrol.

On September 15, 1976 Hank Hillin was covering the supervisor's desk at the Resident Agency (RA) in Nashville. The first thing the supervisor does in the morning is check the mail. When Hank came to an Airtel from the Chattanooga division he became excited. The Chattanooga RA advised that Marie Ragghianti, chairman of the Pardon and Parole Board, had contacted the District Attorney in Cleveland TN who in turn advised the Bureau. She had only been chairman for about four months and had uncovered what she believed was corruption in the operations of the Board. Hank could see this was a very important case and could be one in a career for the agent assigned to it. He was tempted to assign the case to himself, but to do so would be a violation of an unwritten policy of not assigning a case to himself while he was acting as supervisor. He decided to assign it to Phil Thune an experienced and no-nonsense, hard-working agent.

Hank talked to Phil and they agreed he should move on this case immediately. Phil contacted Marie Ragghianti and interviewed her on three different occasions. She gave him extensive information that pointed to corruption at the highest levels of government and right to Governor Blanton's Pardons and Parole Board as well as extraditions and commutations. Marie's believed bribes were occurring in Governor Blanton's administration that she was part of.

The information was passed on to SAC Joe Trimbach in Memphis. The SAC recognized this as the most important case in the Memphis division. When Hank came to Memphis Trimbach got right to the point, "Hank, I am reassigning the pardons and parole investigation to you." Hank replied, "Joe, I assigned that case to Phil myself. If I get the case back, it could be misunderstood in the Bureau. Why don't you at least give him a chance?" Trimbach shook his head. "There will be no further discussion of the matter. I am the SAC," he said with finality. "I want you on the case. I expect you to keep me advised on any progress you might make." Hank knew that Joe had just given him the biggest case of his career, but all he felt was frustration.

On October 8, 1976 Hank and Phil met Marie and her attorney Bill Leech at a remote state park on a gravel road. Hank could see that Marie matched perfectly the description that had been given him. She was in her 30s, attractive, and tastefully dressed in a flowered print dress. Her dark hair was pulled up on top of her head, and she was wearing a pair of oversized, wide rimmed dark glasses. To Hank she definitely did not look the part of a parole Board chairman. She was younger and much softer than he had expected. Her attorney Bill Leech was lanky, over 6' 3", distinguished looking, holding his lawyer's briefcase.

Marie told Hank and Phil about her suspicions of what was going on in the Pardon and Parole Board. She gave Hank a sheaf of papers which she said came from the file she kept on clemency cases when she worked in Sisk's office. She said, "I know it sounds strange but when I was working for Eddie, I wasn't suspicious. I was just learning the job." She said her suspicions were that Board member Charles Traughber was involved in the mysterious activities." "Traughber?" Hank said with surprise. "I thought we were talking about Sisk."

Leech interrupted, "Fellows, you need to remember that Mrs. Ragghianti feels a natural loyalty toward Mr. Sisk. She has three young children to support and he helped put her in her present position, and she doesn't want to leave that position. Frankly, she doesn't think Mr. Sisk is involved in this, and I have to tell you I have known him myself for years, and I have a hard time believing it." Hank told Marie, "Eddie Sisk is our man. Traughber can't put people on the street. Sisk is the one with the power through the governor's office." Marie said, "I know it sounds bad, but you don't know Eddie, he's so nice. He has a wonderful wife and children. I know his wife Claudette. They are such a nice family. " Hank replied, "It sounds like we are talking about two different people.

177

I'm telling you, Eddie Sisk is corrupt. "

Hank then suggested, "Marie, there is one way to resolve it, you can wear a tape recorder and record your conversations with him. Tell him you want to go along with whatever he wants, and see if he'll open up to you about these suspicious cases. Let's get his voice on tape, one way or the other." Marie said, "No I can't, I won't." Hank urged her to cooperate, "I don't think you realize how important it is, and what an important role you could play. If you really want to do what's best for the Board and state government, and help us put a stop to Sisk, wear a recorder." Leech joined in, "Marie, I think you should do it." She shook her head and said, "I just can't do that." Hank, though disappointed, thanked her for what she had given him and they went their separate ways.

On October 12 the Board held a hearing on a very sensitive case. George Edwards, a young black man, had been serving a 15-year sentence for armed robbery when he was chosen as one of the inmate trusties to work at the governor's mansion. He was the maître'd, responsible for seeing that the first family was properly served at mealtime.

In the summer of 1976, Blanton had commuted Edwards' sentence to time served. Once out of prison Edwards went to work for a political crony of the governor's in a new liquor store in Nashville. There was only one catch; state law made it illegal for a convicted felon to work in a liquor store. Within days, the Pardons and Parole Board received a request from the governor's office to consider George Edwards for a full pardon, which would clear his record. Marie was the Blanton administration's representative on the Board, and her fellow Board members Charles Traughber and Joe Mitchell looked to her for guidance on how the administration wanted them to vote. There was confusion on Traughber and Mitchell's faces that day when Marie announced she was voting against the Edwards pardon because he did not meet the Board's criteria. Following her lead Mitchell and Traughber voted no also.

The vote went unnoticed for two days. Then Sisk called in a rage. Edwards had to have this pardon. He spoke with each of the Board members and a few days later Mitchell and Traughber changed their votes, and Edwards was pardoned.

Hank didn't know exactly which way to turn so he called Marie, figuring that in light of the Edwards pardon the Board would be in turmoil. Hank asked her how she and Eddie were getting along. She replied, "He's not very happy with me." "Have you talked to him lately?" he asked. "Yes, he came by my house last night." "What? He came to your house?" Marie said Eddie was under a lot of pressure right now. "He drops by often to talk to me. He said he was upset because I am causing him so much trouble."

Hank said, "Listen Marie, we're getting nowhere like this. You need to wear a wire, especially if he's coming over to your house at night." She said, "Hank, I couldn't talk to him if I were wearing a tape recorder. Eddie would know something was wrong. Believe me, Eddie's not a bad person. He just has a lot of people putting demands on him. I still don't believe he is involved in this." Hank then proposed that he hook a recorder up to her telephone and talk to Sisk. Again she refused. Marie said she wanted to be honest with Sisk, and with everyone else. She said if she had her way she would hold a press conference, and announce she had blown the whistle, while explaining the irregularities she had uncovered. Hank pleaded with her, "We want to keep this investigation secret as long as possible."

By the middle of October, Hank was getting nowhere with the Tennpar investigation. Marie told him that Sisk suspected an investigation was underway and had thrown a temper tantrum. He had accused her of initiating it, claiming "his source in the federal court house" had told him that Marie and her attorney had gone to the FBI about a matter relating to commutations. Marie denied it.

On October 21, 1976 Hank got a tip from a TBI agent friend that the Blanton administration was aware of the investigation and were destroying incriminating documents. Hank went to the Nashville US Attorney Charlie Anderson and convinced him to convene a grand jury and subpoena Sisk, Marie and Murray Henderson, commissioner of corrections, to bring with them their office records pertaining to extraditions and pardons, dating back to 1975.

The next day Hank assembled all the Nashville agents and they served the subpoenas simultaneously and carried away records from the respective offices. In the coming weeks they organized and reviewed the documents and gained valuable evidence for a federal grand jury.

A month later Hank was prepared to seek indictments against Sisk and possibly Blanton. Despite having more evidence the US Attorney and Department of Justice decided it was insufficient to seek any indictments.

Hank received a disturbing phone call from Marie a few weeks later. She once again wanted to call a press conference and announce she was the one who started the investigation into the Pardons and Parole Board. He told her this would sabotage his investigation. He asked her if she had discussed this with her attorney Bill Leech. She admitted she had and he was against her plan. Hank, Leech, and Phil Thune met with Marie and convinced her to stay away from the press for now.

Marie continued to go her own way as chairman of the parole board to Sisk's dismay. But as long as Sisk controlled Traughber and Mitchell's votes he could override Marie's no vote on the hearings for prisoners he wanted released.

On March 28, 1977 Charlie Benson contacted Ed Bell, a young attorney who was an extradition officer in the Secretary of State's office, a law school classmate. Benson offered him $500 if Bell would report to the Secretary of State that there was no legal basis to extradite his brother-in-law's son to Georgia where he was facing auto theft charges. Bell went to Hank and told him about this contact and agreed to record future conversations with Benson.

On April 13 Hank met with Bell to finalize his next meeting with Benson. But before he sent Bell off Hank wanted to inform Bell's boss, Secretary of State Gentry Crowell. Hank asked Crowell not to tell anyone else about what was happening, especially not the governor nor anyone in his office, or in Eddie Sisk's office. Two days later Bell met with Benson at Nashville's Hyatt Regency Hotel in a room that Hank rented and set up with audio recording. Benson spoke at length about what he wanted Bell to do. Bell eventually agreed but said he needed $1500 for his part. Hank and Bell agreed to wait until April 20 for the next meeting. On April 19 Gentry Crowell felt he could no longer sit on the information. He wanted to tell Blanton. When Hank heard this he immediately called Crowell to the FBI office.

Hank played the April 15 recorded conversation between Bell and Benson for Crowell. After he listened to the tape Crowell said he felt he must tell the governor. Hank said in an angry voice "Telling the governor is like telling Benson, you heard him on that tape. If you tell Blanton, the first thing he will do is call Sisk, and that will be the end of the case. I can't make you do anything, Mr. Secretary, but if you do this, I will do everything in my power to indict you for obstruction of justice."

On Friday, April 20, 1977 Bell had a second recorded conversation with Benson. Again they talked about the extradition matter and set a date for the hearing.

Over the weekend Hank listened to the tapes over and over and reread the transcripts several times. He decided that not only did the case against Benson have merit on its own, but it also was evidence of the criminal conspiracy being run out of Sisk's office.

Bell called Hank the following Tuesday morning and said, "We've got a problem. I just talked to my supervisor John Beasley. He found a note on his windshield from JP Bradley, Crowell's chief assistant. It said, "You should check with me and Gentry because the governor knows what you are doing." Hank immediately went to Crowell's office to confront him about the leak. Crowell denied he had told the governor about the investigation. He said he was summoned to the governor's office the previous morning to meet with Blanton and Sisk. Blanton already knew what had happened. After telling them what he knew, Blanton said he was suspending Benson and ordering a special TBI investigation into the alleged bribe.

During the course of the next several weeks the entire story unfolded in the press following Benson's actual suspension. The TBI conducted an investigation of the Bell-Benson case and reported to the governor they could not find sufficient evidence to charge Benson with a criminal act. Benson was subsequently reinstated with full back pay.

In early May 1977, Hank learned the US Attorney Charlie Anderson had decided to transfer the Tennpar case to the public integrity section of the Justice Department in Washington. He told Hank it was the only way to guarante the investigation would not be undermined. Anderson said, "We've got Eddie Sisk's old roommate, Hal Hardin coming in to replace me and I would be derelict in my duties if I didn't press for the case to be transferred." Anderson was an appointee of the previous Republican administration. With Jimmy Carter elected president, Hardin, a Democrat was the newly appointed US Attorney for Middle Tennessee. Anderson feared that Hardin would be reluctant to pursue the Democratic governor of the state.

On May 11 1977 Hank received some bad news. Marie called and said, "I don't know how to say this but I was arrested last night for DUI."

For the past six months Marie felt she was under increased scrutiny. She believed, but could not prove, that Eddie Sisk was behind her being stopped by Nashville Metro Police, for allegedly weaving on her way home from a Democratic party reception. She didn't score high enough for a charge of DUI, only reckless driving. Marie told Hank she had been "set up" and asked Hank to check into it. Hank reviewed the arrest report and talked to the officers involved. He could find no evidence of anything irregular about the traffic stop.

A couple of days later Hank received a call from a Justice Department attorney, Andy Reich, of the public integrity section. Reich and another department attorney, Steve Pitt, were coming to Nashville to take over the prosecution of the Tennpar case.

Hank picked up the attorneys at the airport and drove them back to the FBI office. The attorneys were already very knowledgeable about the case. He began to have a good feeling some indictments were forthcoming.

On June 3, 1977 the federal grand jury wound up the day's testimony in the Benson-Bell case. The two recordings of the conversations between Benson and Bell remained the crux of the case. When the grand jury had gone home, Reich, Pitt and Hank sat down to decide what to do. Hank argued that the Benson-Bell case was part of the overall conspiracy because it was one more indication that corruption was a fact of life in the legal counsel's office. Reich told Hank he wanted to give the case to the local DA, Tom Shriver's office. He said he couldn't establish enough of an interstate angle to the bribery. His boss at the public integrity office agreed with him.

Two months later, Marie was stopped again under suspicion of DUI on her way home from a Democratic fundraiser after which she had been drinking at a hotel bar. Even though she thought she was targeted by the police at Sisk's direction, this time she did register high enough to support a DUI charge. Hank checked again at her behest but found nothing amiss in the arrest.

In September 1977 a third grand jury was convened to hear evidence in the Tennpar case. No indictments were returned. Attorneys Reich and Pitt declined to comment about the year-long investigation, except to say, "It is continuing and that useful testimony had been heard this week."

A few weeks later SAC Trimbach visited the Nashville RA and had a private meeting with Hank and told him he was suspending the Tennpar investigation. "There is entirely too much adverse publicity involving the governor and this investigation," he said. "We can't seem to get any support from the US Attorney or the Justice Department. It seems like the FBI is taking all the heat." He told Hank to dictate an Airtel to the Bureau to that effect. Hank said, "I can't do it. It's not right, it's the wrong thing to do. I want nothing to do with any document saying that. You can do it if you want, you're the SAC. You can take the case away from me, but I am not going to put my initials on anything that would stop the investigation." Trimbach stared at him, taken aback as Hank stood up and walked from the room. Outside the room he could hear Trimbach, dictating the Airtel he had wanted Hank to sign. Hank later received a copy that he filed away and forgot. Hank continued with his investigation notwithstanding Trimbach's putting the case in abeyance.

After three grand jury sessions, Andy Reich and Steve Pitt were preparing to return to Washington in July to draft a prosecution memo, a document that states the upside and downside of an investigation. Hank told Andy, "We don't need a memo. We're ready to go the trial. What else do you think we need that I haven't already given you?" Reich replied, "I know you've worked hard, but we need to proceed cautiously. This is a very sensitive case. Everyone in the department is watching us. We have to make sure we've got our ducks in a row."

Hank was dejected, believing that with all his work he was no closer to getting any indictments. They all knew Blanton was continuing to hand out clemencies but didn't know how many were sold, favors to political cronies, or legitimate.

Andy Reich flew in from Washington for the October 4, 1977 grand jury session. He told Hank Tom Henderson, the head of public integrity, was reviewing the case right then and it would not be long before indictments would be returned. None were.

On January 30 1978 Reich called Hank, "We have a real problem, Tom Henderson doesn't think prosecution is possible with the testimony of a prime witness (Bill Cole) who is in jail." They discussed it for a while and Reich said, "Henderson has killed the case."

In a last ditch effort to keep Tennpar alive, Hank, SA Irving Wells from Chattanooga, SAC Trimbach, along with SAC Hal Swanson of the Knoxville office, traveled to the Justice Department in Washington to plead with Tom Henderson. Hank outlined the entire case including the evidence against Bill Thompson and Eddie Sisk. After some consideration Henderson said, "This case is much more substantial than I or anyone in public integrity realized. What we need here in integrity is a flowchart. We want to show the different acts by Sisk and Thompson in chronological order, so they can be traced and the conspiracy tracked. We also need a few more witnesses interviewed, and Andy, you will provide their names." The contingent then returned to Nashville believing that new breath had been breathed into Tennpar.

On March 30 Hank received a call from Andy Reich, "Hank, I've got bad news again and this time it's final. The public integrity section has declined prosecution and we are in the process of sending a letter to that effect to Sisk." Hank said, "So it was a con job, after all." He couldn't believe the prosecution had been declined.

Letters went sent to SAC Trimbach and Sisk's attorney advising there would be no further investigation. Hank's hands were now completely tied. There was no way to describe his disappointment.

It is important to understand that the very thought of the federal government/FBI investigating high levels of a state government was an extremely sensitive undertaking. This was a unique case. Local sheriffs were routinely targeted for malfeasance but not governors. Also after three grand juries had convened and deliberated without returning indictments, the justice department's public integrity section had to consider whether a continuing investigation would yield positive results. This section had the ultimate power. Had Marie Raghiantti worn a wire and recorded her conversations with Eddie Sisk early on as asked, the government would have a prosecutable case.

Back in Memphis I had been following the progress of Tennpar and was astounded that Justice had closed it down. I was running an all-agency drug enforcement, organized crime task force (OCDETF).

In early April 1978 the Memphis Police Department moved an undercover officer, Joe Hoing, into the topless nightclub operations of Arthur Wayne Baldwin. The officer was so good he rose quickly in the organization, eventually becoming Baldwin's main confidante.

Hoing, among other things, made a federal case against Baldwin for distributing cocaine. Baldwin was tried and convicted on several counts. Baldwin's attorneys wanted him to be sentenced only for the conduct he was convicted of---not anything additional Hoing may have discovered. The US Attorney agreed since he wanted to get Baldwin to cooperate and first hand tell them everything. The USA thoroughly debriefed Baldwin. Every word was taken down by a court reporter and transcribed into six volumes.

Now the US Attorney had to find an agency to "work" Baldwin. The FBI hadn't been part of the Hoing investigation and was reluctant at first to take on Baldwin as a CI. With encouragement from AUSA Hick

Ewing (Hick said "I had a nose for the ball'), my supervisor assigned me as Baldwin's control agent. I realized at once Baldwin's potential and we were off and running.

Baldwin grew up in Northeast Arkansas not very far from Memphis. He left the Midsouth in the 1960s and moved to the Seattle area. He soon was working for a reputed mobster, Frank Colacurcio, who owned several clubs in the area. Baldwin, who turned out to be a good businessman, rose in the ranks to become Colacurcio's number one manager. Baldwin didn't look or act like a thug most of the time, but if someone crossed him he would retaliate with a vengeance. He stood just under 6 feet, probably 170 pounds, blonde hair, approximately 40 years of age, not particularly intimidating for a man of his reputation. He reportedly left Seattle after the IRS charged him in a tax case. I wondered later if perhaps he had a falling out with the Seattle mob.

In late April I was debriefing Baldwin at one of his topless nightclubs. He said Ernest Withers, a state ABC agent, had been visiting his club on a regular basis. Withers demanded pay-offs in connection with Baldwin's liquor sales and wanted free table and lap dances from the strippers. He also expected a bottle or two of liquor to take home. This is the same Ernest Withers who Sammye McCrory had negotiated with in her attempt to get her husband released from jail the year before.

I told Baldwin about my previous experience with Withers and that I knew Withers was operating in Memphis as a recruiter for people willing to pay money to have a loved one released from prison.. I gave Baldwin a small recorder to hide on his body. I told him the next time Withers came to his club, somewhere in their conversation, tell Withers that some friends of his had a son in the Shelby County Jail who was about to be transferred to the main state prison at Brushy Mountain. They were extremely worried about him, having read stories about prison life, and were ready to get him out by any means. They were rich and could pay whatever it took.

When Baldwin next saw Withers he told him the tale I had spun. "What can you do for him?" Baldwin asked. Withers replied, "That depends." Baldwin told him that money was no object; they would do whatever needed to be done to free their son. "Let me go to Nashville and talk to my people," Withers replied. "I'll be in touch with you later."

Next I started searching for the name of an inmate that Baldwin could give to Withers, if Withers agreed to work with him. I had to have a real name and story to put forth. From working a case with the MPD I knew a prisoner named Steve Hamilton who was facing a 10-year prison sentence in the state system. Hamilton was still in the Shelby County Jail awaiting transfer to the state.

On June 8, 1978 Baldwin reported he had a tape discussing with Withers the possibility of paying for Hamilton's release. I listened to the recorded conversation. When Baldwin brought up the subject of needing help for an inmate Withers asked for details. Baldwin told him that a friend of his son was being sent to state prison and the boy's family was concerned and gave Withers a rundown of the current situation. Withers said, "I can't help the boy unless he's in state custody or has a state number. But you tell me when they send him up there and I'll see what I can do."

Throughout the summer I kept Hick Ewing up to date on the progress Baldwin was making with Withers. We surveilled their meetings, with audio and video, from an adjoining motel room. Other times they met at GiGi's Angels, Baldwin's premier topless club. What we wanted to do eventually was cut Withers out of the loop and see if he could introduce Baldwin to his contact in Nashville. Baldwin told Withers, "I need to look the man in the eye, I can't lose the family's money on a scam." Baldwin assured me, "Don't worry about Withers. I can handle him." Baldwin had all the credentials for an underhanded negotiator. He favored open–necked shirts that showed off all his gold chains and flashed hundred dollars bills the way other people showed fives. He had mob connections and was a convicted felon. I could tell from the conversations that Withers looked at Baldwin as if he were the mother lode.

"Look," Baldwin said, "You say that man's going to be here in three or four days. I'd like to shake his hand and call him by his name. This Hamilton kid is only the beginning. I represent big bucks." He told Withers in the future he would sort of be his silent partner. Withers went for that proposal, the thought of all money and no work was irresistible. He told Baldwin his contact in Nashville was Fred Taylor, the highway patrolman on the governor's security staff, driver for Blanton's brother Gene, the same Fred Taylor who had recommended Charlie Benson for his job in the legal counsel's office assisting Marie Ragghianti.

Near the end of August, I called Hank Hillin and asked him, "Hey, do you know a state trooper named Fred Taylor?" I told him that was the name Withers gave Baldwin as his man in Nashville. He said the name evoked a dim memory. There may have been a Fred Taylor in one of his firearms classes sometime ago.

Hank began checking Fred Taylor out which was difficult since no one in the Highway Patrol seemed to know what he was doing. Our files in the Memphis office contained an application Taylor had made to attend the FBI National Academy in Quantico, a regular eight-week course for local police officers. Taylor had been a member of the Tennessee Highway Patrol for 17 years, though his record was unimpressive.

I wanted Art to ask Withers to call Taylor who in turn I hoped would call Baldwin, the man with the money, so Withers was no longer the middle man.

Apparently the plan worked because in late August 1978 Fred Taylor called Baldwin and set up a meeting for just them in Memphis on

September 4, Labor Day. We immediately began making preparations for our guest. I decided that in keeping with Baldwin's reputation I would rent a limousine for the occasion. I asked my good friend and colleague SA Dick Gray to act as Baldwin's driver; we even rented him a chauffeur's uniform complete with a hat. Dick was a perfect actor and loved playing this role. He was very gregarious, could talk to anyone on just about any subject. He was a true "bull shitter" which made him a perfect choice for this job. He liked to talk about sports which always seemed to be a good conversation starter. This "job" also required him to hang around the topless clubs.

In the meantime, during July and early in August, while I was working Art Baldwin against Ernest Withers and Fred Taylor in Memphis, Hank in Nashville was still trying to breathe some life into Tennpar by covering leads as they came up even though the Justice Department had given up on the case.

On August 9, 1978 a very excited AUSA Joe Brown called Hank. Joe Brown, first assistant USA in Nashville, had been put in full control of Tennpar. US Attorney Hal Hardin recused himself from the case because of his prior contact with Gov. Blanton and other members of his administration. The same thing had happened in Memphis where US Attorney Mike Cody had recused himself and put first assistant USA Hickman Ewing in charge of the Memphis Tennpar investigation.

Joe told Hank he had just received a call from attorney Lionel Barrett. Joe said, "I don't know the details but there's somebody in his office right now who's ready to buy somebody out of prison." Hank was in the lawyer's office within ten minutes. Even though the Justice Department in Washington believed there was not a prosecutable case, the local US Attorney's office and FBI could pursue this lead since it was possibly new evidence.

Hank asked Barrett, "When can I meet your client?" Barrett said,

"Right now," but warned Hank that his client Sheryl Leverett was reluctant to talk to the FBI. Sheryl had medium-length brown hair and was wearing a loose blouse and tight jeans as she sat alone on Barrett's couch, drinking a soft drink. She looked at Barrett and said, "I should never have told you." Hank said, "Mrs. Leverett, I don't know what exactly it is you have to tell me. And I'm not going to make any promises I can't keep. But I'll tell you that if you cooperate, the FBI we'll do everything in its power to see you get what you want." Leverett replied, "I want to get my husband out of prison." Hank told her he could not promise that but could promise he would look at the situation and see what he could do.

After some coaxing Leverett told Hank her story. She and her husband John had been arrested with 35 pounds of marijuana in their possession. John had previously been convicted of armed robbery but was released on probation after serving one year of a 6-20 year sentence. She was able to make bond on the drug charge, but John's probation was revoked and he was sent to prison.

With John in prison Sheryl became increasingly desperate and decided it was time to act. She contacted an attorney, Dale Quillen a well-known lawyer with a reputation for handling controversial cases. He told her that he could give her the help she needed. Quillen was a big man—6'3", at least 200 pounds—with a booming voice and a shaved head. He was known around Nashville as "the Kojak of the court room."

Sheryl told Quillen she wanted to get John out "anyway she could." Quillen told her he had once had a client convicted of murder and that for $15,000, a portion of which went to Charlie Benson, the client was placed on work release. Quillen said Benson could be "dealt with."

Quillen told Sheryl to contact Benson and set up a meeting but not discuss money at first, but rather fill Benson in on the details of John's situation. He told her that he would work out the other arrangements himself. She was going to have a meeting with Benson the next day. Hank told her he wanted her to record her conversation with Charlie Benson. After some hesitation she agreed.

Hank could hardly believe that this lead had dropped into his lap. At last he had a good chance to prove what he knew was going on in the Blanton administration. And I had the Memphis case involving Fred Taylor that was going the same way.

Hank went immediately back to the Federal Building and met with USA Hal Hardin and AUSA Joe Brown. Hardin said, "Dale Quillen is one of the toughest criminal lawyers in Nashville. If what she says is true, we are going to be stirring up a whole new hornet's nest." Hank acknowledged this, "That's why we need voices on tape." "Right," said Hardin, "Corroboration, if we don't get that, all we have is her word against the word of a veteran attorney." Hank agreed, "I just want to make sure we all agree that Tennpar is back on track." "No question about it," Joe Brown replied.

The next day Sheryl had her meeting with Benson which she recorded. The conversation was all above board and Benson only asked about her husband's situation in prison.

Dale Quillen was out of town for a week or two but when he returned Hank began receiving information from Sheryl about telephone conversations with Quillen. At the end of August she called Hank with big news: Quillen had talked to Benson, and it appeared he would help. The cost: $10,000. She said they had arranged for her to pay the money on the Tuesday after Labor Day

Hank asked SAC Joe Trimbach in Memphis for $10,000 for Sheryl to pay Quillen. He said there would be no money until Quillen produced signed clemency papers for John Leverett. Hank told Joe, "I am not sending that girl to see Dale Quillen with nothing. I have given her my word. She's done everything we've asked, and we can't hang her out to dry." They talked about the problem for a while and finally Joe came up with a solution. He had recently sold a private airplane and had some money in the bank.

They decided Joe Brown would put $9500 in a passbook account in Sheryl's name and Hank would come up with the first down payment of $500 in cash. Sheryl would take the $500 and passbook, showing a balance of $9500 in savings, to her meeting with Quillen. She would give Quillen the $500 as a down payment until John's release from prison. When John was out, she would go to the bank and withdraw the $9500 as a final payment. They didn't know if Quillen would go for this but it was the best they could come up with.

In Memphis we were preparing for Fred Taylor's September 4, 1978 visit with Baldwin. I knew that Baldwin never went to the airport to pick up anyone. Dick Gray, in his chauffeur's uniform driving the limousine, would get Taylor at the airport and go to the Hilton Hotel where Baldwin and he would have a meeting.

Dick picked up Taylor, who had no luggage with him, at the airport. Dick noticed right away that Taylor's nerves were definitely on edge. There was no good–natured conversation in the car as Dick chauffeured him to the hotel, where Baldwin had taken a room for the night. While SA Woody Enderson and I watched and listened to their conversation from the room next door, Taylor asked Baldwin about his driver. My pulse started racing as Baldwin casually dismissed Taylor's fears. They agreed to hold off discussing business when Dick was around. After Dick had booked Taylor into a room for the night and brought them bottles of Jack Daniels and Chivas Regal, Baldwin sent him off to have some supper. It was obvious from what we were seeing and hearing on the TV monitor that Taylor and Baldwin had become friends. They relaxed and started talking.

I had briefed Baldwin prior to the meeting and told him to get as much information from Taylor as he could but use his judgment about how hard to push him. I couldn't have written a better script.

"B" is Baldwin and "T" is Taylor:

T: All right, right, number 1, the commissioner of corrections is my cousin. OK? Number 2, I can handle the Pardon and Parole Board. They're not kin to me but they're my people. You told me you had one individual name.

B: I had talked to Withers once before about it but at that time the prisoner hadn't reached the state system. That's what we were waiting on, yeah. The boy is at jail east now. He's got his state number. He took a guilty plea and got sentenced from five to ten.

T: First one? *(first conviction)*

B: Uh huh.

T: What's his name?

B: Steve Hamilton

T: Five to ten for what?

B: Uh, I think he got, I think he got two armed robberies. I'm not sure whether he pled guilty to. I don't know whether he had to plead to both of 'em or whether he just pled the one.

T: What do you propose? What do you want to do?

B: I want to get him cut loose.

T: All the way?

B: As much as I can. Now the boy's father. I never met the boy's father until this came about. The boy's father came to me and he says do whatever you can for my son, like I would and like you would, if in the same position.

T: Everything you can?

B: Said do whatever you can for my son. I said, look, I said, I'm, I'm just making some preliminary inquiries and I says, uh, I don't know whether I can do nothing or not. I says but if I can't then whatever money you give me, I'll give your money back. I said you ain't gonna lose a quarter. And the man trusted me, enough, you know, and like I said, you talk to a hundred people and you'll never find one that'll say I've told 'em a lie. I lot of 'em might say they don't like me cause I don't take no shit from King Kong.

T: I don't either. I said now on a deal like me coming down here and you paying my damn expenses and stuff, I expect that. Other than that if I take $500 as a binder, I'm either going to do what I tell you or get your $500 back. That's the only fucking way my mother taught me.

Later during the same conversation Baldwin said he was working on getting $15,000 from Hamilton's family for his release. Baldwin told Taylor he would keep $5000 for himself and give Taylor $10,000. Taylor said, "$10,000 for my man?" Baldwin said he didn't care who Taylor was dealing with and as far as he was concerned the $10,000 was for Taylor himself.

Baldwin then queried Taylor about his job in Nashville and his background. Taylor told him he was in the governor's office on the security staff, he was from Newport TN and had been with the highway patrol for 17 years.

I called Hick Ewing and gave him a summary of the meeting. He agreed we were getting to the upper level players in the bribery scheme.

Hank and my investigations continued on their parallel tracks. The following day, September 5, 1978, Hank, Joe Brown and Sheryl Leverett met to prepare her for her afternoon meeting with attorney Dale Quillen. They gave her five $100 bills (the serial numbers and denominations recorded, called "marked bills") and the passbook in the name of Mrs. John Leverett showing $9500 in the account. She was nervous as she got in her car. Hank followed along with two other agents who were parked nearby.

Sheryl Leverett wore a wire to record her conversation with Quillen as well as a transmitter so Hank could listen in.

Quillen said: "I just told him *(Charlie Benson)* this. I said the lady *(Sheryl)* has got ten thousand dollars, on the phone, and that was all was said. I didn't, shit, I'm not gonna give the money to him. Ah, I mean I'm not gonna violate the law myself. But, he said well you get it in your hands and I will see what I can do."

Leverett told Quillen she had the money together. He said he would give her a receipt for it. "Well, I want it made clear to you that I'm not gonna, I'm not gonna lose that fucking law license (pointing to his framed license on the wall) for anybody. I think I know what's going on and I think it's going to be very legal. If not, I ain't gonna have anything to do with it."

Quillen next asked Sheryl where the money was. She replied she had $500 in cash and showed him the passbook in her name with a balance of $9500. He wanted her to go to the bank and withdraw it and she said she would. But she wanted to know what was going to happen next. He said the judgment against her husband would have to be final first.

Sheryl was worried that Benson would get the money and not do anything. Quillen told her, "I'm not gonna let him. He's not gonna get it till the boy is out. I think it's just as safe as it can be. If it weren't, I wouldn't be messing with it."

Sheryl was supposed to meet Quillen with the remaining cash the next day but she put him off for nearly a month. Hank renewed his plea to SAC Trimbach that he had to have the cash. Trimbach maintained his position that the FBI wouldn't put forth any cash until the signed clemency document was in hand. Hank made a compromise with him: the Bureau would give $6000 immediately and the remainder when she had the document.

On October 10 Sheryl returned to Quillen's law office. He told her,

"You see, I wouldn't give anybody a damn penny. I'm not going to start giving Charlie Benson or Eddie Sisk or Governor Blanton, not a penny to do anything. It's a violation of federal law to do it, and they would rather have me in jail, you know, than have your husband in jail." Sheryl gave Quillen $3500 in cash and he gave her a receipt, with "Representing executive clemency" written on it.

Quillen told Sheryl he had a meeting with Charlie Benson scheduled for October 17 and would have a firm release date for her husband by 1:30 that afternoon. After the meeting, Quillen called Sheryl with the news. Benson had said his release date would be by Christmas. On October 18, Sheryl gave Quillen another $3000 so he had now received a total of $7000 for his "fee."

Again Hank put forth a plea to SAC Trimbach: "I want the money for Sheryl to pay the remaining $3000 to Quillen within the next week. I don't think we should wait. If we do, it would queer the whole deal. They're not going to take action until Quillen has all the money. I think we should go ahead and play along now. Get the ball rolling." Trimbach replied, "Absolutely not. The FBI will not buy someone out of prison. It goes against everything the Bureau stands for. Our job is putting people in prison, not getting them out. I'm shocked you would suggest this."

Hank had no choice but to tell Sheryl he could do nothing further for her without the additional money. He had hoped that with all of the "fee" paid, Quillen would produce the signed clemency document as he had promised. Quillen was eventually indicted on Tennpar bribery charges.

On September 25, 1978 Taylor called Baldwin. He had checked Steve Hamilton's record and discussed the case with his contact. "The man said what he could do is get him a time cut, make him eligible for parole, put him on work release in Memphis…and he'd be paroled within one year."

Baldwin told Taylor that sounded good to him, but first he'd have to check with the boy's family. Then Baldwin mentioned another name, one that we had given him, Larry Gillespie. Taylor told him he would check on Gillespie's prison record and the conditions of his sentence, to find out whether he met the basic criteria to be released. Taylor called Baldwin back a week later and said Gillespie could be worked out. They agreed to meet the following week with Baldwin providing airline tickets for Taylor's flight to Memphis.

Hank had arranged for SAs Frank Christina and Tom Gruel to be at the Nashville airport for the Piedmont afternoon flight to Memphis on October 9, 1978. They watched as a nervous Fred Taylor dry–cleaned himself (made sure no one was following him) as he prepared to board the flight. He was all decked out in a three-piece suit and aviator glasses. At the last moment Gruel boarded the plane and slipped discreetly into a seat up front.

Our chauffeur Dick Gray picked Taylor up and deposited him at the Executive Plaza Hotel to meet with Baldwin. We were set up in an adjoining room and recorded and videotaped the men's conversation. Taylor spent some of the time boasting about the deals he had made.

Baldwin paid Taylor $2000, in marked bills as always, as partial payment for Hamilton's release. We observed Taylor count out the money, place it back in the envelope and then place the envelope in his left front pocket.

The following day Dick Gray took Taylor to the airport where he boarded his flight to Nashville, unbeknownst to him accompanied by SA Susan Marley. In Nashville she saw Taylor being met by Charlie Benson in a beige Pontiac. Later that afternoon Taylor called Baldwin at his home and advised that his "main man" wanted more money up front before they went any further on the names Baldwin had provided since "they had never done business" with Baldwin before. Taylor said they normally never proceeded with less than one-half the agreed amount in advance.

On October 18, 1978 Taylor was back in Memphis to meet Baldwin at the Executive Plaza Hotel. After discussing the Hamilton and Gillespie prisoners Baldwin gave Taylor $3000 in cash.

T: Yeah, well see the, I can have the damn board consider the case whether they are meeting or not. But we can tell when a man is interested when he gives you something. And if he gives…hell yeah, I want to do business and he gives you something up front, then we can put his name in the mill. Now if it's now, if he don't follow through with his and then the governor just don't do it.

B: That's right.

T: 'Cause I control the signature.

B: Whichever one you move on, uh, I'll bring the money to Nashville.

T: We'll do both of these together. We're gonna do 'em at the first, first time they interview 'em and the next time they're out, you know.

B: Okay. The same week that that happens I'll get in touch with you and make arrangements to come to Nashville and get it squared away.

T: Absolutely.

This was a quick turn-around trip. When Taylor arrived back in Nashville that same evening FBI agents saw Charles Benson meeting him in his state vehicle.

After the October 18 meeting I decided we needed to move things along a little faster. I wanted to see just how far Taylor and company would go. My thought was to propose a $100,000 deal for the release of a notorious outlaw. I got my fellow Tennpar agents, Dick Gray, Woody Enderson and Harold Hays, together. We started kicking the idea around. Woody said, "I have a candidate who would be perfect, Ed Hacker who is in Brushy Mountain State Prison." We all recognized the name of the inmate who had led the escape attempt a few months before with James Earl Ray who was serving life for killing Martin Luther King Jr. Hacker had been arrested for armed robbery and bank robbery and was considered capable of any crime. I talked to Hick Ewing about this plan and he said, "Go for it."

There was nothing in Hacker's record that would recommend him for early release, actually quite the opposite. We discussed whether putting forth Hacker's name would "spook" our friends in Nashville but decided this group was so brazen they would likely go for it with a $50,000 pay off to them.

I considered the options and decided to break the deal down into payments of $25,000 each for Baldwin and his "partner" who brought the deal to him, leaving $50,000 for Taylor and "his people." This was "show money" that was intended to never be given to anyone, only to prove Baldwin was the "real deal." Agents didn't have any trouble getting show money although we did copy the serial numbers in case the bills got away from us.

I briefed Baldwin on the plan and told him to "play it by ear" with Taylor at their next meeting. I instructed him to just mention a big deal, maybe $100,000 he was working on but not to give any names. "Just see what his reaction is. Feel him out at first, Art," I said. "Find out what they can do and how far they are prepared to go."

On November 1, 1978 Taylor telephoned Baldwin. They discussed how the pending cases were progressing.

B: No, huh, you, you indicated me it was gonna' be done the next two or three days when we talked about it the last time.

T: That's my error then because the man ain't gonna do nothin' till after this election's over. (He was referring to the upcoming Tennessee gubernatorial election; Blanton wasn't running for re-election.)

During this conversation Baldwin mentioned a large money deal which would involve an inmate at Brushy Mountain State Prison.

On November 14 Taylor and Baldwin met in the Holiday Inn Motel on Lamar Avenue in Memphis and Baldwin brought up the big deal again.

B: Ok, I don't even have the man's name but I can give y'a all the circumstances. Uh, the deal originated out of Oklahoma City. It's a $100,000 deal; Uh, 25 for me, 25 for the man that's gonna hold on to the money, and in fact, the man's got money now, and 50 for gettin' it done. Now this guy, he's in Brushy Mountain, uh, I think he's doin' life or somethin' like that, and he just wants to hit the ground.

T: What's he in for? You don't know?

B: Unh, unh. But it's got, you know, got to be bank robbery, murder or something.

T: Wouldn't be bank robbery or the state wouldn't....federal woulda done it instead of the state. It's gotta be drugs or murder.

B: And I think that he might have a federal hold.

T: Or rape.

B: I think he's got, might have a federal hold, too. So, it, uh you know, if there'd be a way, I don't know how, you know, as far as the, you know, maybe somebody could let the wrong man out on, you know, the door could be left open or, all, if he just you know, gets 30 minutes, then our end of it's OK.

T: He needs to escape.

B: Yeah, he needs to go. That's right.

T: He'd be satisfied with gettin' by God, I can get 'im out.

B: Yeah, if, uh, somebody can find an excuse to take 'im out to .... or whatever. I think that'd be the easiest way to do it.

T: Not only that, hell, I'll get 'im out and give 'im a date.

When I listened to this part of the tape I realized that Taylor was suggesting that prison guards or officials could be bribed to let Hacker just walk away. This went way beyond what I thought Blanton was capable of.

The next morning the two men met in Baldwin's room for breakfast and over bacon and eggs continued their conversation.

T: On the big one. He said, he said we could, we could do whatever we needed to for that price, you know.

B: Okay, like I said, but you keep in mind it don't make no difference, whichever way…you know, that you can get the most money and the least heat.

T: We'll look at it and see. We might be better off going legal than we would be in escape from up there…unless we could go ahead and transfer him to Nashville and do it from there…We'll work on it. So there's several ways we can go at it.

B: I'll just put some question marks by that. I'll get the name for you and then, and I'll just tell them people it looks like it's a 90% chance that it will be done.

And that, that the money is okay on that..okay. You, you said that Blanton knows and already given his okay.

T: Yeah, yeah…yeah, he's okay on it…He's given me the green light to, you know, for my judgment.

B: Well, what about the guy who has the power of attorney? Does he know Blanton okayed it?

T: Yeah, yeah, yeah.

B: Okay, in other words if you bring the documents to 'em then he's got to sign 'em.

T: I mean he's already been told to sign the documents we present to him…Uh, huh. So there ain't no problem there.

B: They ain't but one of those people is there? You don't have to worry about somebody else….

T: No, no one…shit no. He's the only one that can sign that.

B: Yeah, it'd be just my luck that they'd have two or three power of attorneys running around the day before we was supposed to do something and then blow up everything.

T: Kid …makes all his appointments has got his power of attorney sitting right there in the office right there.

Then Taylor made a telephone call and asked "Is my main man there, C.B? By this afternoon before we can get a name…There's many ways we can do. All he wants is out. He don't give a shit. He wants 30 minutes." (We assumed CB to be Charles Benson, and "main man" Eddie Sisk.)

Baldwin told Taylor he was leaving for Oklahoma City later that afternoon. When they next met Baldwin would provide the name of the inmate he wanted out for $100,000.

The two AUSAs, Hank and I agreed that we would soon be ready to make some arrests. Before that could happen the Public Integrity Section in Washington had to give its okay. This time the dreaded section chief Tom Henderson, the one who had shut the case down before, came to Memphis. After he looked at the transcripts of Baldwin's conversations with Taylor Henderson didn't hesitate to give permission and we were on our way to breaking wide open an unprecedented investigation.

On November 28 Taylor flew to Memphis to meet with Baldwin again. I had secured $50,000 in marked bills for Baldwin to use as "show money" to Taylor. Woody Enderson and I watched and listened from an adjoining room at the Executive Plaza Hotel as Baldwin showed Taylor the money. Taylor's eyes brightened as he looked at the stack of bills. He said, "Give me a name." Baldwin showed him a piece of paper with the name "Larry Ed Hacker" written on it. "Twenty-five years for armed robbery, went in '72."

Taylor made a few calls from the room. The first was to the legal counsel's office in Nashville. He gave the name, number and description of Hacker, his conviction and sentence. In another call Taylor said,

"Our only concern is what we can do. Man wants, says he's got to know something pretty strong about, no later than 2 o'clock and like I said I'm holding, you know. Yeah I just looked at it here but I don't wanna carry it. That's solid you know. You need some consultation? Where is it? Call him at the office. Huh? Now, yeah but I don't, you know I don't..I'll explain that later. It's solid, you know. The same deal we talked about, yeah…Call him at the doctor's office and, uh, call me back. Uh, oh, wait a minute now, Morgan County got a detainer on him? Is that jurisdiction of the DA? Who's the DA? Man may not know about that. 'Course that's not going to bother them anyway. Yeah, call him at the office and run that by him briefly and call me back. Now, how long do you think it will be before you call me? Okay."

Woody and I looked at each other and couldn't suppress a smile as Taylor repeated Hacker's criminal status:

T to B: He escaped November '76, stayed gone until April of '77. And escaped in June '77 and was gone two days. They don't show whether he returned voluntarily or not on what he's got there. It shows his federal detainer, Greenville, South Carolina and got a state detainer on him in Morgan County which is up in uh, Wartburg, I don't know.

Not long after Taylor returned to Nashville, a clerk in the FBI office told Hank that Fred Taylor was on the phone and wanted to know the status of his application to the Bureau's National Academy. Hank was astounded at first, then suspicious. Did Taylor know about the investigation? Was his call a ruse? Hank had the clerk tell Taylor he needed to speak to SA Ben Hale in the Memphis office who was the recruitment coordinator. When Ben called Taylor he expressed his earnest desire to attend this school for outstanding police officers who are on their way up. "How's my application coming? Do you have a place reserved for me?" Taylor inquired. "Well, Lt. Taylor," Ben answered wryly, knowing exactly who Taylor was and the part he played in the pardons and parole case, "There's a good possibility we might."

We all had a good laugh about this, a laugh well-deserved after such a long, tense and sensitive investigation.

In early December SAC Joe Trimbach decided Tennpar needed to come to a close before Christmas. Since several of the inmates getting clemency for cash were scheduled for release by Christmas, he wanted to make sure this didn't happen. The paper work began: Hank and I had to prepare lengthy affidavits in support of search and arrest warrants. I went to Nashville and we worked long into the night to get them done. Mine ran to 62 pages.

Agents from the nearby field offices had to be assembled and briefed to execute the search warrants. We anticipated seizing documents from the legal counsel's office and the pardon and parole board in the Capitol in Nashville. In the end over 50 agents were involved. The target date was December 15, 1978.

But we wanted to have in our hands signed clemency documents obtained with marked cash before the warrants were executed. Baldwin and Taylor had another meeting scheduled for December 13. Woody and I checked out the $50,000 in show money again as well as $10,000 Baldwin was to pay Taylor to be applied to the first of the other deals that went down.

With this much cash at stake I realized there was a possibility for a "rip" like in a drug deal where the bad guy gets the cash ripped off from him by an unrelated third party who is in the know. So we had agents stationed in critical places in the Holiday Inn to observe and intercede if it came down to that. We also had the connecting doors between our control room and Baldwin's room rigged so if we had to make a sudden and unannounced entry all we had to do was open the door in our room and kick the other door open.

We watched and listened on December 13 as Taylor told Baldwin he wanted to put Hacker on the street just before Governor Blanton went out of office on January 19. The commutation document would show Hacker's sentence commuted to time served as of January 15 or 16 whichever day "the man" decides on, Taylor explained. Taylor said they were drawing up several commutations, probably 8 or 10, which would be filed in the Secretary of State's office, as required by law, around January 16-18 as Blanton was leaving office. Hacker's would be one of these.

B: Well, is this gonna, is this gonna, this will handled out of the governor's office, then.

T: Yeah, governor'll sign it, yeah.

B: Will he sign it or will it be a power of attorney thing?

T: No, well, it'll be a power of attorney sign it. He never signs, he never has signed one that I know of.

Baldwin then gave Taylor an envelope containing 100 $100 bills for Hamilton and Gillespie's release. At first Taylor miscounted and came up with only 99. Baldwin smiled. Taylor recounted by carefully turning each bill so Ben Franklin faced the same way. There were 100 which I knew was the correct amount since I had put the marked bills in the envelope. This was "buy-walk money." We needed to let the money walk. We might or might not ever see it again but it was necessary to make the case. In case the bills did reappear I had recorded the serial numbers.

Next Taylor made a call to Benson's office at the legal counsel office and told whoever answered to cut a legal document with everything but the date. He then told Baldwin he was going to move more quickly and get on an earlier flight back to Nashville that afternoon.

Before Taylor left Baldwin flashed the $50,000 again. Taylor's eyes sparkled at the sight of so much cash. They agreed Taylor would return in two days, on the 15th, with the signed clemency documents. Baldwin said he would then contact his principal to say the documents were in his hands and give Taylor the $50,000.

Our chauffeur Dick Gray took Taylor back to the airport. When he arrived in Nashville SAs Burl Smith and Jim Harcum were watching as Charlie Benson met him. The two men talked excitedly as they hurried to a shiny state car, driven by a man who closely resembled Eddie Sisk. These agents reported back to Hank who in turn called me right away. December 15 could not come soon enough for us.

Early on the morning of December 15, 1978 I went to US District Court Judge Harry Wellford with my 62-page affidavit in hand seeking an arrest warrant for Charles Frederick Taylor. Judge Wellford had no qualms issuing the warrant so I then assembled the agents who were to cover the Baldwin-Taylor meeting scheduled for later that morning.

Baldwin, who thrived on late nights and the wee hours of the morning, was not particularly happy to meet at 10 a.m. especially when he was hung over. As usual I met him in his motel room before Taylor's scheduled arrival. I said, "Art, we've got one requirement. We have to have *signed* release papers. That's what you want to see: Ray Blanton's signature on a clemency document. Send him back if he tries to flim flam you." I counted out the marked $100 bills for Baldwin to give Taylor as the phone rang, "He's here," the surveilling agent said.

"You know the drill, Art," I said. "Keep it simple and watch your language. Remember, one of these days, a jury is going to be watching your debut on television." I closed the door behind me and went to the room next door where the videotape equipment was ready to roll.

Taylor came in Baldwin's room and without any conversation handed him a piece of paper. It was a single unsigned clemency document containing the names of Steve Hamilton, Larry Gillespie and

Larry Ed Hacker.

Baldwin said, "My man ain't gonna go for this thing not being signed...this don't mean nothing here." Taylor replied, "I could have got it signed I guess I should have got that clear with you...That's my fault. I should have gone ahead and got it signed."

Baldwin told Taylor his man with the money was in Memphis but would be leaving early in the afternoon and he had to have it signed. Taylor said he could call Nashville and have a signed clemency document flown to Memphis before the man left. In fact, he could call Nashville and if the document could be signed that morning he would fly to Nashville himself, pick it up and return to Memphis with it.

After Taylor made a call to extension 3621 (Benson's number) in Nashville, Baldwin asked, "What's the guy's name?" Taylor replied, "Eddie Sisk is the legal counsel."

Taylor then made arrangements for a new document to be drawn up with the governor's signature on it. Baldwin interrupted Taylor in his telephone conversation and said it would be better to have two clemency documents, one for Hamilton and Gillespie, and the other just for Hacker.

As soon as Taylor got off the phone, it rang again. Baldwin answered, "Hello. Yeah. It's about time. Thought you was gonna sleep all day or something." It was me calling him pretending to be the money man. "You're doing good Art, tell me about the deal," I said. Baldwin laid out the situation to me. He explained there had been a mix-up over getting the documents signed and Taylor was going back to get the documents signed and return by early afternoon. I told him we wanted to have the signed clemency documents as close to 2 pm as possible. This time frame was important because Hank and I wanted his team in Nashville to begin executing the search warrants and possible arrests of Benson and Sisk at the Capitol no later than mid-afternoon on this Friday in

December. But the Nashville team needed to know the situation with Taylor first. We hoped once we confronted Taylor he would flip and cooperate; if not we'd play it by ear. Either way it went Nashville had to know before they could proceed.

Baldwin said to me, "I understand. Yeah. I want to get it over with. I'm tired of fucking with it. I'm tired. Well, let me ask. Why don't you call me back in 10 minutes?"

After Baldwin hung up he told Taylor to check his airline schedule. "My man says 2:00, 2:15 is the latest he's doing business today. We'll have to do it Monday if it's gonna be any later than that. I'd like to get this thing over with." Taylor replied, "Yeah, I would too."

Taylor discovered after checking with the airlines that the timing was going to be very difficult to arrange. The quickest he could return to Memphis was 2:28 pm. I called back, Baldwin explained the situation to me and I said, "Tell him to go ahead. But tell him I'm changing my reservations and this is it. If he can't get the documents here by three, the deal's off."

Baldwin passed the word on to Taylor who immediately went to work, booking flights. More bad news. The time of the flight to Nashville had been changed due to the Christmas holidays. There was no way he could make the round trip and be in Memphis by 3 pm.

B: Do you have anybody up there, can just catch the flight and bring it down here maybe?

T: Yeah.

Taylor called the familiar 3621 extension in Nashville and learned that Benson was in an extradition hearing and said:

"Let me holler at him again, will ya? Where is he? Yeah, he said to call him out of it, uh hum. In a extradition hearing...(pause)...Hey all right. Are the things prepared? Okay now. I tell what we need to do. If we don't get this out of the way today and it's partly my fault and you know lack of understanding on my..but it's gonna be delayed and I. I wanna get rid of this fuckin thing. Tell ya what do. Tell 'em, go ahead and get 'em done immediately. Make ya a reservation on that 1:10 pm Southern flight out'a there. I'll meet 'ya in the airport lobby when you deplane. Now, no, you'll have to be out'a there at 1:10 pm. Go ahead and expedite whatever in the fuck you're doin'. You gotta be out'a there at 1:10 pm because this man on this end made two strong commitments and he's got to go... Have someone call me back and confirm."

Trying to keep the pressure on Taylor and wanting to know the other end of Taylor's Nashville conversation, I called the room again in my role as the money man. Baldwin explained to me that Taylor was having someone in Nashville fly the documents to Memphis and they would be here before 2 pm. "We need to know who's flying them down here," I said. "I don't want some secretary bringing them down. Get some assurance that the man who's bringing them down knows what the hell is going on, and isn't going to blow the whole deal." Baldwin replied, "Yeah, I'll yeah he's real careful, but I'll check. Uh, he knows the man knows what he's doin'...I'll talk to him about it. Yeah...We'll have it done by three."

When Baldwin hung up he told Taylor what I had said. "I understand his apprehension. I'd be the same fucking way."

While the men waited for confirmation of Benson's arrival in Memphis they discussed various other deals they were working. Baldwin once again quizzed Taylor about when Hacker would be released, January 19. He thought his money man might get nervous having to wait so long.

The phone rang again, Benson calling Fred Taylor. He couldn't get there until 2:57 pm. What to do? Baldwin said, "Tell him to go ahead," Baldwin responded and Taylor quickly repeated the message over the phone, and the courier was on his way. We couldn't believe our luck that Charlie Benson would be the one to arrive with a signed clemency document in his possession; this was a real slam-dunk for the prosecution.

At 11:26 a.m. after the men continued their small talk Baldwin pulled out an envelope with $6000, divided into two equal stacks of $100 bills. He took one of the stacks and handed it to Taylor.

B: See if that ain't thirty, now takes care of Gillespie.

T: All right. (counting money)

B: There's thirty, takes care of Hamilton.

It was nearly 11:30 a.m., we now knew it was decision-making time as to whether we arrested Taylor then and tried to flip him. We were running out of time to advise the Nashville agents to serve the search warrants that day. Also Benson would be on his way to Memphis soon with the signed documents. We didn't want him to leave Nashville if Taylor refused to cooperate.

AUSA Hick Ewing was in the control room with us (me, Woody Enderson and Harold Hays) that day. It was such a sensitive case, perhaps leading to the arrest of the governor of Tennessee, Hick wanted to be on the scene for the confrontation of Taylor. Also only Hick could assure Taylor of what kind of help he would receive from the government if he were to make a deal.

Taylor continued counting the money, then slipped the envelope into a coat pocket. After pocketing the bills he picked up the clemency paper and said, "I think I'll burn this fucking thing."

Baldwin said, "Well you better just tear it up. I wouldn't have no smoke in here." Taylor began tearing the paper into pieces, walking toward the bathroom.

As soon as we heard Taylor say he would burn the document, Woody, Harold and I ran from the control room to Baldwin's room and knocked on the door. We wanted to stop Taylor from destroying the document.

The time was 11:30 a.m., Taylor dropped the pieces of the clemency paper in the toilet and answered the door. When he did, Woody and I entered.

"Mr. Taylor, we are with the FBI," I said. "We're investigating a conspiracy to sell executive clemencies out of the state Capitol." Taylor stared back at me without speaking. Art Baldwin stepped around the group and out the door. As Taylor watched him go the first signs of recognition were beginning to show on his face. Harold Hays raced into the bathroom and came out with the wet remains of the unsigned clemency document.

"We'd like to talk to you about what happens next," I continued. "We'd like your cooperation." Taylor wasn't saying anything. Woody and I worked on him for another minute, then Woody suggested we go into the next room. We seated Taylor in front of the television monitor, and he looked around the room at the sophisticated surveillance equipment as Woody rewound the videotape. Hick Ewing watched with anticipation.

"I want you to watch right here," I said, and pointed at the screen. The picture came on of Taylor counting the payoff money Baldwin had just given him. "We've got you, Mr. Taylor," I said. "The only question now is how hard you make it on yourself."

Taylor looked at me, "What do you want?"

"We want you to wear a wire against the people in Nashville. And we want your testimony on the witness stand."

Taylor thought for a minute, then spoke, "I want total immunity."

I looked at Hick who shook his head. "Not for what you've done, Fred," I said. "We'll do what we can to help you, and you'll be a lot better off with our help than without it. But we can't promise total immunity."

Taylor crossed his arms and looked straight ahead. He wasn't going to have any more to say. But I was. "You are under arrest, Taylor."

Before we took Taylor to the federal building I called Hank and told him we didn't get any cooperation and had Taylor under arrest.

State Trooper Taylor was a bagman who had bragged incessantly--- and unknowingly---to a hidden videotape recorder about his past and current exploits in freeing convicted felons. He had offered money-back guarantees. The Tennpar case had been stymied for a long time and my informant, a topless club operator with a criminal record, played an Oscar-winning role without a written script, to blow it wide open.

As soon as the Nashville agents learned Taylor refused to cooperate they headed to the airport to intercept Charles Benson before he boarded the flight to Memphis. With Hank in the lead they found Charlie in a corridor leading to the gate. Hank came up behind him and said, "Charlie, you are under arrest for violations of racketeering laws." Charlie Benson was astonished, he thought it was a joke. It was not a laughing matter when he was transported to the FBI office.

Hank told him to empty his pockets. Benson had just gotten his state payroll check cashed and had $364 in cash. He also had a bank passbook, a Piedmont Airlines ticket to Memphis, cards, notes and messages. Then he pulled out the contents of his right pants pocket and Hank sat back with a sigh of satisfaction. There was a roll of hundred dollar Federal Reserve notes, bound with a rubber band. There were 33 of them, all 33 were on the list of serial numbers of the bills Baldwin had given Taylor two days before. In his briefcase Benson had three copies each of two signed clemency documents, one for the immediate release of Larry Ed Hacker, and the other to release Hamilton and Gillespie.

Hank and AUSA Joe Brown tried to convince Benson to cooperate with the government but as with Taylor it was a futile effort. Brown said, "All right. We move on the Capitol."

At 2:40 p.m., on Friday, December 15, 1978, FBI agents entered the legal counsel's office asking for Eddie Sisk. Hank had arranged for two beefy agents, Burl Smith and Darrell Hamar, to serve the warrants on Sisk. Sisk was a big man and known to be physically aggressive so he didn't want to take any chances. The agents went into the inner office as Sisk was coming out from behind his desk. Hamar said, "Mr. Sisk, we are agents of the FBI, and we have warrants to search your office and your person." A search of Sisk's billfold found 13 $100 bills. Hamar recorded the numbers and called the office; 12 of the 13 numbers matched bills passed from Baldwin to Taylor on December 13. Sisk was arrested on the spot and transported to the federal building where he and Benson appeared before a magistrate. At the same time Taylor went before Judge Wellford in Memphis. All were released upon posting bond.

The media had a heyday with the news of the arrests. Of course speculation and rumors abounded: How high up will this go? Will the governor be charged? Local and national newspapers printed portions of Hank and my affidavits. Agents in Nashville were combing records and following leads as people came forward with stories of paying cash for prisoners' releases. Other agencies of the Blanton administration came under scrutiny for payoffs for favors in road building and liquor licenses. The state of Tennessee was at a low point in its history.

With the exception of testimony in the event of any trials, my part in Tennpar was finished.

The aftermath of the investigation continued in Nashville however. A list of 13 names was found in Eddie Sisk's desk, and identical ones in the Pardons and Parole Board office and Benson's office. Hank believed this was the master list of inmates who were soon to be released in return for payoffs. The ones Baldwin worked, Hamilton and Gillespie, were on the list.

Early on the morning of Monday, January 15, the state Attorney

General Bill Leech (the same Bill Leech who represented Marie Ragghianti when he was in private practice) issued an opinion that Blanton's term of office terminated officially at 12:01 a.m., Tuesday, January 16, and the incoming governor Lamar Alexander didn't have to wait until January 20 to be sworn in.

Blanton began signing as many clemency documents as he could before his term legally ended at midnight. He told his legal counsel, "Get together as many cases as you can." The signing began at 9:20 pm and ended two hours later. Blanton came out of his office and told the waiting reporters, "Remember, this administration is under a court order to reduce prison overcrowding."

The following day, Tuesday, January 16, newspapers carried the list of 52 commutated inmates: 24 murderers, 15 armed robbers, and 13 convicted of burglary, assault and nonviolent crimes. Under pressure Lamar Alexander agreed to be sworn in on January 17 to stop Blanton from doing more harm.

One of the new governor's first acts was to order the Capitol be sealed so no further documents could go out of the governor's office. Despite the order the new legal counsel Robert Lillard was still at work, people outside waiting for a commutation miracle. Lillard finally capitulated and left, leaving 30 clemency documents on his desk, yet to be signed by the governor. One of these was for Eddie Denton, an inmate who had served only three years of a sentence for murdering three people. His family or someone close to him had reportedly paid over $85,000 for his immediate release.

During his tenure as governor Blanton granted 656 executive clemencies. The previous governor Winfield Dunn granted about 100 in his four-year term of office.

Roger Humphreys was one of the most egregious commutations that Blanton approved in January before he left office. On May 11 1973

Susan Garrett Humphreys was found lying in a pool of blood in her apartment in Johnson City Tennessee by police officers. Near her on the floor in another pool of blood was the nude body of her lover, John Roger Scola. The police department received a call about 1:45 PM from the next-door neighbor who reported hearing shots in the apartment of Roger's wife Susan Humphreys. Susan was shot 12 times in the back and John was shot six times with what appeared to be the same weapon.

Within hours, Humphreys had been arrested by police." I probably did it," he told the arresting officers and was immediately charged with the double murder. Humphreys had a two-shot Derringer in his possession when arrested which proved to be the murder weapon. In order to shoot the two victims 18 times, Humphreys had to stop and deliberately reload the Derringer eight times.

Roger Humphreys was found guilty on two counts of second-degree murder and in 1975 began serving a term of 22 to 40 years. He was the son of a Blanton political crony.

On the day of the mass commutations, January 16, Humphreys' release paperwork was hand-delivered to the prison within minutes of Blanton's signing it. The now ex-inmate was rushed to an apartment near the prison where his new wife was waiting with her bags packed. By midnight Roger was out of town and never seen again.

On March 15, 1979 a 41-page indictment was returned on Eddie Sisk, Charles Benson, Fred Taylor, Dale Quillen and Bill Thompson, charged with conspiracy, extortion and bribery in accepting cash to block extraditions and gain freedom for state convicts. Trial preparation began in earnest. AUSA Hick Ewing was temporarily assigned to the Nashville division to second chair Joe Brown.

Bill Thompson was indicted in Memphis for failure to pay tax on income of $43,067 in 1972-73. This charge might help the government convince him to plead guilty in Tennpar and testify for the prosecution.

A senior US District Judge, Charles Neese from East Tennessee was appointed to hear the case. Jury selection began on July 16, 1979. The judge required that all 142 government witnesses be present and be seen by the prospective jurors. I was on standby, out in the corridor, in case any last minute investigation was needed.

Quillen's attorney made a continuing motion that the charges against him be dismissed which the judge ultimately did.

I took the stand on Friday, August 3. Judge Neese had a heart attack that evening. Eventually Judge Gilbert Merritt III, a judge on the Sixth Circuit Court of Appeals, was appointed to continue the trial. After reviewing the status he declared a mistrial in early September 1979. It was too complex a case to just continue. He wanted a new jury and to start the trial anew. There was a delay of nearly a year as Sisk, Benson, Taylor and Thompson filed motions and then appeals to have the charges against them dismissed, arguing that another trial would put them in double jeopardy.

A bizarre incident occurred on August 31, 1979. A 190-pound bomb was found in a parked car next to Classic Cat II, a topless club in downtown Nashville about two blocks from the federal courthouse owned by Art Baldwin's ex-wife.

After extensive investigation by ATF Baldwin was charged with the attempted bombing and went to trial in federal court in Memphis on March 17, 1981. The trial was in Memphis because he and his co-defendants were also charged with arranging fire bombings there in 1979. Baldwin claimed he was "framed" by his co-defendants and that arson was not his way of doing business.

I was called as a witness by the defense in an attempt to convince the jury of Baldwin's truthfulness. I had been involved in this case in 1979 when I tried to recruit Baldwin to record conversations with Jack Bowie, the main arsonist. Baldwin refused when I told him he would work with ATF since it was their case. He said at the trial, "I felt comfortable working with Hart and I felt like the fewer people you work with, the less danger you're in." All I could say at the trial in answer to a question about information provided by Baldwin was, "I would say it was reliable in most every instance." The jury convicted Baldwin.

After the double jeopardy appeals ran their course and failed, US District Judge James Churchill of Detroit was appointed to replace Judge Merritt in late 1980. He set a trial date for March 10, 1981. Hank Hillin had retired from the FBI by then but came back on board as a consultant.

On February 6, 1981, Bill Thompson pled guilty to the charges against him. Prior to his plea he provided agents with extensive details of his involvement with Sisk in commutations for cash beginning in October 1975. He recounted the Sammye Lynn McGrory deal I was part of, saying it fell through when she couldn't come up with the money.

When the case was ready to go trial against Benson, Sisk and Taylor, Judge Churchill made it clear there would be no plea bargaining once the trial began. At once there was a furious series of conferences between the government and defense attorneys. No attorney can look in a crystal ball and tell his client exactly what the results of a trial would be, only his best guess based on the evidence and his experience. We believed our case was so airtight at least one of them would plead guilty.

The next day, March 11, Sisk and Taylor pled guilty to count one of the indictment, in return for the government dismissing count two, with the clear understanding they would testify truthfully and fully against Benson. When Sisk took the stand to enter his plea, he danced around his admission of guilt. He said he had received a series of "loans" from Bill Thompson totaling $10,000 and claimed they had been paid back. We knew and Sisk knew these were payoffs but he couldn't bring himself to admit it fully, only that the "loans did induce me to attempt to participate with Thompson on those matters" whatever that meant.

When Fred Taylor entered his guilty plea he admitted taking money for clemencies which flowed to Sisk through a pattern of racketeering.

Now we had only Benson going to trial. We were confident with the addition of the testimony of Sisk and Taylor he would be convicted. The trial was set for April 1, only a few weeks away.

As is always the case with government witnesses, Sisk and Taylor were interviewed by the US Attorneys prior to the trial.

Sisk demanded that Hank Hillin not be present at his interview. The prosecutor and agents talked it over and decided to agree to Sisk's ultimatum. Hank gave a word of caution, "Better tape the interview. You can't depend on Sisk to tell the truth."

So the interview was taped, and true to Hank's prediction, Sisk said, no, he didn't know anything about a statewide clemency-selling scheme in his office, he didn't take any money, he didn't know anything about Benson taking money. An arrogant Sisk said he had money in his pocket the day he was arrested because Benson had loaned it to him to give to Taylor who would buy something for Sisk at the Magnavox plant in Greenville Tennessee. This was a far-fetched story, actually a bold-faced lie. Sisk denied everything and had no value as a government witness against Benson.

When Taylor came in for questioning it was a similar story. Plus it was obvious to Hank that he was wearing a recorder. Taylor was nervous and uncomfortable. Hank said, "Are you wearing a body recorder?" Taylor stared at him a minute and then nodded his head. He admitted he wore it to have a record to help Benson in his upcoming trial.

AUSA Joe Brown and the agents went out of the room and discussed what to do next. When they went back in, Hank said, "Get your gear and get out and don't come back until you decide to tell the truth." Taylor and his attorney were back the next day. But Taylor was just as evasive as Sisk had been. He also double-crossed us and was of no value.

Now it was time for Charles Benson to have his day in court. The trial started on April 1, April Fool Day, which turned out to be a fitting title for what transpired. For the next three weeks, the government put on proof detailing the conspiracy and Benson's role in it. More than 60 witnesses testified. I spent almost a week on the witness stand, producing the videotapes of Taylor and Baldwin and explaining how the payoffs were orchestrated. Bill Thompson, who had become a government witness, testified, "I never gave any money to Charlie Benson. I know of no wrongdoing by Benson." Another betrayal.

After weeks of government testimony Benson's attorney Gordon Ball began. The star witness was Charlie Benson himself. Benson came across to the jury as friendly, his cherubic face did not fit the image most people would have for a professional racketeer. He insisted that he had simply been Eddie Sisk's boy. He said he knew nothing about the deals Sisk had going on. No, he said, he had not taken the calls from Fred Taylor on December 15, when the payoffs were made. He replied, "You will have to ask Fred Taylor about that.

Benson admitted he had $3300 in $100 bills on him the day he was arrested. He said perhaps some serial numbers of the bills may have matched those the FBI paid through Baldwin to Taylor in Memphis, but he knew nothing of that–he was merely holding the money for Taylor. As to the commutation documents for Ed Hacker and the others that the FBI had found on him–he was just doing what he was told to do, delivering some documents.

In the end Charles Benson was acquitted. One of the jurors interviewed by a Nashville newspaper after the trial said, "We all believed he was involved in what was going on but the government didn't lock him into the crime." On that day one of the principal players in this conspiracy walked away a free man.

Eddie Sisk and Fred Taylor were sentenced on July 1, 1981. Sisk, with an audience of 80 members of his church, gave a 20-minute plea, no longer proclaiming his innocence. He was asking for the same clemency that he had sold. Both were sentenced to five years in federal prison. Sisk sobbed openly, Taylor's face remained a blank.

While the FBI was working the pardons and parole case the Internal Revenue Service in Nashville was looking into the issuance of state liquor licenses.

Rumors spread that a license could be had with money paid to the Blanton administration, that it was more than the usual Blanton political patronage system that thrived unchecked. In 1981 Ray Blanton was tried and convicted of bribery and income tax evasion related to state liquor licenses. He was sentenced to three years in federal prison and fined $11,000.

In retrospect my part in Tennpar was enjoyable. I got a kick out of orchestrating a scenario and script for Baldwin with Taylor. And that got results fairly quickly. If the Sammye Lynn McGrory – Ernest Withers investigation had gone better, this might have yielded results as well. Hank Hillin had constraints on what he could do with the intervention by the Justice Department's Public Integrity section although he kept on despite them. I didn't have this problem. In the end we both suffered to an extent by not getting the convictions we anticipated and expected. But how many times have I said: It's our system of justice, our jury system that has persisted for over two centuries. It's the American way and we live with the consequences, whether or not they are as we wanted.

Eddie Sisk served his time and returned to Nashville where, at last report, he was employed at a mattress store. Charlie Benson returned to his hometown of Newport Tennessee where he, at last report, operates a sporting goods store. I can't locate any update on Fred Taylor.

My chief and fearless informant Arthur Wayne Baldwin died on September 7, 1997 in Memphis at the age of 59. He had been released from federal prison in 1987 after serving time for income tax evasion and bombing the Follies Nightclub. He allegedly spent his remaining years trying to overcome his criminal past. In the mid-1990s he opened Chariots of Fire Christian School with his father and sister in Earle Arkansas. His sister stated at the time of his death, it was "sad that the public will never know the sweet and caring man who spent his last years lecturing young adults." He claimed he became a Jehovah's Witness and studied accounting while in prison. I believe he was getting older and had lost everything. It was quite possible he had had a religious conversion.

Chapter 13
Fraudster from the British Isles

S tarting in 1977, banks across the United States were being victimized by a phony loan scam that was costing them hundreds of thousands of dollars.

A con man who by all appearances was well educated, articulate and knew his way around the financial world would pick out a bank loan officer he believed would be vulnerable to his illegal plan. The ideal target was a banker who had personal financial problems. First the con man called the loan officer about obtaining a substantial business loan and explained why he needed the loan and the collateral he had to put up that was enough to secure the loan.

The con man usually called the banker several more times to discuss the loan and get personal information from the banker. He was trying to feel him out to see if the banker might be amenable to what would turn out to be a scam.

Once the con man was comfortable he would make his pitch, "Look, I know you are in somewhat of a financial bind and could use a sizeable amount of cash to help you out with this temporary cash flow problem. If I were to get, say, a $100,000 loan from your bank, I would kick back $25,000 to you."

He would then assure the banker he had a business deal that would net him at least $200,000 when it closed so he could easily repay the loan. The con man would assure the loan officer he would provide documents to establish collateral for the loan that would pass an initial scrutiny by any loan committee but wouldn't be good enough if the loan went into default. But of course that wouldn't happen since "he had a sure thing going." The con man would convince the loan officer that he would be covered because he made the loan on the basis of what he thought was legitimate collateral. Of course any bank loan officer who was honest would not fall for this. If the loan officer refused the con man, he moved on to another likely candidate.

If the con is pulled off successfully, the con man pays the banker, takes his money and fades into the sunset. When the loan goes into default the bank checks the collateral and discovers it is fake and the bank has a worthless loan to write off. If the bank becomes suspicious of the loan officer, it refers the case to the FBI.

In the first two cases I worked the bank became aware of its loan officers who had larceny in their hearts. In both cases, after my investigation, the bankers were prosecuted. I never identified the con man in either case.

This scam apparently achieved international interest since in the spring of 1978 the head of security at Union Planters National Bank in Memphis advised me of a likely scam to defraud the bank of $100,000 by an individual in London, England. Robert Wilson, a loan officer at the bank's downtown branch, had received a call from a person who wanted to get a loan with some very suspicious terms.

Wilson told me the man, Rene Greville, had a British accent, seemed to be charming and knew a lot about Memphis. He claimed to have an import/export business with interests in Tennessee. He was looking for a loan in the amount of $100,000, secured with collateral in Tennessee. The banker told Greville he would call him back.

I told Wilson he should wait a few days to make the call and I would return with a recorder and witness the call. In the meantime I contacted the legate (FBI agent attached to the embassy) in London and gave him the name Rene Greville and that he purported to own a bookstore in downtown London. The legate called me the next day with the con man's full name, Rene Brooke Fulke Plantagenet Greville, and confirmed he owned a bookstore. He didn't have a criminal record.

I returned three days later and Wilson made the call. Greville seemed to know a good deal about Wilson's employment such as how long he'd been there, what his job history was. Greville said he had heard Wilson was inventive in making loans. He said he was lining up a real estate deal that would clear him $250,000 but he needed to spend $100,000 on improvements to the property to complete the sale. Wilson told him he needed more information and would give him a few more days to get his documents together. Wilson told his secretary that if Greville called and I wasn't there, to tell him he was out of town and he would call him back.

A few days later Wilson received a FedEx package from Greville with the promised collateral, an interest in a Nashville business and some real estate near Collierville, Tennessee. For tax purposes, Greville said, the documents were in the name of a business partner. I checked the collateral and as I anticipated it was bogus and worthless.

Wilson called Greville, again in my presence, and asked him whether the collateral would hold up under casual scrutiny. He replied it would but might not withstand an in depth examination and reiterated that he would make enough on the real estate deal to easily pay off the loan. Greville assured Wilson the bank wasn't taking any chances. He would complete his deal within two months and repay the loan in full. Further, he said, to make the loan go faster and reward Wilson for his efforts, he would give him $25,000 of the proceeds. Wilson said he would think about it and call him back in a few days.

I asked Wilson if he had any financial problems since I knew from the previous similar cases that the victim/eventual collaborator had been handpicked. Wilson replied he was going through a divorce that was going to hit him pretty hard in the pocketbook but he wasn't desperate for money.

Instead of Wilson initiating the call, Greville called him in a few days. The secretary told him Wilson was out of town on a business trip and would return the next week. Wilson called Greville the following Tuesday and told him he could make the loan but Greville had to come to Memphis to fill out the paper work.

One day later Greville called and said he had made travel arrangements and would arrive in Memphis in 24 hours. Wilson told him to bring the original collateral documents since he could not use copies. Greville agreed and said he planned to check into a hotel and then call Wilson once he was in town. At about 3:30 p.m. the next day he let Wilson know he was at the Crowne Plaza in downtown Memphis. Wilson replied that it was too late to do the loan that day but to call him about 9:30 in the morning and he should have everything prepared to make the loan. When I learned that Greville was supposed to be at the Crowne Plaza I confirmed he was a registered guest.

I arranged for two adjoining rooms at the downtown Holiday Inn, only a few blocks from the Crowne Plaza, and got SA Harold Hayes and his crew to wire one of the rooms for sound and video so Harold and other agents could hear and see from the adjoining control room. I had already told Wilson I would impersonate him and handle the final transaction. I couldn't let Wilson have a face-to-face meeting with Greville being unsure of what his reaction might be to what I hoped was his arrest. Wilson had prepared loan documents for Greville to sign and a cashier's check in the amount of $100,000. I needed to personally witness Greville signing these.

At 9:30 the next morning Greville promptly called Wilson. Wilson told him to meet him at 2 p.m., at the Holiday Inn since they couldn't meet at the bank to sign the documents and receive the cashier's check. We knew Greville had set up a bank account at another Memphis bank, the National Bank of Commerce a few months before and could cash the check there. Wilson told Greville he would go with him to NBC for Greville to cash the check and pay him his $25,000. Greville said he would wire the remaining $75,000 to his London bank the next day and return to London.

At about noon SAs Harold Hayes, Chuck Allison, Ellis Young and I went to the Holiday Inn and checked out the sound and video equipment. Harold taped the lock on the door between the rooms so they could gain immediate entrance into the meeting room if needed. I waited for Rene in the room.

He arrived on time, we introduced ourselves and sat down at a table facing each other. He bragged that his full name was Rene Brooke Fulke Plantagenet Greville and he was descended from British royalty through the Plantagenet family. I played the part and acted impressed.

I said, "Do you have the original documents?" "Yes," he said, opened his briefcase and showed them to me. I removed the loan documents from my briefcase, handed them to him to read over and sign. I wanted to get his fingerprints on these but didn't want to hand over the check yet. He took the papers, looked them over briefly and signed them in the proper places. We talked again about how he was going to pay me off. I said, "Okay." I offered him the check; he took it and placed it in his briefcase.

The signal to the other agents was his taking the check. They came in the room, identified themselves as FBI and advised him he was under arrest for bank fraud. They stood him up, searched him and took some identification from him. He was shaking like a leaf.

I asked him to sit down again, identified myself and told him I had checked the so-called collateral for the loan and knew it was worthless.

I said, "We obviously know you were attempting to bribe Mr. Wilson since we have you on tape several times offering him $25,000 for negotiating the loan for you." He was advised of his Miranda rights, asked if he understood them to which he replied, "Yes." I asked him if he would explain to me what this loan was all about. He said, "I have nothing to say and want a lawyer."

Chuck and Ellis handcuffed him and took him to an interview room at the FBI office. I went by AUSA Dan Clancy's office and told him what had happened and he authorized an arrest warrant for Greville. I then joined the other agents and Greville and told him a warrant for his arrest was being prepared.

Once served with the warrant Greville went to the Shelby County Jail with a hold put on him by the U. S. Marshal. I wonder what he thought of our American jail.

The next morning Greville, represented by the federal public defender, appeared before U. S. District Judge Harry Wellford. The judge found probable cause for the arrest and bound him over for a preliminary hearing. After arguments from AUSA Clancy and the public defender the judge set a bond of $25,000. As far as I know Greville didn't have to give up his passport. He was then transported back to the jail.

The following day the defense attorney made a motion to reduce the bond to $10,000, arguing his client was not a flight risk and would return for trial. Dan Clancy argued strenuously for no reduction saying that Greville had every reason to jump bail and return home to England. I was stunned when Judge Wellford agreed to the bond reduction. He then set a preliminary hearing for the following week. Greville posted bond late that afternoon and was released.

When the day for the hearing came the defense attorney appeared alone. He said he couldn't get in touch with his client and didn't know where he was. Judge Wellford issued a bench warrant for Greville's arrest.

I contacted the legate in London with the news and asked for his help in locating Greville. He called me the next day. Scotland Yard determined Greville had passed through customs at Gatwick Airport the day after his missed court appearance. A Scotland Yard officer made a pretext call to Greville's bookstore and verified that he was back at work.

AUSA Clancy contacted the U. S. Department of State and advised them of Greville's fugitive status in England and began preparing documents for an extradition hearing.

Two weeks later Judge Wellford received a message from Greville, expressing his outrage that anyone in America would dare to prosecute him. He sent a letter that was tied with a ribbon and claimed he was not in the United States when the alleged acts occurred:

"Any alleged act that took place in the United Kingdom is solely within the jurisdiction of my Sovereign Lady, Elizabeth II, by the Grace of God, Queen of Great Britain and Northern Ireland, and I place myself under Her Judiciary and Law.

" If there were such a crime in this country, which there was not, I claim that I would be answerable only to a prosecution brought by the British Authorities and tried in an English Court of Law.

"I still most stoutly maintain my innocence of these charges and my refusal to appear is in no way an admission of my guilt.

(The FBI) used an "Agent Provocateur and self-confessed criminal, who has been handsomely rewarded by the prosecuting Authorities for his base and cowardly actions" to "seduce, entrap and entice" (me.).

The charges "are scurrilous and malicious and strike not only at my liberty but at my whole life and character. If it were that the American Government could prove legal jurisdiction to charge and try me, which I assert they could not, then I would still feel that I could not expect a fair and just trial in the true tradition of democratic justice."

I couldn't imagine what Judge Wellford was thinking when he reduced Greville's bond. I had testified as to the scam Greville tried to put over on the banker and had tape and video recordings of the transaction at the hotel. Here was a man with a passport who could leave the country if he chose.

Dan Clancy spent the better part of a year dutifully compiling sworn statements of the charges and the government's proof for use by the Justice and State departments in getting Greville extradited. The British authorities refused to hand the fugitive over. Dan said, "I can't understand why not."

There were reports Greville may have used the influence of highly placed friends to defeat extradition. No one knows for sure. Dan Clancy said, "He's not coming back unless he wants to----and he doesn't."

In late 1982 I traveled to London on another case along with others from the task force. Two Scotland Yard officers were our hosts and took us on a special tour of all the sights. On the third day I told them about Greville. "I know where his bookstore is located in London. I'd like to walk in there while I'm here and confront him."

They nearly had a heart attack. They said the Home Office (England's version of our State Department) would have them fired and there would be an international incident. They reminded me I was a guest in their country and they were my minders. I had a good laugh and told them I was just kidding, which I was.

In 2012 a person with the exact same name, Rene Brooke Fulke Plantagenet Greville, was a defendant in a British civil case. He was charged with failing to pay some debts. It just may be the same person. As a matter of fact I would bet money on it and I bet he won't try to return to the USA. If he tried to enter the United States he would be arrested on the outstanding warrant.

Chapter 14
Underbelly of the Mid-South

James "Jimmy" Allen Whitten, originally from Hernando, Mississippi, was a topless nightclub owner, with ties to Art Baldwin and Danny Owens. His father owned a bail bond business located across the street from the historic courthouse.

Over the years Jimmy gained a reputation for prostitution, drugs and other offenses. When the topless nightclub business took hold in Memphis, he soon recognized the money making potential. He befriended Art Baldwin and became manager of one of his largest and most successful clubs. Our task force sent informants to the club who soon found out Whitten was selling drugs to the dancers and club patrons.

In November 1981, Whitten and topless nightclub owner Danny Owens were charged with assault and intent to murder. Whitten had left his job with Art Baldwin and was managing a topless club called The Pink Garter Lounge for Owens. Jimmy and Danny had gotten into a fairly minor fracas with four or five customers, later identified as Outlaw motorcycle bikers, and threw them out of the club. These patrons returned a few minutes later to continue the fight. Whitten and Owens armed themselves with baseball bats that were concealed under the bar. They waded into their opponents and beat them so severely that all five of the tough bikers ended up in the hospital with serious injuries. That assault case was pending in Tennessee state court, while we were investigating Whitten.

About nine months later, a Memphis Police detective assigned to the task force investigated a rape complaint made against Jimmy Whitten by one of his employees. The victim was a 16-year-old girl who worked for Whitten as a topless dancer. Whitten was charged with statutory rape and arrested a few days later. "Statutory" in Tennessee then meant that consent is not an issue when the victim is between the ages of 15 and 18 and the perpetrator is more than five years older than the victim. Whitten was then 27. Whitten posted bond and was released.

We continued to work on Jimmy Whitten hoping to make a drug case against him. Sgt. Mitch Donavan from the Shelby County Sheriff Office was a member of the task force. He had an informant who believed he could purchase cocaine from Whitten. Mitch was in his early 40s, a handsome ladies man. He wore his dark hair slicked back on the sides and was always impeccably dressed. We had worked many cases together in the narcotics task force.

On September 10, 1982, Mitch's informant arranged to purchase two ounces of cocaine from Whitten at midnight in the parking lot of The Late Steak Club in Southwest Memphis.

Before sending the informant to make the purchase from Whitten, we searched the informant's vehicle and person. I once had a case where neither the informant nor his vehicle was searched before he went to meet the person to make the buy. On cross-examination, the defense attorney asked me if it were not possible that the informant already had the drugs on him that he claimed he had purchased from the defendant. On the stand I had to agree that this was possible. The jury acquitted the defendant.

Upon confirming the informant and his vehicle were clean, we equipped him with a concealed recorder to record the transaction with Whitten.

We had surveyed the parking lot that afternoon and selected positions where we could park our vehicles and surveillance van to cover the buy. The drug buy went down like clockwork and Whitten was arrested after he passed the cocaine to the informant after paying for it. Whitten was brought to the surveillance van where Sgt. Donovan, and I were waiting to interview him.

Jimmy was tall and slender, dressed in a shiny leisure suit with an open necked shirt. His dark receding hair was not as neatly combed, as was his usual habit. He wore dark-rimmed glasses and had a moustache and Van Dyke type beard. The arresting officers had already frisked Whitten and removed a loaded .38 caliber pistol from his pocket. In another pocket we found the buy money and confirmed that the denominations, serial numbers, and series of those bills matched the ones given to the informant.

We advised Whitten of his constitutional rights and confronted him with the evidence we had against him. An officer called for Sgt. Donovan to come outside for some reason and he left me alone in the van with Whitten. Whitten showed me a sizeable gold ring with a 6-karat diamond he was wearing that he claimed was worth several thousand dollars. He offered to give me the ring he said I could sell easily for $4000. In return, he wanted me to destroy the cocaine in my possession. Before replying, I keyed up my walkie-talkie which would transmit our live conversation to the dispatcher and be recorded. I then told Whitten that this drug case belonged to Sgt. Donovan and if we were going to destroy the evidence he would have to okay this offer. I got Mitch back into the van and asked Whitten to tell him what he had just told me. Now there would be a witness to the bribe. He repeated his offer and said we could sell the ring and split the $4000. I then advised Whitten that he was under arrest for distribution of cocaine as well as for attempting to bribe a government official.

The next day a complaint was filed in federal court charging Whitten with the firearms violation, the illicit drug charge, and attempting to bribe a government official.

That same day Whitten appeared before two Criminal Court divisions, one on the rape, the other the assault to murder charge. Once court was over the secured bond totaled $200,000 on the state charges. Very quickly Whitten posted the bond and was released from custody. I would guess that Whitten's father had connections with Memphis bonding companies that enabled him to speed up the process.

We had made arrangements with the Shelby County Jail captain to notify us if Whitten posted bond on those charges. We got a call and were at the jail when he was released. Before he could leave the building we arrested him on the federal charges.

Later that afternoon, Whitten was taken before the US Magistrate for an initial appearance and bond hearing. AUSA Tim DiScenza laid out the details supporting the charges. Tim pointed out to the court that Whitten was facing up to 15 years in a federal prison if convicted and also explained the serious charges he faced in state court. In an effort to avoid Jimmy being released again on bond, DiScenza told the magistrate, "At this point, Mr. Whitten presents a substantial risk of flight and a clear and present danger to the community because of his absolute disregard for the law."

Whitten's attorney Glenn Sisson contended during the hearing that DiScenza and Assistant District Attorney Dan Newsom, who was representing the state of Tennessee, were merely stockpiling criminal charges against his client to drive him out of business. He said Whitten was attempting to sell his interest in several nightclubs because, "He had been a source of embarrassment to his family." The prosecutors asserted that Whitten was trying to liquidate his nightclub interests so he could leave Memphis permanently just like Danny Owens who had fled the country to avoid prosecution after being indicted by a federal grand jury. Since Whitten and Owens were business partners there was likelihood that Whitten might follow the same path. The judge set a bond of $50,000 that Whitten immediately posted and was released from custody.

Whitten's attorney told the press he was going to trial on all three cases, "There are defenses for all these cases."

Referring to the statutory rape charge, Sisson said the 16-year-old girl involved in that case was a dancer in one of Owens' topless clubs and she had in her possession a forged identification card showing she was 19. "The state will have a difficult time getting a conviction in this case," Sisson said, adding that the only prosecution witnesses are the girl and an investigator for the Attorney General's office.

The girl's father, James Paul Henderson of Greenwood, Mississippi was indicted on charges of using a minor for obscene purposes. Prosecutors contended that Henderson brought his daughter to Memphis to get her started in the topless dancing business. He took most of her earnings and left her with little money of her own. Henderson was a frequent patron of Whitten and Owens' topless bars.

Sisson said the alleged victims in the assault to murder charges were in his words, "Troublemakers from a motorcycle gang and were causing a disturbance at the Pink Garter Lounge when the incident occurred." Sisson said he would contend that Whitten was acting in self-defense.

On January 14, 1983 Whitten's lawyer worked out a plea agreement with both the state and federal authorities. Whitten would plead guilty to the federal charges and the state charges against him would be dismissed. He was later sentenced to 12 years in federal prison.

Nearly 30 years later, in January 2012, Whitten was charged in DeSoto County Court with murdering his 24-year-old live-in girlfriend, Sara Dabney Jones. Sara's body was discovered along Oak Grove Road in the early morning hours of December 22, 2011.

Police said it was the middle of the night when Whitten and Jones got into a fight at Whitten's house. He had arranged her bond on drug charges she was facing. She ran out of the house, jumped on a bicycle and rode down the street trying to get away from him but he followed her in his pickup truck. Officers said he hit her with the truck and left her body in the ditch. A passing motorist saw a mangled bicycle and what appeared to be a pile of clothing along the roadway. He stopped and realized that what he saw was a body. He asked if she was all right. She was dead.

Authorities found a cell phone on Sara's body that contained photos of her and Whitten, which led to the 55-year old's arrest. A witness who lived on the same road said he heard a truck "with a loud exhaust" strike what he thought was a mailbox around 1:45 that morning. Further investigation revealed that Whitten took his damaged Escalade to a repair shop that same morning. A broken headlight was found at the scene.

At his initial court appearance Whitten was placed under a half-million dollar bond, ordered to have no contact with the victim's family and be outfitted with a GPS device that he had to pay for as well as its monitoring. His attorney had argued that Whitten comes from "one of the largest families in DeSoto County" and his family ties and business interests would keep him from flight. People in the Hernando community were outraged that Whitten was granted bond, which once again he posted. "He is a dangerous sociopath felon known to associate with Danny Owens' dangerous mob friends." In 2012 Danny was in federal prison in California.

As a convicted felon Whitten was prohibited by law from owning, operating or working for a bail bond company. When his father died in 2007 he inherited the bonding company building and was the landlord. Many thought despite this prohibition he was illegally writing bonds.

In mid-February 2013, while awaiting trial on Sara Jones' death, Jimmy Whitten was arrested on drug charges for possession of meth and heroin and being a felon with a weapon. On May 6, 2013 Whitten pleaded guilty to a reduced charge of leaving the scene of an accident that caused death.

DeSoto County District Attorney John Champion explained, "Investigators felt they could prove the charge of leaving the scene of an accident causing death. Jimmy Whitten's trial was for next week, but after reviewing the evidence I knew it would be difficult to prove that it was an intentional homicide. You try to get the next best resolution on the case, and I felt the best and most provable charge was leaving the scene of an accident causing death."

Sarah Jones's mother said that Jimmy Whitten was a predator who preyed on young girls. He would go after young girls and bail them out of jail and get them hooked on drugs and then if they didn't do what he wanted he threatened to revoke their bond, she said. She said her daughter stood up to him and he admitted leaving the scene that caused her death.

Another local person said, "Whitten not only illegally writes bail but goes into the Hernando jail to recruit his victims, usually young white girls. He addicts them to heroin, meth and other drugs, holds them as sex and forced labor slaves in his house by locking them in with no hope of escape."

Whitten, dressed in a yellow jumpsuit and shackles, was sentenced to 20 years in the Mississippi state prison system for the hit-and-run. The drug charges had yet to be resolved.

Chapter 15
Mahar: Thief, Convict & Overall Good for Nothing SOB

Roy Daniel Mahar, a convicted bank robber, had been out on parole only eight months when he thought up a scheme to rob a jewelry store in the Frayser area of Memphis. Frayser had once been prosperous but now was a seedy, crime-ridden part of town. Mahar had approached my informant Danny Haley to join him in the robbery. I had jammed Danny up when investigating a large marijuana grow and distribution network in North Mississippi run by a local attorney.

I knew Mahar from a bank robbery case in 1975. Mahar looked the part of the career criminal he was. There wasn't anything in particular that I could describe about him but I just knew it. I doubt he ever worked an honest job in his life.

Danny owed Mahar $20,000 for cocaine that had been "fronted" to him, drugs given him with the understanding Danny pay him when he sold the coke. Instead Danny squandered the money. Mahar told Danny he would forgive the $20,000 if he would assist in robbing the jewelry store. Danny Haley and Abbott, the store owner, were cousins. Abbott was involved in more than jewelry since Danny had delivered cocaine to him for Mahar.

Abbott's Diamond Enterprises was located on a major east-west road more or less by itself. There were convenience stores and gas stations scattered around it. It was a small, low-end jewelry store compared to others in Memphis.

The plan was for Danny Haley to arrive at the store just at closing time. He was to subdue Abbott with a chemical, probably mace or pepper spray, and then let Mahar and his cohorts Charles P. Fisher, Bill Pegram and William E. Sides into the store to steal the diamonds and money in the safe. I told Danny to stay in touch with me and record any telephone calls to or from Mahar with a simple recording device I gave him.

On January 28, 1982 Danny told me he was to meet Mahar and the other three at a restaurant the next afternoon. I had already briefed the recently formed Organized Crime/Drug Enforcement Task Force about the planned robbery and we put together a plan to equip Danny with a Nagra recorder to record the meeting. The Nagra is a high-quality device, when concealed on the person's body at about chest level, picks up a conversation. I didn't think Mahar would check Danny for a wire since they had been criminal partners for so long. If he found the recorder we were prepared to swarm in and rescue him. We covered the meeting that was uneventful except for the conversation.

We took the tape from Danny and went to a nearby motel room to listen to it. Mahar told Danny they had to kill Abbott to prevent any heat from coming down on Danny. Danny was to subdue Abbott and then give him a lethal dose of Scopolamine Hydrobromide (a sedative). Mahar said the death would look like the result of a heart attack or some other natural cause. Mahar showed Danny three handguns and assured him he would not be harmed because he and the others were professional killers. Two days later Mahar and Sides met Danny in the parking lot of a bar in South Memphis. They discussed again that Abbott must be killed to protect Danny. Mahar said he was robbing the jewelry store to get enough money to buy cocaine outright instead being fronted the drugs. The robbery was planned for the following night.

Task force officers took up a position near Abbott's store and waited to hear from the surveillance teams who were in Horn Lake Mississippi waiting for Mahar to leave his home. Danny and I entered the store at 9 pm as if we were customers. Danny approached Abbott and told him he had someone he wanted him to meet. I walked over, gave him my name and told him I was an FBI agent and showed him my credentials. I explained to him that four men were prepared to rob his store shortly after closing time, that the criminals' plan was for Danny to overpower him and let the others in through the back door. I told Abbott we needed his cooperation to arrest these people. He agreed to help us in any way he could.

I told Abbott to close the store as usual and for him and Danny to come to the back room. After 10 minutes he was to open the back door to let me and other officers in. Another officer dropped us at the back of the store and left the area. As planned Abbott opened the door and we went inside. I immediately hooked up a recorder to the telephone in case Mahar tried to call Danny. At 9:15 the surveillance units in Horn Lake advised that Mahar and Fisher were on the move towards Memphis. Nothing happened until the surveilling units reported they had Mahar's car at a Circle K service station about two blocks from the store. Fisher was in the car and Mahar was talking on a pay phone. After about four or five minutes Mahar hung up the phone and returned to his car.

At about one in the morning Mahar called Danny and I was listening on the extension. Mahar said he was having trouble locating Pegram who had the equipment to open the safe. He told Danny he didn't want to snuff a man for only what was in the showcases and was considering calling the deal off for the night. I handed the extension to another officer and told him to put a note in front of Danny telling him to keep Mahar talking as long as he could. Walter Hoback from ATF and I hurried out the back door, got in my car and headed for the Circle K where we hoped Mahar would still be at the telephone booth. I wanted to avoid a car chase if possible. As we turned into the parking lot of the station I could see Mahar in the booth on the phone. I pulled up directly in front of him, and with my weapon in my hand rushed to the booth. Mahar didn't see me until I opened the door and I heard him say, "We're busted" and hung up the phone. I covered him and identified myself telling him that he was under arrest. Walter pulled him out of the phone booth and walked him toward my car. We ordered him to put his hands on the roof and spread his legs. Then I searched him. In his right front pocket I found a 9 mm semiautomatic pistol. The other agents grabbed Fisher just as he opened the passenger's door. He was also armed. I told Mahar to keep his hands on the top of the car and not to move while I took the pistol from his pocket.

Four officers took Mahar and Fisher to the county jail and booked them on charges of conspiracy to cross a state line to commit a crime of violence. The rest of us spread out to search for Pegram and Sides. We arrested Pegram at his home in Mississippi about an hour later without incident. Early in the morning we spotted Sides' vehicle in front of an apartment complex where we knew he lived and arrested him without incident.

The subjects made an initial appearance before federal Magistrate Aaron Brown in late afternoon. At the end of my testimony AUSA Dan Clancy detailed for the judge the extensive criminal background of the subjects. Pegram's lengthy record included postal and bank burglaries, theft from interstate shipments, and assaulting federal officers during a shootout at a roadblock. Sides had a long record of arrests and convictions and had escaped custody several times. Clancy advised the judge the suspects were a danger to the community with great potential for violence and should all be subjected to strict bond measures to keep them from fleeing. He said they had every reason in the world to not want to be here. Magistrate Brown responded, "I'm sure they would all agree they would rather not be here." Brown refused to set bond for

Mahar, Pegram and Sides, and set a $250,000 secured bond for Fisher.

As the Marshals were leading the four subjects from the courtroom Pegram pointed to me and said, "I'll remember you buddy boy and you know what I mean." I considered this a veiled threat, though not enough to charge him with threatening an FBI agent. When I got back to the office I told SAC Bill Beavers. He wanted to assign one or two agents for my protection. I pointed out that Pegram was being held without bail and as long as that didn't change there was no danger. He agreed and told me to ask the US Marshal to tell him if Pegram were ever released from custody.

I was not concerned as long as Pegram remained behind bars but should he be released I would be. His arrest record dated back to 1940 and if cornered and had a chance, he was known to shoot it out with law enforcement. One ironic thing is that he had a relative Tom Pegram, a fellow FBI agent in the Memphis office.

Since Mahar was being held without bond pending his trial I figured I had heard the last from him for a while but that was not to be. About three months after the attempted robbery and killing, a source of mine who lived in West Memphis Arkansas called and said he had something he wanted to talk to me about but not on the phone. I told him to meet me at three that afternoon in the parking lot of the Greyhound racetrack in West Memphis, just across the Mississippi River from Memphis.

The informant told me about a middle aged couple he'd known for years who contacted him and wanted to talk to him about a job they might need done. They told him they were Roy Mahar's relatives and wanted to hire someone to help him escape from the US Marshals. Mahar had been subpoenaed to appear as a witness in an upcoming trial in US District Court in Alabama. They could find out when the marshals would be transporting Mahar and wanted someone to intercept the marshals on the trip and free Mahar from federal custody. He was then being held at the Federal Correction Institution in Memphis. The source told them that was way beyond his ability but he knew of a couple of big time criminals who would probably do it for enough money. I told him to wait a couple days then tell them he had a man who wanted to talk to them about the job. If they were interested he was to set up a time and place for me to contact them.

It was a few days later before the source called and said the couple wanted to meet me. I told him to set up a meeting the next morning at 9:30 at a famous country breakfast restaurant in West Memphis. He called back in a few hours and said the meeting was set up.

I went to the US Marshal's office in Memphis and explained to them the information my source had given me. That afternoon I met with three marshals, four task force members, and the FBI resident agent in West Memphis and informed them about the planned escape. We then prepared a plan for the officers to cover me during the next day's meeting.

I equipped myself with a Nagra recorder and we all drove to West Memphis arriving at nine. This gave the covering teams time to locate a place to set up their surveillance. The CI and I entered the restaurant at about 9:25 and selected a table near a window that would allow the surveillance teams to observe us.

At a little after 9:30 the husband and wife arrived. The CI introduced me and then left saying he had to go to an appointment. After the CI left I asked the man to tell me how he and his wife expected to get their relative sprung free of custody from the US Marshals. He told me Mahar was a close relative and some months back had given them a large amount of money in case he wanted them to do something for him.

The husband did all the talking. He said that during a previous visit to Mahar in jail he told him he had been subpoenaed as a witness in an upcoming trial in Alabama and the marshals would drive him there when his testimony was needed. He wanted his relatives to find someone who could waylay the marshals and free him during this trip. He told them to use the money he had given them to pay for his escape and keep $2000 for themselves. Mahar told him he would be in prison for the rest of his life if convicted on the current charges and pleaded with him, shedding tears. The husband agreed to be the go-between in Mahar's escape plan.

Mahar told him to go to a certain person in Memphis who would give him a 9 mm pistol he owned. They were to buy a small suitcase, put the pistol, clothing, other supplies and $500 in cash in it. The person hired to free Mahar was to bring the suitcase for Mahar when he escaped. He told me they had already purchased a suitcase and put in the items Mahar specified along with a box of 9-millimeter ammunition.

The husband wanted to know what it would cost to get the job done if I agreed to take it. I told him that taking a prisoner from two US Marshals would be a risky job and would require hiring a partner to help me. The price would be at least $15,000 depending on whether I could find someone to assist and what he would charge. He said they could come up with $15,000 but that was all they could lay their hands on. I told him I needed to think about it for a few days. I gave him my beeper number and wrote down his home telephone number and told him I would be in touch later.

We all returned to the US Marshal's office and decided I should tell the man I would take the job. Later that day I made a recorded call to the husband setting up a meeting at the Greyhound racetrack at three in the afternoon the next day. Again the meeting was to be surveilled. The next afternoon I drove to the Southland Greyhound parking lot and the surveilling units selected their spots after I parked my car in a deserted area.

Shortly after three one of the surveillance units advised they had the subject's car in sight and there was only the driver in it. The husband parked near me and got out of his car, carrying a small suitcase. He got in my car and told me he had brought the suitcase in case I had decided to take the job. I told him I had found a partner and we agreed the price would be $15,000 and I needed $5000 upfront. He agreed to this arrangement but he didn't have a firm date yet. He would let me know as soon as he knew one and left the suitcase with me.

I didn't open the suitcase until everyone involved was back at the Marshal's office in Memphis. The suitcase contained men's clothing, toilet articles, $500 in cash, a 9 mm pistol and a box of 9 mm ammunition.

We discussed where we were in the case and decided it was about time to take the subject down. One of the assistant US Attorneys joined our discussion. If he agreed we had a good case, we were ready to arrest the subject. From what he could see we had a prosecutable case only against the husband. He pointed out the wife hadn't joined the conversation during my meetings with them. Even though the husband implicated her in his talks with the CI and me we had no proof other than his word that she really was. Privately we had already come to that conclusion.

After several ideas to implicate wife were put forth and rejected we decided to arrest the husband, put him in the Craighead County jail in Jonesboro Arkansas and put me in the jail with him as a co-conspirator. Someone asked me if I really wanted to spend a few days in jail. I said I didn't but would if we had a chance of making a case against the wife.

The next morning I took the 9 mm pistol to the Memphis Police Department weapons unit. The armorer (a person who maintains weapons) rendered the pistol inoperable but in such a way a casual inspection couldn't detect it. That done, I put it back in the suitcase with the other items.

The agent from the West Memphis RA went to the US Magistrate in Jonesboro and obtained an arrest warrant for the husband. This agent and two from Memphis arrested him at his West Memphis home and brought him to the jail in Jonesboro. Two hours later they brought me in and booked me on the same charges as the husband.

I had been in many jails before but now I was on the wrong side of the bars. The jail didn't have separate cells; we were all in a common area, even to sleep. There were 10 or 12 other inmates in addition to the subject and me. I was mostly confident that no harm would come to me but my worst nightmare was that someone I knew would recognize me. I grew up in Trumann, Arkansas, not more than 15 miles from Jonesboro and played sports all over the adjoining counties. I knew a lot of people and kept up with some of them over the years. Plus I had many relatives still living in the area, a few of whom I will admit, were not the most law abiding citizens.

In addition many people who knew me in the area also knew I was an FBI agent. My concern was that someone who knew me and my occupation would blurt it out before I could stop him. I might be roughed up by other inmates before the jailer could get to me. None of the jail personnel knew my true identity. I was booked as Joe Ray Stewart.

We were put into the general population and when I could get the husband aside I asked him if he knew who snitched us off. He said he had no idea who could've done this. I replied the only people who knew what we were planning were the man who introduced me to him and his wife.

He assured me that his wife wouldn't do that and besides she didn't know a whole lot about the plan. He said he couldn't vouch for the person they first contacted who introduced me to him.

Since I was the last person booked into the jail that day all the other inmates had already chosen their cot and bedding. I ended up with a damp mattress and didn't want to speculate how that had happened.

Over that night and the next two days I didn't get any more information from the husband. On the second afternoon I called the West Memphis agent and told him to come get me out. In the mornings they served cold coffee and oatmeal with one slice of bread. Lunch was a bologna sandwich and dinner was some kind of microwave dish. I had had enough and wasn't getting the information for which I had been willing to go to jail.

Within the hour the agent arrived and told the jailer he was returning me to West Memphis to lodge me in the county jail there. We got outside and he asked me what I wanted to do. I said I wanted to go to the best restaurant in Jonesboro and have dinner. Which we did.

When I drove back to Memphis I stopped in Trumann to visit my parents. I debated about whether I should tell them about my jail time but in the end I did.

"Mom, I just got out of jail, the Craighead County one, about an hour ago."

"Son, what have you done to be put in that terrible place? You're not a criminal."

I knew she would get all worked up so I didn't let the ruse go on long. My parents knew the horrible reputation of that jail.

Mahar and the husband were indicted on charges of conspiracy to plan Mahar's escape from a federal prison. The relative received a five-year prison sentence. Mahar also pled guilty. Sentencing was deferred until the other charges against him were resolved. He was subsequently found guilty along with the other three in the jewelry store robbery attempt and all received lengthy prison time. An additional five years was added to Mahar's sentence for the conspiracy to escape charge. Now this *was* the last time I had any connection with Mr. Mahar. He died in a federal prison in Texas in 2004 at age 66.

Chapter 16
Drug Dealer Ron, the Cousin and the Trooper

R on Lucas was a big time dealer of cocaine and marijuana in the small community of Camden Tennessee. SA Jerry Bastin, the RA out of Jackson, knew this but couldn't make a buy from him. Jerry's informant, a prostitute and Ron's customer, told him she could easily introduce an undercover agent to Ron. Jerry called me and we began an undercover case that ended with the arrest of a Mississippi State Trooper.

The CI previously worked as a prostitute in Jackson and met Ron through her job. She was in her mid-20s, slender and good-looking and no doubt still a prostitute. She met Ron about two or three years before and became a steady customer as had her friends she hooked up with him. To her knowledge he had never engaged in any violence, was married and had two small children.

After I met her she chose the time for me to meet Ron. She had told Ron I was a major drug dealer in Memphis. On a Tuesday I picked her up in Jackson and we headed to Camden. When we arrived at Ron's home he and his wife invited us in.

It was a nice, neat house just outside the city limits of Camden. He was a white male, about 35 years old, 5'10" with a chunky build. The CI introduced me as a big dealer from Memphis who was looking for a steady supply of cocaine, marijuana and pharmaceuticals. We sat in his living room and chatted with Ron and his wife for about an hour. I eventually brought up the topic of what dope he could sell me, what his prices were and what quantity he could deliver. He said he wanted to think about it and would get back with me. He was a country boy, but a savvy one.

In another two or three days the CI called and told me Ron wanted to talk to me at his home again. I said we would meet him at his house at 10 a.m. on Saturday and let Jerry know about the meeting.

On Saturday morning I picked up the CI and we went back to Ron's. We talked in generalities for a while. When he mentioned drugs, I could tell he was feeling me out to see if I really knew anything about the dope business. After a while he told me he had talked to people in his area but didn't know anyone in Memphis to check me out. Despite not knowing much about me he decided I was okay and we could do business together.

Soon Ron asked me to come into the kitchen to talk in private. I was pretty sure what was coming next. Ron laid out a short line of coke and inhaled about half of it. He handed me the straw and told me to taste the rest so I could confirm it was "good stuff." I knew the real reason was to test me to see if I would do the coke. Most dope dealers believe that undercover police wouldn't, which is true. I told Ron I once got strung out on coke, lost about 20 pounds and was starting to get careless about my business so I quit cold turkey and made myself a promise not to mix business and pleasure ever again. He seemed okay with that but asked me to show him my driver's license. I agreed since I knew the Joe Ray Stewart license would check out. If he had a friend in law enforcement nothing would be questionable.

After some more talk he agreed to sell me 10 pounds of marijuana when he could score it from his supplier. He'd let me know when I could pick it up at his house. I gave him my undercover beeper number and told him to call when he was ready to deal.

I returned to Jackson, dropped off the CI and met with Jerry. We decided to take the CI out of the equation since I felt I could talk to Ron one-on-one. I gave him a quick run down of the meeting and then headed home.

Not many days later Ron was ready. I agreed to meet him the next afternoon at his home. Jerry and another agent would be nearby to cover the buy. This was a "buy walk," the dealer is allowed to walk away with the money. The next day I wore a concealed transmitter in my cowboy boots so Jerry and his partner could hear the transaction. I also was wearing a reel-to-reel recorder. The transmitter was for safety. I met Ron as planned and after I looked at the marijuana we discussed price and arrived at a figure I thought was okay.

I then paid him with FBI "buy funds," money that came from an account the FBI had established for these kinds of transactions. I made Ron count the money out so the covering agents could hear and record him. I told Ron I needed four ounces of powdered cocaine if he could find some. He assured me he could and would call me.

I called the CI and told her about my purchase from Ron in case he should check with her. I said it looked as if I could take it from here and she should stay as far away from Ron as possible.

A couple days later I called Ron and told him I was going to take a break for a few days and come to Camden with my bass boat to fish on the Tennessee River. He said to come on, that he knew all the good spots and would go with me.

I let Jerry know my plan and said I would call him with the name of the motel where I was staying. He wanted me to call him from a pay phone at least once a day to keep him updated. I then hooked up my boat to my personal pick up truck with license plates registered in my undercover name.

I headed to Camden and checked into a motel near the river at about 3 p.m., called Ron and told him where I was. He said he had the package I wanted and would bring it to me. I said, "Hold onto it. I can't be driving around with it and can't leave it in my room for some nosey maid to find." "Okay, I'll see you in a little while." He came over and we set a time to go fishing the next morning. Fishing is my hobby so I could just be myself.

We met at the boat ramp at about 7:30, put my boat in the water and headed upstream. Right away my outboard motor started giving me a problem. We fished until early afternoon, and then headed back to the ramp. Ron left for home and I returned to the motel. I took the carburetors from the motor and brought them to my room to clean and adjust. Ron dropped in unannounced around 5 pm. I was still working on the carbs and had parts scattered all over the room. He was somewhat surprised but I think it bolstered my cover as just an ordinary, although drug dealing, man.

We fished together again the next day with no motor problems. That night I called Jerry and told him Ron and I had agreed to meet at my motel the next morning to do the dope deal. At about 10 Ron arrived with the cocaine. I was wearing the transmitter as well as the recorder again so Jerry and another agent could listen.

To verify that the white powder was really cocaine I took about a half teaspoon and put it in the heavy test bag that held three small glass tubes of chemicals. With my fingers on the outside I broke the tubes for the chemicals to mix with the powder. As I suspected the substance immediately turned bright blue meaning a relatively pure batch of cocaine.

Ron and I haggled over the price for a few minutes. When I gave him the money I had him count it as before. Ron left and I checked out of the motel about 30 minutes later and met Jerry in Jackson to put the coke in an evidence bag.

Jerry and I decided to wait to reconnect with Ron so we could plan what steps to take next. After a week I called Ron and told him I hired two women who easily sold the 4 ounces. Now if he could get me more of that same high quality dope I wanted a kilo. He said he would check on it and call me in a few days.

Two days later Ron called and said he had the kilo for me. I told him I was real busy. "If you can bring it to me in Memphis I'll add $500 for your trouble," I said. He agreed and I told him I'd meet him in the lobby of the Holiday Inn at Poplar and I-240 at two the following afternoon.

This time Jerry and I planned to make a 'buy bust.' We would arrest Ron after he delivered the coke and took the money. I rented adjoining rooms at the hotel. The technical agents wired the "deal room" with video and audio and fed it into the adjoining control room. Four or five agents in the control room would follow the transaction. The connecting door was rigged in such a way that it could be opened only from the control room. This was a safety measure in case Ron tried to rob me. We also had a surveillance team outside who had the description and license number of Ron's car to let us know when Ron appeared.

I met Ron in the lobby about ten minutes after two and we went up to the room. Ron had the cocaine in a paper grocery bag. I tested it and said it was okay. I gave him the agreed upon amount of money, I believe it was $30,000, and asked him to count it as before. When I heard a knock on the door I left the room. SAs Ed Young and Jack Sampson were in the hallway. Ron didn't react when Ed entered the room since he was dressed casually. Jack, in a coat and tie, followed and when Ron saw him he took a few steps back with a look of shock and surprise on his face. They identified themselves and told Ron he was under arrest for dealing cocaine.

The agents searched him, advised him of his rights and began questioning him. At first Ron said nothing. The agents told him they had him on video dealing the cocaine. He said he didn't know for sure what was in the grocery bag, that he had been paid $500 to deliver the bag to this room.

They then told him he had just sold a kilo of cocaine to an FBI agent. He said, "You must be lying. There was this guy named Joe who I met several times. He once had his outboard motor taken apart and spread all over his room in a motel. I don't believe he's an FBI agent. If he is FBI, bring him in here and let me see him and show me his ID and I will talk to you."

I was in the control room and heard Ron's words. I went back into the other room and showed him my FBI credentials. He looked at me, "You son of a bitch. You really fooled me!" He then agreed to give a signed statement admitting to the three buys I made from him.

When we got back to the Memphis FBI office Ron wrote out a statement in his own words and handwriting. He said he had no anger towards me, "You were just doing your job and I got caught." I gave him a ride back to his car and told him to start thinking about making some buys from his suppliers. I said, "The more cases you make the more the AUSA handling your case will be able to tell the judge. This will make a difference in any sentence you might receive. Call me when you are ready to go to work."

About a week later Ron called and said he had something lined up. I said I'd come to his home the next day at 3 p.m. When I arrived both Ron and his wife greeted me like a family friend. Nearly the first words Ron said were, "I know your real name is Corbett but is it okay if we call you Joe? That's what we know you as." I said, "That's actually a good idea. That way if we're doing a dope deal, you won't mess up and call me by my true name."

Ron arranged for the purchase of half a kilo of coke from a guy he had dealt with several times in Nashville. I left Ron's house and made a call to Jerry and told him what we had. He said he would call the Nashville RA and get the dealer checked. Nashville would decide when to do the deal. I went back to Ron's and had dinner with him and his wife. I told him Nashville agents were checking out the dealer and would let us know when they wanted to move. Ron had already told me he usually met the dealer at a shopping center parking lot to make the exchange. I checked into the Camden motel again.

Jerry called me the next morning. Nashville had found a record for the target dealer. He had one federal conviction for distribution of a controlled substance. Nashville wanted to make the buy the next day and gave the name of a shopping center they preferred if the subject would agree. If not there, we were to give them the location as soon as we knew it.

Ron came by my motel room later that day and I told him we wanted to make the buy at two or three the next afternoon and the location. This was to be another 'buy bust.' I put a recording device on the motel phone and Ron placed the call. The seller agreed to meet us at the spot Ron suggested the next day at 2 p.m. I called Jerry and told him the deal was on. The code for the agents to move in and make the arrest was when they heard me say on the transmitter, "This looks like good coke."

Ron and I got to the designated place a little before two. The seller showed up about 15 minutes later and got into the back seat of my car carrying a paper grocery bag. After some discussion I asked to see the cocaine. The seller passed the bag to me and I took out one of the four plastic baggies and looked at the coke. I tested a small amount of the coke and gave him the money he wanted and asked him to count it to make sure it was the correct amount. He said he didn't need to count it, that he trusted Ron. I said, "Okay. This looks like some good coke." The seller said, "Yes it's good stuff. Call me when you need more."

He had just gotten the back door open when two cars came to a screeching halt alongside the rear doors. Agents jumped out with their IDs in one hand and pistols in the other. The subject was arrested without incident. Ron and I quickly drove from the scene and met Jerry and two other agents. I weighed the coke, put it in an evidence bag, initialed it and gave it to Jerry. At that time ½ kilo was worth wholesale $15,000 to $20,000; that amount would have retailed for up to $100,000 or more depending on how much it was cut.

In the next month or so Ron set up three more 'buy busts' that went down like clockwork. After the fourth Ron had exhausted his Nashville dealers. Ron once told me about a dealer he often did business with in northern Mississippi. According to Ron this person had a cousin who was a Mississippi state trooper. The guy told Ron that he and the trooper had worked a scam many times that made them a lot of money.

Ron explained to me how the scam worked. The trooper's cousin would arrange the sale of 1-5 kilos of cocaine to another dealer. The cousin would pick up the buyer at a parking lot and say they were going to a motel room his wife had rented for a day to keep the coke. The cousin/seller would drive the buyer to the motel. The cousin would go into the motel room, come back with cocaine, show it to the buyer and let him check it. The dope would be exchanged for the money while they were in the car.

The seller then would head back to where the buyer had left his parked vehicle. Somewhere on the way the trooper, by prior arrangement, would stop them. He would check the driver's license of the driver and ask him if he had been drinking. The driver/seller would say. "Only a couple beers a few hours ago." The trooper would tell him he stopped him because his dispatcher reported that a citizen had called in a drunk driver with a description that fit this vehicle.

Then the trooper would tell the driver to park his car well off the road and lock it up. Now that the men were out of the car the trooper would handcuff them and tell them he was taking them to the county jail for a breath test. While they were en route to the jail a confederate of the cousin and the trooper would break into the cousin/seller's parked car and take the money and the cocaine. Eventually the trooper would determine the driver was not over the limit and return the men to the parked car. The driver would discover his car had been broken into and to make it look legitimate would ask the trooper to take a report on the burglary. Of course he couldn't tell the trooper what was missing.

The cousin/seller would take the unsuspecting buyer back to his vehicle with some conversation about what a bad deal this had been but "things just happen." Next the cousin would meet the trooper, pay him a previously agreed upon sum for his services and the cousin and confederate would divide up the money and he would keep the cocaine for another scam.

Jerry and I talked and decided to make some buys from this Mississippi cousin/dealer Bobby Rice, then try to flip him and get an introduction to the trooper named Clayton. Now that we planned to work a case in the FBI northern Mississippi division Jerry let the Oxford MS resident agent know what we had and asked them to check out the dealer and the trooper. A few days later SA Wayne Tichenor called Jerry. The suspected dealer, Bobby Rice, was known to local law enforcement but the trooper had a clean record.

Jerry, Ron, Wayne and I met at a south Memphis motel to set up the deal. Ron had a phone number for Bobby Rice and felt confident he could buy drugs from him. We put a recorder on the motel phone and had Ron make a call. He got an answer on the first attempt and after some discussion made a deal to buy two ounces of cocaine from Rice two days later at a parking lot in Southaven, MS, just over the state line. This was to be a 'buy walk' transaction, covered by Jerry and agents from Oxford.

Ron and I met Rice as planned and made the buy without incident. A week later we made a 4-ounce buy from him. These buys were recorded, the cocaine tested, etc. just as we did in Tennessee.

Now we had to decide how far to go with Rice and whether we could eventually get the crooked trooper. Jerry and I met with Wayne Tichenor to discuss where we were and what the next step should be. In our opinion we had solid evidence against Bobby Rice. The lab report identified the drug as 76% pure cocaine, which is normal range. If it had come directly from Columbia it would have been 100%. Since Rice had a prior criminal record we knew he would be facing a lot of federal jail time, a fact that favored our being able to flip him.

We decided to make another two-ounce buy that would be a 'buy bust' this time. About 10 days later Ron set up the purchase for the next afternoon. Rice showed up, got in the back seat of my car, passed the cocaine to me and I paid him. I said the code, "This looks like good stuff" which brought four agents down on him like a swarm of bees. Rice was arrested, advised of his rights and the charges against him.

We took Rice to the Oxford RA office and interviewed him for about two hours. After discussing the evidence we had against him and the range of prison time he was facing if he didn't cooperate, Rice agreed to do whatever he could.

Rice didn't hesitate to identify his current supplier although at first he was reluctant to confirm what Ron had told us about his arrangement with his cousin the state trooper Thurman K. Clayton. Upon further consideration Bobby Rice told us he could set up a deal with the trooper just about any time. I asked if he could introduce Ron and me to Clayton so we could deal directly with him. Rice said he didn't think this would be a problem since he and Clayton were kin and had pulled the scam several times earning him and the trooper a lot of cash.

After about a week Rice called Trooper Clayton and arranged to introduce Ron and me to him. Two days later we were to meet him in New Albany, Mississippi, near Tupelo, Elvis Presley's birthplace. We met as scheduled, the trooper remaining in his cruiser, and we in our vehicles. The trooper nodded to us, indicating we should follow him. We drove for about 30 minutes and followed him through a farm gate that he unlocked and across a pasture to a thick stand of pines. We spotted the trooper's parked cruiser concealed in the trees where it couldn't be seen from the road. I had previously told Rice that once the introductions had been made he was to leave and have no further part in this and not to talk to Clayton about it from this point forward.

Clayton was casually leaning on the cruiser's fender. He was about 5'11", 185 pounds, starting to gain a little around the waist, about 40-years old. He was dressed in his full uniform with holstered pistol at his hip. Introductions were made and Clayton suggested we sit in his cruiser so he could listen to the highway patrol dispatcher on his radio since he was on duty. All this time I was wearing a recorder in my cowboy boot but not a transmitter. Clayton never checked to see if I was wearing a wire. After the formalities were taken care of Rice said he was leaving and would not be a part of the operation from this point on. While I didn't know for sure, I suspected he and Clayton had already come to some arrangement to share in the bribe I would pay Clayton. It would be normal for Rice to get some of the money since he had hooked me up with Clayton.

Ron and I continued to talk to Clayton for a while about how much he wanted as his part of the scam and how it would work. Since we were in his cruiser I was not only recording the conversation but also the Mississippi Highway Patrol (MHP) dispatcher talking to other units. I told him I was trying to set up the sale of five kilos of cocaine but the purchaser had not yet committed. We agreed to meet again to plan the "rip" when I had the sale cemented. I asked Clayton not to talk to his cousin Rice about it since I didn't want any more people involved than absolutely necessary. He agreed this was the way to take care of business.

The next day agents and supervisors from the Memphis and Oxford offices met to listen to the taped recording of the meeting with Clayton. Everyone agreed that the way the conversation went there could be no successful entrapment defense if it were raised at a trial. We also jointly prepared a script for me to use at my next meeting with the trooper. There would be no coverage of the meeting; I would only wear a recorder to capture the conversation. It was too risky to have other agents nearby. We knew how surveillance conscious a cop would be and I didn't feel I was in any danger from Trooper Clayton.

Ron and I met with Clayton a few days later at the same location in New Albany. I told him I had the sale arranged for two days later if it fit into his schedule. He said that was okay, he'd be working second shift that day. I told him we'd drive south on U. S. 78, leaving Memphis at about 8 p.m. He suggested a pull over just south of Potts Camp for the stop, a wide spot in the road without even a stoplight. I agreed and asked how much he would charge for his part. He said that with five kilos involved he wanted $10,000. We agreed he would meet me at a motel in Southaven at 2 p.m. the afternoon of the stop for me to give him the cash.

Clayton arrived at the motel in a civilian vehicle, that a quick check verified as his. He took the money and I asked him to count it out since I was wearing a recorder but he said he trusted me and had to get to work. For security reasons we had not told anyone in the MHP about this case. Two agents from Oxford planned to advise the commander and his chief about the upcoming operation late that afternoon and have them waiting at the county jail with other agents once we arrived with Clayton under arrest.

I selected Jack Sampson, a first office rookie agent from Memphis to ride with me as the prospective dope buyer. He was a fast learner and a hard charger and could dress and act the part of a drug dealer. At an earlier meeting at the office agents were assigned their roles in the take down. A Bureau plane would be up to surveill the area and keep agents on the ground advised of what was going on.

We left Southaven a little after 8 p.m. The surveillance units had left earlier to take up their positions. When we went through Potts Camp I saw the trooper's cruiser parked between two buildings and saw him swing out and start following me. Just before we got to the turn out he turned on his blue lights and I pulled over at the designated spot. Clayton came to the driver's side of the car and asked for my driver's license and proof of insurance. I said, "Why'd you stop me?" He gave me the old line of someone calling in about a drunk driver and a description that fit my car. He told me to park my car in a safe position in the turn out which I did. The trooper asked about our drinking and we said only a couple of beers. Clayton said he could smell alcohol and was going to take us to the Benton County jail in Ripley. He handcuffed us and put us in the back of the cruiser, which had a screen between the front and back seats. He didn't search either of us. We weren't armed since it wouldn't have been a good idea and I didn't have any fear of him.

Clayton drove us towards Ripley, a 20-minute drive. When he pulled into the driveway alongside the building I could see my good friend and fellow agent SA David Baldovin and SA Steve Overly standing on the steps to the jail. The FBI didn't want any agents formally booked into a jail if there was any way to avoid it.

Baldovin and Overly had to think up a ruse, a reason to be at the Benton County jail with the sheriff at the time the trooper brought us there. Dave knew the sheriff and the trooper were friends so they couldn't let him know the real reason for their presence. Whatever they told him it worked. Clayton had just gotten us out of the cruiser when Dave and Steve approached him, identified themselves and placed him under arrest for bribery.

They turned the tables on him, placing him under arrest and released us. "The poor sheriff," Dave said, "was bewildered, having no clue or idea what was happening." Dave told me, "This was the first time I ever 'unarrested' an FBI agent."

After Clayton was arrested and handcuffed the MHP commander, his chief and the captain for the district drove up to the scene. They got out and told Clayton he was relieved of duty. They took all his MHP equipment from him including his pistol, mace etc., a routine procedure.

I heard Clayton tell his captain that if he would take the handcuffs off and give him his pistol back he would walk out into the dark and end this right here. His request was obviously denied. But it was an inferred admission of guilt.

The captain told him he was going to search his cruiser and remove everything and inventory it. I watched as the captain popped the trunk and began. He opened a metal briefcase on the trunk floor. I was standing next to him and could see a large stack of U. S. currency inside that I was certain was the $10,000 I had given Clayton earlier. The captain removed the money from the briefcase and handed me several individual bills that I verified as being on the bait bill list. The captain put the currency in a plastic evidence bag, sealed and initialed it for me.

Dave Baldovin and Steve Overly put Clayton in the back of their car and took him to the Oxford RA while I rode with SA Wayne Tichenor.

Wayne Tichenor was successful in getting Clayton to admit to his guilt. Clayton gave a signed confession in his own handwriting. Two U. S. Marshals were on standby and took Clayton to the Lafayette County Jail. The next day a hearing was held before the federal Magistrate who bound Clayton over for trial. Clayton posted the $50,000 bond and was released the same day, August 3, 1985.

Despite his unequivocal admission of guilt, Trooper Clayton chose to go to trial on the charges before a jury in the U. S. District Court in Oxford on April 7, 1986. Big John Booth Farese, a flamboyant and renowned Mississippi attorney represented Clayton. Farese was a short man, gray hair thinning on top, probably in his mid-60s. He carried himself with authority although his dress was usually sloppy.

I testified about my meetings with Clayton and played the recorded tapes. I related my witnessing the MHP commander taking the cash out of Clayton's briefcase. Another agent testified that the serial numbers, denominations and series of the bills matched the list I had prepared of the bribe money. Wayne TIchenor introduced into evidence Clayton's signed confession.

Ron was on the stand for at least half a day. Ron testified about the meetings with Clayton and the latter's willingness to engage in the scam. Most of the time Ron was being cross-examined by the hard-hitting attorney Farese but the cross-exam never got anywhere. John Farese treated every prosecution witness the same.

While Farese didn't raise the defense of entrapment I could tell from his questions that his plan was to convince the jury that Clayton was led into the scheme by the FBI. The defense didn't put on any witnesses to testify as to the facts, only character witnesses who said they had known Thurman Clayton for many years and knew he wasn't a criminal.

The thrust of Farese's closing argument was that the big FBI came into rural northern Mississippi and led Trooper Clayton, who didn't have a blemish on his record, down the primrose path to bribery, an act he never would have done without this encouragement. He said that all along Clayton intended to do his own investigation and once the bribe money was paid to him he planned to advise his superiors of the scam I was perpetuating.

Attorney Farese held a Bible in his left hand and raised it in the air when he made a statement alluding to Clayton's innocence. He said, "He who is without sin casts the first stone." People in Mississippi are noted for their fervent religious beliefs. Farese was obviously playing to this local audience, the jury. He even shed a few tears describing his innocent client.

The prosecution gets the final word to the jury in a rebuttal to the defense's closing argument. AUSA John Hailman reminded them of the actual facts to keep them on track after Farese's fabrications. Hailman couldn't actually say Farese was lying but could imply it.

On April 18, 1986 after days of testimony and several hours of deliberation the jury notified the judge they had reached a verdict. They returned to the courtroom and took their regular seats. The judge asked the jury foreman if they had reached a decision. "Yes," he said and read from a sheet of paper. "We the jury find Thurman K. Clayton not guilty on all counts." The judge then polled each juror and asked if not guilty was his/her verdict. Each one answered in the affirmative.

We looked at each other in disbelief. How could the jury come to this conclusion? But the jury had spoken and there is no appeal from a not guilty verdict.

Because of his extensive cooperation with the government Ron was given a suspended sentence with court supervision for three years. The sentencing judge made it clear that any infraction of the law would result in his going to prison to serve the rest of the time.

What did the FBI accomplish even with this verdict? As to Clayton he lost his job and his pension from the MHP. I don't know and can't even speculate as to what ever happened to him after that.

We also shut down the Bobby Rice-Clayton cousins-scam and put many high-level drug dealers in Tennessee and Mississippi out of business. More of them always seem to crop up no matter how many we arrest and convict but at least we made a dent and took some dope out of the supply chain. And I know, if he were still alive, I wouldn't hesitate to hire Big John Booth Farese if I or one of my loved ones got into criminal trouble in northern Mississippi.

Through my contacts in the trucking industry I got Ron a job driving an over-the-road truck, a job he knew. In 1991 after I had retired from the FBI and was working for the Shelby County Sheriff's Office, Ron called me from a truck stop in West Memphis, Arkansas. "They're out to get me. They're going to hurt me." He said. I told him to stay put and would see him in less than 30 minutes.

I headed across the Mississippi River to meet Ron. I could tell immediately that he had been "tweaking." He was jumpy, nervous and paranoid. No one was after him. He had been driving the truck for 10 or 12 hours and had taken some crystal meth to keep him awake. I reminded him of the judge's orders, drug use could send him to prison. "I'll look the other way this time but if I hear anything like this again I'm going to the judge. Get in your sleeper cab and sleep for eight hours." I never heard from or about him again.

Chapter 17
Eric Bovan: King of Cocaine in 80's Memphis

Eric Bovan, a premier drug dealer who brought hundreds of millions of dollars of cocaine into Memphis, became the target of the Organized Crime Drug Enforcement Task Force (0CDETF) that I headed in 1987. We believed he distributed 5-10 kilos once or twice a month. If true, just one load would have a street value of several million dollars. Bovan's notoriety was widespread. Often when a Memphis Police Department (MPD) officer presented anti-drug messages to schoolchildren a student raised his hand and said, "I know you catch a lot of drug dealers but you'll never catch Eric Bovan."

Informants were constantly telling us that Bovan was dealing in kilo amounts but we couldn't learn anything specific about his operation. The problem was he limited his associates to family or very close friends. Eric had six or eight brothers and sisters and many cousins who were dealers or mules, the ones who illegally transport drugs for dealers.

Eric lived with his mother, Sylvia Saulsberry, in South Memphis and appeared to run his operation from her home. Her house was south and west of Graceland in a neighborhood of modest homes on large lots filled with shade trees. She ran a nightclub called Mr. B's in South Memphis that had no connection with drug dealing we could find.

Eric claimed to have dropped out of high school at age 22 which is not likely but that was his story. Perhaps he didn't have much formal education but he was no dummy and had figured out a way to make himself a rich man. He once said he saw cocaine trafficking as a business, one to make money, although with a calculated risk.

Soon we realized that Bovan almost never came into direct contact with the cocaine that came mainly from Los Angeles. He used a family member or a trusted associate from his inner circle to carry the money to purchase the cocaine and bring it back to Memphis. Each trip usually involved 1 to 5 kilos and sometimes up to 9 or 10. Eric kept tight control, sending two or three people who he allowed two days and a night to make the trip one way, driving straight through to California. They were ordered to drive the speed limit, obey all traffic laws, no drinking, no weapons.

For the most part our informants made controlled buys, ones that we covered from start to finish with cash we provided. DEA (Drug Enforcement Agency) Special Agent Henry Baker was the first undercover officer to buy from the Bovans, two 1/8-ounce bags of powdered cocaine from Linda Faye Mims aka "Pee Wee," Eric's sister-in-law. Henry was a tall, slender black man probably about 30 years old. He was street savvy and could walk the walk and talk the talk in the black community. He once made an undercover buy in a house when MPD narcotics officers raided it. Henry slipped quietly into a back bedroom, opened a window and hotfooted it from the neighborhood. This put him in solid with the dopers.

One of my informants told me Bovan employed the "Dog Man," true name Earl Woods, who was not related to any of the Bovans, but Eric trusted completely to transport large amounts of cash and cocaine. The Dog Man made trips to Los Angeles and Henderson Nevada (a suburb of Las Vegas) as one of Eric's mules. He also distributed kilos of cocaine to Bovan's wholesalers and buyers who were mainly Eric's relatives. He didn't appear to be a dealer himself.

In the spring of 1987 my source told me the Dog Man was getting worried about what he had gotten into and wanted to talk to the FBI. The source arranged for me to meet Earl in Overton Park, a large wooded area about two miles from downtown Memphis.

I knew the only way to bring down a closely held organization like Eric Bovan's was to develop an informant from within the upper echelon. There was no way an undercover officer could penetrate the family connections. I hoped that Earl Woods would give us the break we needed.

I introduced myself and showed Earl my credentials. He was about 35 years old, a lifelong Memphian, married with two children. He told me he was into something illegal and was so deeply involved that he was worried he might be arrested. He recently had a "religious experience" and wanted out of the criminal life. I wondered how he had gotten himself into this predicament. He seemed to be a nice guy and intelligent. He was black, poor and without much formal education or any marketable skill beyond training dogs so probably the lure of money drew him to Eric Bovan.

I decided to give him the benefit of the doubt to see what he could tell me about Bovan's organization. I told him if he was honest and wanted to cooperate I would talk to AUSA Tim DiScenza who was part of our Task Force. Anything Earl could do to help us put Bovan and his distribution network out of business, the bigger break he might receive at sentencing, if he was ever charged.

It was obvious that for Earl to be effective in helping us break up the largest ever drug-dealing organization in Memphis he would have to continue to handle cocaine for Bovan. I made it clear to him he was not to do any "freelancing." He was not to sell any drugs nor engage in any acts of violence nor use any illegal drugs while working with me. He agreed.

Earl knew almost all the players, large and small, and could name them. He had met Bovan about two years earlier when he sold him a dog from his business raising, training and selling guard dogs. Bovan seemed to like Earl and they eventually became close friends. Earl wasn't an innocent and knew Bovan was big in the drug scene. Even though Earl was basically a stranger to Bovan he came to trust him completely. Eventually Eric asked Earl if he wanted to work for him and offered to pay him "good money" for his help. Earl quickly agreed to this arrangement, knowing he would be breaking the law every step of the way.

Earl described to me how a typical out of town purchase of cocaine would go down. Bovan arranged for different people to rent a medium-size sedan or borrow a car from a friend to be used on the trip. He would send two or three people and pay their expenses plus $500 to $1000 each to take cash to the cocaine seller. When the couriers returned to Memphis they would contact Bovan from a pay phone and he would tell them what to do next. Earl said Bovan almost never examined the cocaine, consciously distancing himself from the dope.

Earl gave me a list of what he termed "major players" in the Bovan organization. I recognized several but there were a lot of unfamiliar names. I told Earl he was to call me as soon as possible after learning a trip to buy dope was planned and give me all the particulars. I hoped we could follow and/or intercept a load.

Since I was opening up a formal informant file on Earl I needed to give him a code name that would be used in all communication. The task force members would only know him by this name. Two other agents working with me would know his true identity. After thinking about it for a while I decided on the name "Duke" from the song "Duke of Earl," a hit of the 1960s.

As it turned out almost all the information Duke gave me about the cocaine purchases, transporting to Memphis and distribution came after the fact. Circumstances prevented him from letting me know about trips before hand.

On one occasion Duke went with Eric, Janet Mims, Steve McGaha and Charles Lacey in a van to Los Angeles to purchase cocaine. They were carrying a large sum of money he believed to be more than $150,000. Somewhere in the vicinity of Las Vegas, Nevada they experienced mechanical problems with the van. They went to a house at 611 Overland Drive, in Henderson Nevada that Earl believed Eric owned. They couldn't get the van repaired quickly so Bovan told them to rent a car to continue the trip to LA.

Duke and Steve rented a late model Cadillac the following morning and drove to Hollywood, California. They delivered a suitcase of money to an unknown female who lived in an apartment. To Earl's surprise Ernestine Wynn, a Memphis member of Bovan's distribution network, was there too. She directed the purchase of six kilograms of cocaine from a male black. Duke described him as approximately 6' tall and 40-46 years of age with a muscular build. He was later identified as Alex Lowe.

They then drove back to Henderson with the cocaine. Eric Bovan, Willie Bovan aka "Uncle Bo" and Mark Thomas were at the house on Overland Drive when they arrived. Eric instructed Duke, McGaha, Uncle Bo and Mark to load the cocaine in a Toyota van and return to Memphis and deliver the coke to an address on Spiegel Street. At that time a kilogram was selling at a wholesale price of $25,000 to $35,000. It would be worth at least five times that once separated out into ounces or smaller amounts, cut by adding substances to increase the weight and sold on the street. The street value of this load was about $500,000.

Larry Saulsberry, Bovan's half-brother, was at the Spiegel address when they arrived with the cocaine. He instructed them to place the dope in a car parked on the street, driven by Kenny Upshaw. That was the last time Duke saw the coke. Duke explained that Larry was one of Bovan's principal buyers and operated his own drug distribution network. Upshaw was one of Bovan's most trusted cohorts and deeply involved in transporting money and coke for him.

We continued to miss loads and some of the task force members began to suspect Duke was playing with me and was purposely withholding information that would allow us to intercept a big load. I agreed that could be the case since informants are notoriously known to double-cross the agent they were working with. But as near as I could tell Duke was not double-dealing. He continued to give us valuable information not only about the trips to purchase cocaine that checked out but also what was going on in Memphis and identifying additional members of the Bovan organization. To me this represented a great breakthrough in our investigation and I was determined to not give up on Earl.

In mid-June 1987 Bovan instructed Duke to pick up a large quantity of money in Memphis from Larry Saulsberry and Janice Mims. Larry told Duke, Herman DeWayne Saulsberry aka "Chicken Wing," another of Eric's half-brothers, and a male black known only as "Spoon," to drive the money to Eric in Henderson. Then Eric instructed them, along with Ernestine Wynn who was already in Nevada, to head to LA to pick up a load of cocaine, pay for it and return directly to Memphis.

As before, they were told to deliver the coke to the Spiegel address. Saulsberry met them in the driveway and had them put it in Kenny Upshaw's car. Eric was clever in doing this since he ensured the mules never knew the cocaine's ultimate destination.

In late June 1987 I was on vacation with my wife in Steamboat Springs Colorado when I got a message from my office in Memphis to call Duke as soon as possible. When I called he told me that Eric, McGaha and Chicken Wing were leaving Memphis in the next day or two for Las Vegas. Eric had made arrangements to have his new yellow

Corvette hauled by truck to Vegas so he could show it off. He wanted to park on the large circular driveway in front of the Caesar's Palace Casino where he could be seen. Duke believed Eric intended to store a shipment of cocaine in the Corvette for the return trip to Memphis although he had no hard evidence to support his suspicion.

I felt it was worth a shot to fly to Las Vegas and cover this event. I called my supervisor and AUSA DiScenza and ran it by them. They agreed with me. I called the Memphis FBI office and dictated an Airtel to Vegas FBI setting forth the situation and asked for help in surveilling the Corvette once it arrived there. ATF Agent Walter Hoback, my right hand man in the task force, and two other agents would surveill the truck from Memphis to Las Vegas. What I always liked about Walter was his readiness to take on any new adventure and his ability to manage what might turn into a messy situation. We made a good team and proved that interagency cooperation was extremely valuable.

A couple days later Walter advised me they were en route to Las Vegas, following the truck carrying Eric's Corvette. When I arrived in Vegas I learned there was a middleweight championship boxing match scheduled there in the next few days. I figured that was why Eric chose those days for his trip.

We surveilled the Corvette 24 hours a day and watched Eric strut around his car parked on the curved Caesar's Palace driveway. I could tell from a distance that he was adorned with his gold jewelry including a highly visible large gold pendant on a chain around his neck. Some of the Vegas agents walked right past him. I couldn't get close since he would recognize me.

On the day after the fight we watched as Eric's Corvette was loaded back onto the truck for the return trip to Memphis. Part of the time the Corvette was in a parking garage where it was impossible to keep an eye on it so a load of cocaine could have been put in it.

I joined Walter and two other officers on the drive back to Memphis tagging along behind the Corvette. The first night the truck driver stopped at a motel and we set up the two officers to surveill the truck while Walter and I visited the local police department. We hoped to arrange for a drug detection dog to check the vehicle. At about 2 a.m. two dog teams met us and worked their dogs. The results were negative. Too bad. It was another waste of money and manpower but it had to be done.

In early July 1987 Duke told me he frequently picked up large sums of money for Bovan at a residence on 2483 Monette Street in a neighborhood of low to moderate priced homes in North Memphis. Duke said Janice Mims' sister "Peewee" Mims lived there; the Mims family was related somehow to Eric. I got a court order to place a camera on the utility pole directly across the street from the house. This camera would operate day and night giving us a record of individuals and vehicles entering and leaving the home. Every two days an officer or agent, dressed as a lineman, would remove the film from the camera under cover of darkness, and insert a new film.

Later that summer Duke told me Ernestine Wynn was concerned Bovan had been "going around her" in purchasing his cocaine directly from her source in LA. Previously Bovan was paying her $500 per kilo and her source paid her another $500. So Eric was cheating her out of $1000 for every kilogram.

Duke, Eric and Janice Mims went to PeeWee's house on Monette, the place where we had the camera, on September 17. They counted out $130,000 in cash and put it in a canvas bag. Cash in bags like this was usually in $100 bills, rolled up and held by a rubber band, most likely $5000 to a roll. They placed the bag of money in a new Jeep Wagoneer that Bovan owned. They later turned the money over to Kenny Upshaw who Eric directed to drive to LA to pick up a shipment of cocaine. The film from the camera for September 17 confirmed absolutely what Duke told me so we had visual evidence to support his story.

When Upshaw headed out to LA Eric told him to put the dope in a plastic bag and then pour coffee grounds over it all. He was then to place that bag inside another plastic bag and seal it tightly. Many dope dealers thought that covering the cocaine with coffee grounds would mask the scent so drug detection dogs couldn't detect it. That was a fallacy since the dogs were better than the bad guys thought. Another deception tried was to include several dryer fabric softener sheets among the bricks of cocaine and then seal the whole thing in a large plastic bag. Again the dogs couldn't be fooled.

In late September Duke called and said he was holding $47,000 in cash for Bovan until he needed it. At about 10 p.m. I drove to Duke's home in one of our older model undercover cars. Duke took me to the bedroom closet. A large paper grocery sack was sitting on the floor filled to the top with mostly $100 bills. Duke said Bovan knew how much money was in it to the last dollar and would check when Duke returned it to him. I took several photos of the money. If I had had time I would've recorded the serial numbers but that would have taken hours.

We identified three more members of the organization in California when Duke sent Western Union money orders to Alex Lowe, who was the person who delivered six kilos of cocaine to Ernestine Wynn in Hollywood back in June; Warnaco Knox; and Shirron Knox, who was the LA source of cocaine. I sent this information to the LA FBI office. Through DMV the agents obtained drivers licenses for all three so now we had photographs.

As the weeks and months went by, Eric Bovan continued to send couriers, mostly to Los Angeles, who purchased kilograms of cocaine ranging from 4 to 10 kilos per trip. Duke went on most of the trips and would tell me before they left. We tried each time to seize the mother lode when it arrived back in Memphis, but were unsuccessful since Duke was never alone. Once he called me from a pay phone when he got back but we were still too late to intercept the load. If we ever could intercept and seize one of these shipments we could have traced the cocaine back to Bovan and ended the investigation.

In January 1988, an officer with the Shelby County narcotics unit made two undercover buys of cocaine from Anthony Bovan, Eric's brother. A few days later officers served a search warrant on Anthony's home. They seized detailed records of narcotics transactions involving several persons over an extensive length of time. When Anthony was confronted with the evidence he agreed to cooperate and gave us a lengthy statement about his brother's operation.

Anthony said Eric began his cocaine organization known on the street as the "B Team" sometime in 1984. The main players were Eric and Anthony Bovan, and their half-brothers Larry Saulsberry and DeWayne Saulsberry aka "Chicken Wing," He told us that each load of cocaine coming from California averaged about 15 kilograms, at about a total cost of $375,000 to $525,000. That is a lot of cash to have on hand on a regular basis. At some point Eric got a money-counting machine. It had to save time.

In late April Duke told me that Eric, Larry Saulsberry and Steve McGaha were planning a trip to Henderson Nevada in the next few days. They would be driving a blue Chevrolet Cavalier and he believed they would be carrying a large amount of cash. Eric would probably stay in Henderson and send the other two to pick up a load of cocaine in California. Duke said he'd let me know when they left Memphis.

Our task force talked it over and decided I would fly to Las Vegas on the day Eric and the others left. I planned to contact our agents in Vegas and arrange for help in surveilling the Cavalier. I wanted to get a tracking device from the Vegas office to be placed on the car if at all possible. Then when the car headed west I could arrange for the Las Vegas agents to help me surveill it to California, where we could hook up with agents from LA. Then I assumed the Cavalier would head back east with LA agents and me surveilling it. I had my task force members primed to get on the road to meet us on the return trip to Memphis. I figured I would have no problem getting an aircraft up as well. I thought we had a good chance with the tracking device to finally trace a load from its origin to its ultimate Memphis destination.

Two days later Duke called me in the morning and said Eric and crew had just left his mother's house in the blue Cavalier. I called the Vegas FBI office and gave them the information and said I was arriving in Las Vegas that evening.

Expecting the drug dealers to drive straight through I anticipated they should arrive at about eight the next morning. The local agents had checked out the Bovan residence at 611 Overland Drive in Henderson. It was a stucco house located in a small subdivision of modest homes with only one way in and out. There was a gas station/convenience store on the main road leading into the subdivision, about one-half mile from the subdivision entrance. A vehicle had to pass this station in order to enter or leave the area.

We set up at the store the next morning at seven and one of the agents drove by 611 Overland and reported there were no vehicles parked there. At about 11:30 a.m. we saw the Cavalier drive past the store. We waited a while, and then one of the Las Vegas agents did a drive-by and saw the Cavalier in the driveway and no one outside the house.

The local office arranged for their tech agent to meet us at the store at 2 a.m. and then go to the Overland address and place a tracking device on the Cavalier. He came as anticipated and covertly installed the tracker on the car.

This tracking device was of the old vintage, not nearly as compact as later versions. It was a plastic rectangle about 6" x 3" x 3" high, with an antenna about 6" long. A strong magnet attached it to the vehicle. The unit emits a beep about every minute while the vehicle is stationary that can be heard over a dedicated channel on a Bureau radio. If the vehicle begins to move, the tracker beeps about every 30 seconds and as a vehicle following it comes closer to the tracking device the beeps are faster and louder.

We maintained a 24-hour surveillance at the store for the next two days but the blue Cavalier never moved. After two days the Las Vegas supervisor called and told me he was going to have to pull his agents off the surveillance since they had a special case they had to work on.

I remained as the only one watching until nearly midnight. Then I left for the motel hoping the Cavalier wouldn't move before seven the next morning. Luckily nothing happened in the night.

In early afternoon the next day I heard fast beeps. I expected the Cavalier to pass in front of me shortly but it didn't. After a few minutes it went back to the slow beep. I drove by the house; the Cavalier was there but the tracking beeper didn't increase in volume, as it should have when I got close. I then started driving around the neighborhood and in only a few minutes the volume of the beeps increased. I drove slowly back and forth. Then I spotted the tracker, attached to a large green electric transformer. As far as I could tell no one was watching when I removed the tracker. It was in good shape except for a broken antenna.

I went back to my motel, booked a flight to Memphis for that evening and checked out. Then I went to the Vegas FBI office and sheepishly approached the supervisor with the keys to the car I had borrowed and the broken tracking device. I thanked him for their help and my regret for not catching the dopers in action.

Duke called me in a few days and said Eric had found the tracking device, broken the antenna off and moved it. I never knew if Eric had planned to send his mules for a load of cocaine. If he had he certainly would have canceled the trip after finding the tracker on the car. Another failed mission.

Toward the end of May 1988 I spent five days reviewing our case from the start. Our undercover agents and CIs had made controlled buys from 24 subjects for a total of 34 ½ ounces of cocaine using $22,780 in government funds. I believed we had enough information, and weren't likely to get anything more particularly helpful to bolster our case, to prepare an affidavit for search warrants for all the places we knew related to the storage of cocaine and money, sales of dope and books and records of the organization. The next weekend, with Tim DiScenza's okay, I gathered all the files and moved them to the FBI office conference room to write the affidavit.

Sunday night at close to midnight I was finished with the affidavit that eventually ran to 33 typewritten pages setting forth the probable cause to search a total of 23 residences and places of business associated with Eric Bovan's drug ring.

On Monday morning I left the affidavit and prepared search warrants with US District Judge Julia Gibbons. She called me later that afternoon and asked me to come and pick up the documents. Judge Gibbons was one of my favorites. When she was appointed by Ronald Reagan at age 32 she was the youngest federal judge in the nation. Now she is a judge on the US Sixth Circuit Court of Appeals.

With the search warrants in hand we made a plan to execute all of them simultaneously. To pull this off I gathered almost all the agents in the local FBI, DEA and ATF offices, along with about 30 officers from the sheriff's office and MPD. We decided to send four agents/officers to search each location.

The searches took most of the day and were conducted without incident. We seized 30 luxury vehicles, paid for in cash and in "straw names" such as mothers, sisters etc. We also seized three kilograms of cocaine, cash and in excess of $500,000 worth of jewelry, and books and records of the narcotic dealings of most of the subjects. One of the items of jewelry was the necklace and pendant Eric wore in Las Vegas.

After the searches we decided to confront Ernestine Wynn with the evidence we had against her hoping to get her to make a controlled buy directly from Shirron Knox in California. Ernestine, aka "Steen," was a black woman, mid-30s and a known "Booster," a shoplifter in layman's terms.

We told her that we were determined to bring down Bovan's empire and if she would cooperate with the FBI, AUSA Tim DiScenza had agreed to bring a lesser charge against her and she would receive consideration at sentencing time for assisting the government.

Ernestine thought about this for a few minutes and asked if she could talk to Tim directly. I called Tim and told him what the situation was and handed the phone to her. When she hung up she said Tim confirmed the promises we made. She agreed to cooperate and tell us everything she knew about Bovan's operation and to testify against him. The specter of spending the rest of her life in prison was a potent incentive.

Ernestine confirmed Shirron Knox in Hollywood was Bovan's source for cocaine. Shirron used to live in Memphis and the two women were best friends. At the beginning Bovan would tell Ernestine how many kilos he wanted to purchase and Ernestine would call Shirron and put in an order. Bovan would tell her when his mules would arrive at Shirron's apartment and Ernestine would be there to handle the transaction. She confirmed that Eric had started going around her and dealing directly with Shirron who had the contact with the wholesale supplier in California, a person Ernestine didn't know. Sometimes Shirron would leave the apartment and be gone for an hour or so then return with the cocaine. Sometimes a male black, Alex Lowe, would deliver the cocaine to Shirron's apartment. Her description of Lowe agreed with Duke's.

We believed Ernestine was telling us most if not all the truth. I asked her if she would be willing to place an order for three kilograms of cocaine with Shirron and tell her this was a deal she was doing on the side and didn't want Bovan to know about. She agreed and said we could be assured that Shirron would not tell Eric.

I sent an Airtel to the agents we had been working with in Los Angeles and explained the arrangement we had made with Ernestine. They called me back the next day and asked if I could delay the deal for at least a week to allow them to check out the location and the players.

Less than a week later, the LA agents called and said they had everything ready. I called Ernestine and told her we were ready to start the deal and would be at her apartment in about two hours to make a call to Shirron. Walter and I connected a recording device to her telephone. I had Ernestine give me the phone number to dial and then handed the phone to her. I wanted to make certain that she was actually calling Shirron whose number we had in our records. The two chatted for a few minutes and Ernestine placed an order for 3 kilograms of cocaine to be picked up at Shirron's apartment in four days.

I flew with Ernestine to Los Angeles a day before the purchase was to go down. An agent met us at the airport and drove us to a motel, a few miles from Shirron's apartment.

When we were ready for Ernestine to make the call to Shirron, I placed a recording device on a nearby pay phone. She arranged to pick up the cocaine in about an hour. I gave her the number for one of the agent's beepers so she could call, using a code, to let us know the deal went down while telling Shirron she was calling her mules. The LA agents had a signed search warrant to enter the apartment once

Ernestine sent the signal.

The covering agents saw Ernestine enter the apartment at about 2 p.m. About 45 minutes later a late model Mercedes drove into the parking lot and parked near the building's entrance. A young black male generally fitting the description of Alex Lowe went into the apartment building carrying a medium size canvas bag with handles. About 20 minutes later the agent received the coded message from Ernestine.

The entry/arrest team stormed the apartment and a short time later announced all clear over the radio. We were parked nearby but out of sight of the apartment building. When we got there the agents had Lowe, Ernestine and Shirron handcuffed and under arrest. We took them to the FBI office and placed them in three separate interview rooms, still handcuffed with two agents remaining with each.

I interviewed Shirron along with one of the Los Angeles agents in their office in a high-rise building close enough to the beach to get a good view of the Pacific Ocean, quite different from the muddy Mississippi view in Memphis. We told her all the evidence we had accumulated against her and that if she went to trial there was a good chance that she would be sentenced to life in prison. We also explained that if she would cooperate with us she might be considered for a lesser charge. She agreed to help and gave us a signed statement confirming that she had been involved in several shipments of 10-20 kilo of cocaine to Eric Bovan. She said Alex Lowe usually brought the cocaine to her apartment but she didn't know if he was just a runner or the owner of the coke he delivered.

We now had solid evidence against Shirron Knox and Alex Lowe. Again the threat of life in prison was enough to turn a player to our side. She would prove to be a valuable witness at trial and got little jail time after her guilty plea although she did have an issue with truthfulness in her testimony before the Grand Jury.

With all the evidence seized during the searches, records of controlled buys, and interviews with cooperating witnesses I began preparing a prosecutorial report from which AUSA DiScenza would draw up indictments. Tim and I spent more than a week preparing a 21-page indictment charging 26 subjects with various counts of conspiracy to possess and distribute cocaine, tax evasion, and perjury. My testimony before the grand jury in Memphis lasted more than a day. The grand jury returned true bills of indictment on all 26 defendants on November 29, 1989.

The court issued arrest warrants and we began rounding up the subjects. Some were surrendered by their attorneys but some hid from us, including Eric Bovan. Walter Hoback and I looked for him for about three months until one of Walter's informants finally found him and gave us the address for an apartment in South Memphis. The next evening Walter and I parked in a spot where we could see people coming and going from the apartment building. Shortly after 10 we saw a man we believed to be Eric leave the building and start walking towards the parking lot. We approached him, identified ourselves, although he knew us by sight, and arrested him without incident.

The next day I received a call from Eric's attorney. It didn't surprise me that Eric wanted to talk to me without his attorney's presence. It was almost as if we had been playing a cat and mouse game all these years and he knew the inevitable outcome. Walter and I checked him out of the county jail and took him to an interview room in the FBI office. He signed the form acknowledging that he had been advised of his right to remain silent, that he was waiving that right and wanted to talk.

First thing Eric told us he wanted to cooperate in our investigation. He planned to plead guilty with the hope of getting a reduced sentence. He didn't hesitate to agree to testify if this case went to trial. He knew full well what we knew: he would get a life sentence were he to go to trial and be found guilty. I told him we couldn't promise anything but would make AUSA DiScenza aware of his help. His attorney would have to work out a plea agreement with Tim. Eric gave us a long detailed statement of his history in the drug business including the names of all the people who worked for him in his organization. Eric eventually pled guilty to four counts of the indictment and received an agreed upon sentence of 10 years.

Besides Eric Bovan we had 25 more defendants. Already we knew Anthony Bovan, Ernestine Wynn, Shirron Knox and Eric were agreeing to plead guilty. However, their attorneys had a right see everything we had in the way of evidence.

The physical evidence seized in our searches filled three large floats with wheels (those cart-like things stores like Home Depot use to move large items around). With 26 or more attorneys needing to see the evidence I developed a system for five lawyers to view it at a time.

Once I moved everything to the conference room I spread the items out on tables. I tried to answer any questions the lawyers had. Every attorney was somewhat amazed at the quantity and diversity of what we had seized. The jewelry was a show in itself: solid gold large necklaces with pendants bigger than my hand, rings encrusted with gems just to name a few. There were revolvers and semi-automatic pistols. They all closely examined the money counting machine, something I'm sure none of them had ever seen before. It was quite a show.

Under federal statutes the Attorney General can seize just about anything of value purchased with funds generated from the sale of controlled substances. This includes vehicles used to store, transport or facilitate the movement of controlled substances, guns, money, real estate, negotiable instruments, and securities.

Within a week the US Attorney in Memphis filed for forfeiture of everything of value seized except for real property since most of the subjects lived in rentals and those who were owners had mortgages equal to or greater than the property's worth.

The Memphis FBI took ownership of some of the vehicles, and others were transferred to the SCSO and MPD based on their level of participation in the investigation. One of the vehicles our office kept was Eric's yellow Corvette. We had the snazzy yellow Corvette painted black since that was a more appropriate color for an undercover car and it was assigned to me.

Before the trial Eric called and told me about new drug dealers and their locations. I often picked him up, usually in the Corvette, and we would drive around town as he pointed out the dope houses.

Once we had been riding for about 15 minutes when Eric said, "You are driving my Corvette aren't you?" I denied it. "Why would you think that?" I asked. "That's okay," he said. "I recognize it but I'm not mad or anything. I rolled the dice and lost so there are no hard feelings." I could tell he was not resentful. He knew the chance he had taken by being in the illegal coke business and accepted his lot.

By the time the 20+ attorneys filed motions, asked for continuances and did all the wrangling attorneys do in a criminal case we were set for trial in late August 1990.

In the intervening year charges had been dropped against one defendant and 18 pled guilty leaving seven to go to trial. The guilty pleas gave me especial satisfaction since it proved we had such a solid case against them they weren't willing to risk being found guilty and receive the harsher sentences that were possible under the sentencing guidelines.

The usual US District courtroom layout had to be reconfigured to allow room for tables for seven defense attorneys and their clients, young black males who had been caught up in visions of wealth, jewels and fancy cars. Now not one of them could afford to hire an attorney so they were represented by court-appointed public defenders.

The two star witnesses for the prosecution were Earl "Dog Man" Woods aka Duke and Eric Bovan. Tim DiScenza was his usual well-prepared self as I watched his performance from my place at the prosecution table.

Earl laid out for the jury the many occasions he and others handled large amounts of cash and cocaine. He described trips made to Las Vegas and Los Angeles, conversations he was privy to and had overheard. His only weakness was an admission that he had used drugs a few times while he was my informant. I had to take the stand to rehabilitate him and assure the jury that he had been instructed not to use drugs and if he had, to cease.

Eric Bovan, by now 30 years old and still baby-faced, appeared self-assured. He had on an open-necked shirt, his black hair tied in a ponytail. His mother, Sylvia Saulsberry, attended the trial daily. Eric calmly testified, fingering every one of the defendants and their involvement in his cocaine empire, his "risk of a lifetime." As I sat and watched I wondered what these seven young men were thinking. They did Eric's bidding apparently without question and now he was implicitly sentencing them to more years in prison than the ten he had agreed to. Eric said he profited $10,000 on each kilogram of cocaine they procured and transported for him. He admitted he isolated himself from the actual cocaine and let them do his dirty work, just as Earl had told me.

Names that Eric threw out kept the press scribbling on their note pads: Pee Wee, Skinny Pimp, Turk, Scarface, Mc T, Dirty Red, Bubba, Uncle Bo, Spoon and Chicken Wing. Eric was Mr. B.

The jury returned its verdicts on September 7, 1990, after 16 hours of deliberations over three days. Four were convicted, three acquitted, of conspiracy and drug trafficking in what was then the largest cocaine operation in Memphis history.

Tim DiScenza told the press he estimated the cocaine Bovan brought into Memphis had a street value of hundreds of millions of dollars "These people were ferrying carloads and truckloads of drugs with a street value of several million dollars a load," he said. One of the defense attorneys was heard to say, "There is a certain irony to this case. It is a system that operates on somebody of Eric Bovan's stature in the drug world turning around and in direct pecking order testifying against the guys who did the job for him."

This was the last trial I participated in as an FBI Special Agent. I felt like perhaps a football player who retires at the apex of his career. Bringing the end to the Bovan empire was a high (no pun intended) note for me, one I will never forget.

The jewelry we seized was put on the auction block in August of 1992, part of an auction held by the US Marshals Service. The Marshals are charged with selling property seized through federal prosecutions. It was an eight-hour marathon and the prized trinket was described as "a gold pendant the size of a breastplate, bordered by 84 rubies and studded with 229 diamonds that spelled 'Las Vegas Eric'." I knew where that came from. I had held it in my hands after the seizure and knew it weighed at least a pound. A wholesale jeweler from Miami remarked, "Las Vegas Eric threw away a lot of money on something that could never be resold, except to someone named Eric with equally bad taste or someone willing to pick the piece apart and hawk the gems. But not all drug dealers show such poor judgment." In the end the Marshals Service took in about $1 million for about 2,000 pieces of jewelry. Eric's necklace and pendant brought $10,500.

FBI Employee with Bovan's Jewelry

In 1999, after serving his time, Eric Bovan fell into a DEA sting at a medical doctor's office. He was caught going out the back door with 25 prescriptions in his possession for Xanax, Lortab and Hydrdocodone in 10 different names. The doctor was the primary target of a long-term DEA investigation. Eric pled guilty again.

At sentencing in 2002 Bovan's attorney told the judge that his client met the doctor at the hospital where he was hospitalized for one of several strokes he suffered. Allegedly Eric's health problems arose from his "every other day use of cocaine for years." Eric got three years back in federal prison.

Chapter 18
A Crown Royal Bag Leads to Life in Prison

Jim Lee Townsend, aka Jimmy T and J Mack, was a top player in the distribution of cocaine in the Memphis area. He owned the Hawaiian Isle, a club on one end of Beale Street, the street famous for blues music including B. B. King's club and had previously operated other clubs in the same area, J. Mac and Illusions. In mid-1987 the OCDETF decided to target him. This was the same time the task force was working Eric Bovan which wasn't unusual. Agents always had several investigations going simultaneously.

All the task force officers talked to their informants to get information about Townsend's operation and see if anyone could make a buy from him or someone in his distribution network. From this canvas of informants we learned how Townsend operated and the identity of some of his runners and buyers. This was a starting point.

Lieut. Richard Swain, Shelby County Sheriff's Office (SCSO), talked to a criminal informant who told him he could buy cocaine from a woman named Bernice Turner who dealt out of her home. He said she could get as much as one kilogram of cocaine at a time from Townsend. We surveilled Turner's residence for about 12 to 14 hours per day for three days. She lived in a neat, ranch style house on a large lot in South Memphis. The telltale signs of a dope house were there: a great deal of traffic coming and going, visitors only staying inside 5 to 10 minutes. We copied down the license plate numbers of the vehicles to identify the owners. A check of those names in the criminal database found many with prior narcotics convictions.

In September 1987 we put a plan together to make a buy of cocaine from Bernice Turner. Richard Swain was a natural undercover officer; we called him Bear for his long hair and bushy beard. His informant had introduced him as someone who wanted to purchase 2 ounces of cocaine. On the day of the buy we prepared an affidavit for a warrant to search Turner's home in the event Richard was successful. An officer was standing by with the affidavit attached to a search warrant that he would present to a judge for his signature if the buy went down as we expected.

Richard entered the house with his informant at about one in the afternoon. We had four vehicles parked out of sight around the house. We also had a surveillance van in position to record from a transmitter that Richard was wearing. Sometimes when we were running an operation like this and couldn't get the van in a position to receive the transmission we would park a nondescript vehicle in the area with a powerful transmitter in the trunk that would transmit the signal to the equipment in the surveillance van. In this instance the van was in a location where the conversation could be heard clearly and pictures taken of the individuals entering the house.

The buy from Bernice Turner went down as planned and we got the information to the agent standing by with the affidavit for a search warrant. The rest of us stayed in place to watch for activity at the house. When Lieut. Swain gave the prearranged signal via the transmitter, officers knocked on the door and went in. Everyone stay where you are, they were told, a judge has signed a warrant to search this house; an officer is on his way with it. Once the warrant was served on Turner we began our search. We found additional cocaine, drug paraphernalia and a large sum of cash.

Bernice Turner was a big boned white woman in her mid-40s. Her skin had an olive hue, her hair was a mop of coal black. She was dressed in a housedress, slippers on her feet. Since she had a prior conviction for drugs we pointed out to her how much trouble she was in. But if she would help us by telling us who her supplier was we would let any sentencing judge she might face know. She agreed to cooperate and said her supplier was Jimmy Townsend. We asked her how much "weight" (quantity) she was buying from him and she replied anywhere from ounces up to a kilogram. She said all she had to do was call Townsend, put in an order and someone from Townsend's group would bring her the cocaine. He would front her the drugs, to be paid for after she sold them. She must have been a reliable, regular customer to have that kind of arrangement.

We placed a recorder on Bernice Turner's telephone to record the call that she was getting ready to make to Townsend. Actually she gave me the number and I dialed for her. Townsend readily agreed to sell her 1 kg of cocaine and arranged to meet her at a nearby convenience store. We moved our surveillance van and some of our vehicles close to the store to cover the buy. Instead of Townsend showing up, a woman later identified as Hazel Little arrived driving a red Jeep that we had seen before and knew was registered to Townsend's wife. Turner got out of her car and talked to Little in the Jeep. They left in their respective vehicles, returned to Turner's house and went inside. The officers on surveillance could see Little was carrying a package in a plastic bag when she entered the house. In about three minutes Little returned to the Jeep and drove away.

When we figured Little was far enough away, some of us went in the house. Turner told us Little had placed the package in the washing machine. Turner said she had agreed to pay Little $29,000 for the coke

An officer removed the package from the washing machine. He opened it wearing gloves and found what appeared to be a brick (one kilogram) of cocaine. It tested positive in a field test.

About two hours later Turner called Townsend and told him she had distributed the kilo of cocaine and was ready to pay for it. We had gotten $29,000 in US currency (serial numbers recorded as usual) for her. Shortly thereafter Little returned to Turner's driving the red Jeep. In the meantime we concealed ourselves in the house. We observed Turner giving Hazel Little a purple Crown Royal bag containing the $29,000.

Little was young and black, mid-20s at the most, casually dressed. She seemed well acquainted with drug transactions. There were only a few words exchanged between the women.

Little left, driving the red Jeep. She was stopped and arrested about three blocks away by SCSO Lieut. Mitch Donovan and two other officers. They searched the vehicle and found a loaded .38 caliber revolver, several documents in Townsend's name as well, and the Crown Royal bag containing the $29,000. Everything was seized as evidence.

A few days after Hazel Little was arrested, we had a Task Force meeting to discuss what we were going to do with Jim Townsend. He of course knew Hazel had been arrested but might not know for sure we had recorded the calls between him and Bernice Turner. The recordings gave us a strong case against him. The number I dialed for Bernice was his. A conviction would put him in prison for life.

We figured Townsend would at least suspend his drug dealings for a while. The fact he delivered a kilo of cocaine within an hour of Bernice's call convinced us our belief that he was a major supplier was sound. He had to be selling to several small time dealers and operating a major wholesale supply network.

After talking it over we decided to not approach him yet, hoping to make additional cases against him. If we could do this, we would have a better chance of getting him to cooperate and really expand our case.

No more buys were made that could jam up Jim Townsend any

further. Tim DiScenza and I talked about Townsend from time to time and finally decided we needed to act. I reviewed the complete investigation and prepared an affidavit for a search warrant for Townsend's home. But first I wanted to approach Townsend to see if he would cooperate in connection with investigations of other major drug dealers.

Along with three other officers, I went to Townsend's residence on October 23, 1990. One of these officers was ATF SA Walter Hoback. Townsend let us in without hesitation. He was a tall black man, friendly and non-threatening. He could have been anyone's ordinary neighbor in the subdivision of newly built homes. The Townsends had recently moved to the two-story brick house. They had previously lived in the same house on Marynelle that my family and I once owned, an eerie coincidence.

I explained to Jim Townsend the evidence we had accumulated against him and asked if he would cooperate in helping us make cases on other major dope dealers. I told him here's what's going to happen if you don't cooperate:

1. You will be arrested and the government will oppose a bail request.
2. The government will press for the longest sentence possible, which might be life.
3. I will get a search warrant for your house.
4. Your wife will be arrested since we believe we have substantial evidence of her knowledge of the illegal activity occurring in your home.
5. Your young daughter will be taken to juvenile court, as both her parents will be in jail.

I then told him if he chose to cooperate he would enjoy these benefits:

1. He would not be arrested now but at some future date.
2. His wife would not be arrested at all.
3. His daughter would not be taken to juvenile court.
4. The government would file a cooperation statement on his behalf, which might reduce his sentence to 10 years.

I reminded Townsend he had the right to call an attorney but if he did "all deals were off." He chose not to do that. Townsend was still reluctant to cooperate and wanted to confer with his wife. She told him I was "full of shit" and vigorously argued that he should refuse. I even allowed him to read the affidavit I had prepared for the search warrant that detailed the FBI's evidence of his drug trafficking.

Townsend continued to have reservations and asked to speak to Tim DiScenza. They met in the parking lot of a nearby Shoney's restaurant and talked in private for about 20 minutes. Tim essentially reiterated what I had told Townsend.

DiScenza then left and Townsend and I returned to his home. He finally agreed to cooperate and signed a consent to search form and said he wished to give a statement. To cover all bases, I gave him Miranda warnings and he gave me an eight-page statement in which he detailed his extensive drug trafficking activities over the prior several years. Meanwhile the other officers searched his home but didn't locate any evidence.

Consistent with our agreement neither Townsend nor his wife was arrested that day. I had several meetings with him after he agreed to cooperate with the government but he never gave me any useful information. He talked a lot in general about the drug scene in Memphis but not in any detail. I tried to get him to work with me on several large dope dealers that I knew about but he refused, even though he was facing life in prison without parole. After a while I realized he just didn't have the Moxie to go up against the heavy hitters and didn't want to be known as a snitch.

I set the Townsend matter aside for a while until seven months later when I spoke to Tim DiScenza again. I said I didn't believe Townsend would ever cooperate; he was just stalling for time. We decided to go ahead and seek an indictment against Townsend and Hazel Little for her part in the conspiracy. We chose not to seek an indictment against his wife.

On June 5 1991 I presented our case to a federal grand jury in Memphis. The next day an indictment was returned against Townsend and Little charging them with conspiracy to distribute cocaine and possession of one kilo of cocaine with intent to distribute it.

We decided to arrest Townsend and Little on the morning of June 7. We wanted to take them into custody before word of the indictment could leak out. If they heard about it no doubt Townsend and possibly Little would flee the jurisdiction. I knew that if this happened we would have to spend a lot of time finding them. We assumed Townsend had accumulated a large amount of cash that he could use to flee and take care of Hazel Little.

We planned to arrest both subjects simultaneously at their homes to avoid making the arrests in a public place or having to engage in a car chase that usually didn't end well.

At six the next morning I set up on Townsend, parked 75 yards up the street from his house. About an hour later I saw him come out his front door and pick up a newspaper from the sidewalk and return to the house. By eight the two arrest teams were ready to go. I told them I hadn't seen any movement around Townsend's house since he had gotten his paper. We waited until both teams were in place and I gave the go-ahead.

The Townsend arrest team surrounded the house and one officer knocked on the front door. His wife came to the door and opened it. I said we had an arrest warrant for Townsend and that we were going to come in and arrest him. She said her husband wasn't home, having left about an hour earlier and didn't tell her where he was going. She agreed to sign a consent to search form.

We asked her to step aside and entered from the front door and the patio door at the back. We searched the house thoroughly but couldn't find Jim Townsend. While one officer was sitting with the wife in the kitchen I called the team together in the living room where we couldn't be heard. I said Townsend was in the house somewhere unless he had left out the back door and through several neighbors' backyards to the next street over. I didn't believe he left by that route. Further the BMW that he usually drove was still in the garage. That left only one place he could be hiding: the attic.

Some of the task force members stayed with the wife, others covered the exits and the rest of us gathered in the garage. It was typical of houses built in the south in the 1970s for the attic to be accessed by pull down stairs in the garage. I went out to my car to retrieve my flashlight and a mirror on an adjustable handle.

We pulled down the stairs and I climbed to the top but didn't put my head above the opening. Using my flashlight and the mirror, I scanned the interior but could see nothing but pink fiberglass insulation. The two other officers who were on the stairs behind me and I decided to go into the attic and search for Townsend. One of the officers found him about 20 feet from the attic opening covered completely with the blown insulation. Two of us covered him with our weapons and ordered him to get on his feet and keep his hands in front of him. He got up from the floor and looked like a big pink fluffy creature. I read him his rights standing there and told him he was under arrest for conspiracy to distribute and to possess cocaine. Two officers escorted him down the stairs to the garage and let him talk to his wife.

I knew he must be itchy and uncomfortable so I asked him if he'd like to take a shower before we took him downtown and booked him into the jail. He did and we allowed him to shower while two officers were in the bathroom. We then took him to the jail.

Townsend and Hazel appeared before the US Magistrate the next day. Tim DiScenza argued for no bail as to Townsend. He pointed out to the judge the circumstances surrounding his arrest and that the government believed Townsend had sufficient funds to allow him to travel anywhere he wanted making him an extreme flight risk. The judge denied Townsend bail and set a $10,000 cash bond for Hazel Little.

At Townsend and Little's trial in January 1992 the defendants' attorneys filed a motion to suppress Townsend's signed statement and the evidence seized during the search. The judge denied the motion as well as Little's motion to have her trial severed from Townsend's. On January 29, 1992 the jury found both defendants guilty as charged.

The judge sentenced Townsend to life in prison without parole, just as I had predicted, after considering his prior drug convictions in the 1980s. Little was sentenced to five years.

Not long after the sentencing Townsend gave an "exclusive interview" to a local newspaper, from his home at the Memphis Federal Correction Institution. He claimed I orchestrated the charges against him because he refused to cooperate with a plan I had devised to implicate former U.S. Representative Harold Ford in criminal activity. This was an argument his trial attorney had attempted to bring up in her opening statement. The judge ruled that Congressman Ford should not be mentioned during the trial.

Townsend also put the blame for his conviction on a biased jury and general bad press. He said, "I earned my money by successfully operating clubs Illusion and J. Mac. I admit that I was a user of drugs that led to my previous convictions but I never headed a drug ring."

I told the newspaper reporter, "I went over every count of the findings of the grand jury and encouraged Mr. Townsend to cooperate with us. He agreed to help providing evidence pertaining to drug trafficking. I didn't have anything to do with Congressman Ford. My duty as an agent was to end a major drug ring. I did that to the best of my ability. Townsend's indictment was the result of an undercover drug operation, not a conspiracy."

Jim Townsend and Hazel Little both appealed their sentences to the U.S. Court of Appeals. Neither was successful. The last I knew Townsend was in a federal prison in Pennsylvania. I assume Little served her time and is out.

Chapter 19
Exactly *Who* Do You Want Killed?

D oy Daniels said he would rather be dead than go to prison for committing fraud in trading securities but he didn't want to do it by his own hand. Perhaps he was chicken to do it or maybe his family couldn't collect on his life insurance if it were suicide.

It all began in mid-August 1987 when Daniels started on a downward trajectory, losing his investment company and his assets and finally attempting to hire a killer.

Michael Meissner came to the Memphis FBI office after his friend Doy Daniels approached him and offered money if he would kill a witness who had testified against Daniels in a recent hearing in federal civil court. Daniels had to shut down his investment business and all his assets were frozen. He was accused of defrauding investors of more than $400,000 between January 1986 and August 1987. So far it was only a civil case but the Securities and Exchange was investigating and ready to charge Daniels with 14 criminal counts of mail and securities fraud. A conviction would mean jail time.

Daniels, a 37 year-old graduate of Memphis State University, had served a two-year term as a Tennessee state legislator. He lived in Germantown, an affluent suburb of Memphis, and from all outward appearances was a good citizen.

When I met with Michael Meissner he told me, he and Daniels attended the same church and had been friends a long time. Meissner knew Daniels was having financial problems with the SEC arising from his security business. Daniels told Meissner he wanted help in "doing in" his former partner John Harder who had talked to the SEC. He offered to pay Meissner $50,000 in negotiable bonds for doing the job.

I asked Meissner if he would be willing to wear a wire and talk to Daniels about hiring a hit man. He agreed, so I prepared a script for him. If Daniels still wanted to hire a killer Meissner was to say he knew a person on the West Coast who would do the job and was good at his craft. But he was to warn Daniels that if the hit man traveled to Memphis, Daniels would owe him his expenses even if they couldn't reach an agreement.

Meissner called me a few days later. He had a meeting set up with Daniels in Shelby Farms Park for the next day at noon.

I drove to Shelby Farms and selected a picnic table under a large oak tree in a secluded area for the Meissner-Daniels meeting. I called Meissner back and described the location to him. He planned to meet Daniels at noon the next day.

Meissner came to the FBI office early the next morning. I introduced him to the other agents who were working with me so they could recognize him. I equipped Meissner with a small Nagra recorder hidden on his body in a place, which couldn't be found by a quick frisk, in case Daniels wanted to check him out although Meissner didn't believe Daniels would be suspicious.

We then set the plan in motion. A little after noon, one of the surveillance units reported Daniels' vehicle was approaching the meeting place. A white male about 40 years old was driving. He parked near the picnic table, walked over and sat opposite Meissner. From the license plate I confirmed the car was registered to Daniels at his home address.

Later I met Meissner in a nearby shopping mall parking lot. He said Daniels talked freely about wanting a hit man to kill his former partner. Daniels told Meissner to get in touch with the hit man and have him come to Memphis for a meeting. He would gladly pay the man's expenses whether or not they reached an agreement. I told Meissner to wait a few days, then call Daniels and tell him the man from the West Coast was on his way.

I listened to the tape when I returned to the office. Meissner had done a good job in moving forward our case against Daniels. And the surveilling agents had photos of the meeting.

Meissner called me a couple days later. He had told Daniels his hit man was en route. I told him to wait another day and tell Daniels I had arrived and was ready to meet him. Meissner set up a meeting with Daniels and me at a mobile home located in eastern Shelby County.

The day before I rented a nondescript car, and along with other agents, checked the address. We chose two surveillance spots where the surveilling units could see the trailer door. The next evening I followed Meissner to the trailer. He introduced me to Daniels and left. I had a small Nagra recorder in my left cowboy boot. I had taken the boot to a shoemaker and asked him to sew a small pouch on the inside of the upper part of the boot. The Nagra fit into the pouch quite nicely. The other agents took up their surveillance positions.

Daniels looked like a typical businessman, a white male, late 30s, early 40's, about 5'10' and 170 lbs. He was neatly dressed and wore horn-rimmed glasses that made his chubby face look a little more adult. He explained the problems he was having with the SEC and blamed his former partner John Harder for his troubles. Harder had already testified in the civil hearing where the judge ordered Daniels to close up his business. He said he had rather die than go to a maximum-security prison for a long sentence.

"If I have to die, I want to take a couple of other "SOBs" with me," he said. "Huh, what do you mean?" I asked him. He said he wanted revenge for their ruining his life. I knew he had brought everything on himself at the expense of his victims who in some cases had lost the life savings Daniels stole and spent on himself and his family. "I've been thinking about this for a long time," he added.

One of the men Daniels wanted killed wasn't identified by name, only he lived in Salt Lake City, the other was John Harder. His plan was to have the two men killed, then have *me kill him* making it look like a botched robbery. That way his family would collect on a large life insurance policy that he had taken out several years before. He said that he was never going to go to prison.

"That is a crazy plan," I said. "Especially wanting me to kill you." Daniels told me he couldn't face the shame of being charged with a crime and going to prison. The odd thing was Daniels didn't appear to be nervous or at all frightened at the prospect of me carrying out three murders. It was as if meeting with a hit man was an everyday occurrence for him.

"So, what will it set me back?" he asked. We settled on $10,000 for each hit as long as nothing happened to require more than a "normal" killing. Daniels said he had started to delay this meeting and the only reason he didn't was because he wanted to keep his options open. "You know, if I do the job I have to be paid in full in advance." He didn't balk. "Okay," I said, "I need everything you know about John Harder and a good photo." I gave him my pager number to get in touch with me and left.

When I returned to the office, I went to see AUSA Dan Newsom. After he listened to the tape recordings I told him I was concerned about Daniels' frame of mind. He appeared to be very vindictive and under a lot of pressure. Daniels might take it into his head to kill the others himself or find a real hit man who would offer him a lower price. Dan agreed and said we had enough evidence to charge and convict Daniels with solicitation to commit a violent crime.

We arrested Daniels and took him before the US magistrate for an initial appearance the next day. The judge found probable cause to hold him and set a bond of $10,000. Daniels made bond the same day. I suspect the judge set the low bond since Daniels had no prior criminal record, and since his plan to kill witnesses had come to light, he would likely not go any further with it.

It wasn't until June 13, 1988 that the case went before the Grand Jury. Daniels was indicted on six counts of mail fraud, seven counts of securities fraud, one count of bank fraud and two counts of solicitation to commit a violent crime. In the previous nine months the prosecution and defense had been trying to work out a plea deal but were unsuccessful. When we went to arrest Daniels we couldn't find him.

I started contacting his family and friends. I became convinced Daniels had fled the state and was probably somewhere in California but I couldn't get a specific location. Toll records from his home telephone for the previous two months showed several calls to a telephone number in Newport Beach, California

I contacted the Los Angeles FBI office giving them some of the background on Daniels, his mug shot and where I believed he might be. A few days later a Teletype from LA advised that Daniels was arrested without incident on June 16, 1988.

After his arrest Daniels refused to waive extradition to Tennessee so a court hearing was necessary to prove the party under arrest was indeed the same Doy Daniels as named in the indictment.

I had to make the trip to Los Angeles to testify at the hearing. I gave a summary of the case and said I recognized Daniels from my face-to-face meeting with him in Memphis. Daniels was sent back to Tennessee. The Memphis judge revoked his bond and ordered him held in custody until his trial.

Daniels spent three months in the Shelby County jail, the place he so fervently wanted to avoid. On December 8, 1988 I testified at the trial and played the tape of my September 1987 meeting when Daniels set forth his desire for me to kill two men and Daniels himself. The defense argued that he had briefly considered hiring a killer but then abandoned the idea.

Midway through the trial Daniels' attorney approached AUSA Newsom with an offer for his client to plead guilty to the 16 SEC charges in exchange for the government dropping the two counts of solicitation to commit a violent crime. Dan and I discussed the offer and as Dan pointed out, the jury might buy the defense claim that Daniels briefly considered hiring a killer but then abandoned the idea. The plea and the agreed upon 10 year sentence would be a sure thing. Dan said he probably wouldn't recommend more than 10 years even if we went to trial and Daniels was convicted on all counts of the indictment.

On January 20, 1989 Daniels pled guilty pursuant to the plea agreement, was sentenced to 10 years in federal prison and ordered to pay restitution to the victim investors.

The irony of it all is that by attempting to hire me as a hit man, Daniels was exposing himself to being locked up in the maximum-security prison he so feared. A white-collar criminal, on the other hand, goes to a "country club" type of prison.

Chapter 20
What a Woman Will Do to Keep a Man

A frumpy looking secretary in Jackson Mississippi came to the conclusion the only way she could keep her affair with her physician boss secret was to hire a hit man. But she approached the wrong person, a criminal informant for the FBI. The CI went to SA Denise Day in Jackson and she called me,

I met the informant on March 6, 1989 at the Jackson field office. Margaret Madison, 41-years-old, told the CI she wanted Jim Holmes, currently the owner of Metro Pawn Brokers and a retired Jackson police detective, killed. He said Margaret wasn't a habitual criminal, appeared to be a decent citizen, and was unlikely to own or carry weapons. The CI agreed to introduce me to Ms. Madison as Joe Ray Stewart, a hit man from Memphis.

SA Day told the informant to contact Ms. Madison to arrange for a meeting with the hit man the next day, March 7. We decided that 3:00 p.m. in the parking lot of the Metro Center Mall in Jackson would work for the introductions. After sending the informant on his way, Denise and I made plans for surveillance of my meeting with Margaret Madison. I also met some local police officers who were working with Denise on the case. The CI called back that afternoon and confirmed the 3:00 meeting for the next day was a go.

I met the CI, Denise and a couple of other agents and four Jackson police detectives before three o'clock. Plans were laid out to cover my first time meeting with Ms. Madison with in-person surveillance and photographs. We also decided I would wear a transmitter and recording device.

I then followed the informant in my undercover vehicle to the mall parking lot for our initial set up with the seemingly everyday woman who was seeking to place a hit on an everyday civilian. Upon arriving, the informant introduced us; some small talk ensued, and then left. Margaret was a rather plain Jane, the type to wear inexpensive outfits from the local Wal-Mart. A man was with her; I never did catch his name. He didn't have much to say. I think he was there only to give her a feeling of protection.

Margaret explained she had worked as Dr. William Tumlinson, a Jackson physician's private secretary for 18 years. She admitted to a long-running romantic relationship with the doctor. Her victim was to be Jim Holmes, a close friend of her boss/lover. The men had known each other for years. She believed Holmes had been hired to break into her home to get proof of the affair. Recently her home had been burglarized. The only things missing were nude photographs of the doctor and her. Margaret thought Holmes gave the photos to Mrs. Tumlinson who must have hired him.

Margaret wanted to take matters into her own hands so she could continue the affair with the doctor. She also wanted to keep the affair secret, lest it tarnish his reputation as a fine family physician within the community.

Ms. Madison wanted Dr. Tumlinson's wife, Ann, with whom she was fairly well acquainted, to be her second victim. She was specific that I take care of Jim Holmes first, I assume in an effort to keep further proof of the affair from being passed on to the suspecting wife. It was then that I felt Margaret Madison might have not, in fact, lived such an everyday life. She was cold, indifferent, and quite business-like about what she was asking me to do. She showed no signs of nervousness, hesitation or concern as to what my methods for erasing these citizens would be. It was as if she'd met with a hired killer a dozen times.

In a way I felt a bit sorry for her. But I never had a doubt she wanted these two people murdered.

We then discussed my fees. I told her that my going rate was $5,000 per head. I suspected she didn't have a lot of money so I explained my offer was far below the everyday cost of a hit. I told Margaret that because Jim Holmes was a retired police detective, I typically would charge at least $15,000 to cover both hits. The death of someone currently in or retired from local law enforcement would undoubtedly be a huge murder investigation. I told her I could tell she couldn't afford more than $10,000 and though it went a bit against my better judgment, I would take the job.

I had already decided to name a figure I thought she would agree to. If she decided my price was more than she could pay she might turn me down and go to someone else putting Holmes' and the doctor's wife's lives in jeopardy.

As a partial payment I asked Margaret if she could get some blank scrips from the doctor's office. The relief was visible on her face and she agreed she could do that.

I told her I had women working for me who could get the scrips filled and that I'd give her a portion of the money from the drugs as a credit toward what she owed me for the killings. The terms of our agreement were settled then. Margaret would pay me $5,000 for each hit, using the revenue generated from the prescriptions and cash. We set up a meeting for the next day, March 8, for her to pay an initial deposit.

The following afternoon, I met Margaret – this time she was alone - in the same parking lot and received both $500 in cash and five blank prescriptions taken from Dr. Tumlinson's office. She also gave me a photocopy of one of Dr. Tumlinson's signed prescriptions. This meeting lasted only a few minutes. I gave her my beeper number to be reached at any time back in Memphis. We left agreeing that Margaret would contact me once she had gathered the rest of the money.

Then, a week later on March 15, I received a page on my beeper. When I dialed the number, it was Dr. Tumlinson's office and Margaret immediately told me she was unable to speak freely. I assumed this was her attempt to confirm she could reach me. Margaret paged again that afternoon and when I called her back she told me she was at a pay phone and could discuss the portion of my unpaid fees.

"You sure were right to give me that copy of the doc's signature. I had no trouble filling three of those prescriptions for Dilaudid," I told her. "Well, all right," she said with a laugh. "Where's that get me?"

"I reckon I'll give you $800 credit for those." The line was quiet. I then said I was ready to go forward with Mr. Holmes, but that I'd need to receive at least an additional $1,200 to proceed.

"Shoot. All right then. I'll see what I can gather up and get back to you as soon as I have something," she said in a quieter voice and we hung up.

Two days later, on March 17, I received another page and when I dialed the number, I was speaking with Margaret. She told me that this line was her home phone and would be safe. She sounded somewhat terrible and said she had fallen ill with the flu. Her thought was that she would have the money for me by the middle of the following week.

On March 20 I received another page and called back within a few minutes. Margaret told me she had the balance of my money. I told her I would be in Jackson the next day, would check into a hotel, and then call her to arrange for a meeting the following day, Wednesday, March 22. She agreed.

I immediately called Denise Day and described this latest development. Denise said she would select the motel for us, and have adjoining rooms set up for video and audio surveillance. The second or control room was for agents and local officers to monitor my meeting with Margaret. They could quickly decide when to come in and arrest Ms. Madison. When they thought it appropriate they would knock on the hallway door. I would open the door, and the arrest would be made.

I checked into the Ramada Inn later on Tuesday evening, March 21, and called Margaret's home number to give her the room number and phone number of my room. She agreed to a 9:00 a.m. meeting for the next day, March 22.

Margaret arrived about ten minutes late the next morning. She came calmly into the room, made steady eye contact as usual, and we engaged in some casual conversation. I asked if she had the money. She did. She then took out four blank prescriptions from another doctor's office and suggested she pay me $3000 in cash and these prescriptions to close the deal. I started to negotiate with her saying I wanted more cash but after some more discussion agreed to the deal.

Margaret was a common every day, probably law-abiding person for the most part although clearly not moral. I didn't at any point feel even a need to pat her down. Even if she had a weapon I could easily have overpowered her. She had the money and was very business-like about our dealings. I was confident we had a strong case.

She then gave me the $3000 in hundred dollar bills. I told her I would get started on the job in a few days and keep her advised.

It was right then that I heard a sharp knock on the door. I crossed the room and opened it. Two FBI agents and a local officer came in, advised Margaret Madison of her rights, told her what charges she was facing, and handcuffed her. Immediately she almost crumpled to the floor and started crying. It appeared she wasn't particularly hysterical or interested in pleading innocence, but rather just scared to death. In a little over two weeks the undercover case was over.

The following morning at the preliminary hearing I testified for approximately two hours outlining the case and the evidence we had against the woman. The magistrate bound Margaret over for trial in the U.S. District Court of Mississippi, at a date to be determined.

She was charged with one count of using a facility in interstate commerce (the telephone in this case) with intent that a murder be committed and one count of attempting to acquire or obtain possession of a controlled substance by misrepresentation, fraud and forgery. If convicted, Margaret faced up to 25 years in prison and $260,000 in fines. She was released on $5,000 bond with the provision: not to make contact with Mr. Holmes, Dr. and Mrs. Tumlinson, their family, and the doctor's employees.

Holmes told the media, "I don't know what was going on about this whole deal," adding he didn't learn about the alleged scheme until the FBI agents told him Wednesday morning at his pawnshop. "I'm just floored. I just thank the Lord we have people like the FBI."

The local paper reported, "FBI Special Agent Corbett Hart of Memphis testified during a hearing March 24 that he posed as a hired gunman. Madison wanted him to kill Jim Holmes, a former Jackson police officer who operates Metro Pawn Brokers at 1213 Dixon Road, and Ann Tumlinson," the wife of Jackson physician William Tumlinson, Hart said.

Madison, a secretary for William Tumlinson for about 18 years, had a long-term romance with the physician but feared Tumlinson's wife had hired Holmes to investigate, Hart said in the March 24 hearing.

"Pictures of the doctor and Madison in the nude had been stolen in a burglary of Madison's house, and Madison suspected Mrs. Tumlinson had seen the pictures," Hart said at the hearing.

Hart said he asked for $10,000 to kill Holmes and the doctor's wife. Hart agreed to accept part of the payment in blank prescriptions forms that he could have forged for the painkiller Dilaudid. Madison gave him a $500 down payment plus five blank prescriptions from Tumlinson's office and a copy of the doctor's signature at one meeting and five blank prescriptions from another doctor's office at a later meeting.

"That led to the charges of acquiring drugs by fraud on March 8 and 22. She was arrested March 22."

"Madison was charged with use of interstate commerce facilities in commission of a murder-for-hire plot beginning sometime before March 1 and continuing through March 22 because of a telephone call she is accused of making to Hart that day. Hart testified that she met with him several times and called him more times in planning the scheme."

"The drug possession charges accuse Madison of having 11 different kinds of drugs, including the painkillers Demerol and Percodan and Fastin diet pills, on Aug. 28, 1988, and of having 10 Dilaudid tablets in her possession on Oct. 31, 1988."

In early April, I had to laugh when an article in the *Ledger* stated that Margaret had entered a not guilty plea to all charges against her. In addition to providing an overview of the murder-for-hire scheme, the article also detailed the account of Margaret's August 1988 sale of illegal drugs to a different undercover agent, Ron Pitts. He had given her $600 to obtain a bag of 924 prescription pills ranging from barbiturate-codeine capsules to heavy painkillers to diet pills. Besides a good chuckle, the article gave me reason to believe Margaret's trial would go even more smoothly than anticipated.

On Tuesday June 6, 1989 Margaret Madison changed her story and entered a guilty plea to one count of a murder-for-hire charge. Madison's lawyer, Robert W. Sneed, said after the hearing, "She would have had a very difficult case to win at trial. The only possible defense we would have would be an entrapment defense."

Sneed also made an estimate that Madison could be sentenced

somewhere between 37 and 47 months in jail under federal sentencing guidelines. It was likely that, had her case actually gone to trial, she would have faced a sentence up to four times as long if she had been convicted on the murder-for-hire charge and all four drug related charges. It turned out that in exchange for the guilty plea, the drug charges had been dropped.

My thoughts don't often return to clear-cut cases like this one, but one evening about six months later I returned home and found a sizeable UPS package on my doorstep. Opening it, I discovered a gorgeous Stetson Silverbelly 40x felt Cowboy hat. It was clearly top-of-the-line and the sender knew my exact size. In fact, whoever had sent it requested that my full name be engraved inside the brim in gold lettering. I smiled as I looked at a business card that was tucked inside. It was none other than that of the owner of the Dixon Road Metro Pawn Brokers in Jackson, Mississippi – Mr. Jim Holmes. "What a gesture of gratitude," I thought. No doubt the man was indeed happy to be alive.